Vibe-Coding: The Art of Collaborating with AI

Vibe-Coding

The Art of Collaborating with AI

Mark C. Turner MSc, BSc, CFIRM

with Claude by Anthropic

Emsity Limited
Essex, United Kingdom

Vibe-Coding: The Art of Collaborating with AI

Author: Mark C. Turner

About This Book's Creation

This book was written using the methodology it describes. The author developed all concepts, structure, specifications, and editorial direction. Claude, developed by Anthropic, contributed to drafting, research, and iterative refinement under the author's continuous creative direction.

This attribution reflects the book's thesis — that interloquial collaboration between human and AI can produce meaningful work — rather than a claim of legal co-authorship. Where attribution is required, it should be assigned to the human author. The selection, arrangement, creative direction, and final editorial judgement reflected in this work are solely those of Mark C. Turner.

Disclaimer

The information in this book is provided for educational purposes. The author makes no warranties about the completeness, reliability, or accuracy of this information. Any action you take based on the information in this book is strictly at your own risk. The author is not liable for any losses or damages in connection with the use of this book.

Legal information regarding copyright and AI-generated content reflects the author's understanding as of early 2026 and should not be construed as legal advice. Laws and interpretations evolve; consult a qualified legal professional for specific legal questions.

Trademarks

Claude is a trademark of Anthropic, PBC. VS Code is a trademark of Microsoft Corporation. All other trademarks mentioned in this book are the property of their respective owners. Use of these trademarks do not imply endorsement by the trademark holders.

First Edition: 2026

Published by Emsity Limited Essex, United Kingdom www.emsity.com

For rights and permissions enquiries: mark@emsity.com

ISBN 978-1-0676442-0-8 (Paperback) ISBN 978-1-0676442-1-5 (Kindle ebook) ISBN 978-1-0676442-2-2 (PDF)

A catalogue record for this book is available from the British Library.

Dedications

For Colette — my wife and best friend. Thank you for your patience and support through all the years that allowed me to build the knowledge and experience to create this. I love you.

For Colin and Linda Turner — thank you for sparking the fire in 1982 with my first computer.

Preface

This book began as a private reckoning.

In 2025, I completed a large software project built almost entirely through AI collaboration. I am not a credentialled software engineer. I came to software through design and requirement-writing: I could always articulate what systems should do; what I could not do was write the code to build them. That changed. The project existed, it worked, and it had cost a fraction of what a traditional development engagement would have required.

The problem was that I had nearly lost myself in the process, and that when I emerged from it, I realised how little I had understood the risks I had been running. That realisation is what shaped this book's perspective more than anything else.

I came to vibe-coding as a risk management professional. I hold a Fellowship of the Institute of Risk Management. That background gave me something that most AI books lack: a professional instinct for identifying what can go wrong, an unwillingness to accept fluent output as accurate output, and a deep suspicion of any tool that tells you what you want to hear.

AI tells you what you want to hear. It does this because it is trained to be helpful, and it has no stake in the outcome. It will generate confident, coherent, well-structured responses to questions it cannot actually answer. It will produce code that looks correct and behaves incorrectly. It will agree with your framing even when your framing is wrong. The faster you build, the less time you have to notice any of this.

The books being published about AI collaboration are almost exclusively written by technologists or academics. They describe capabilities without consequence, opportunity without obligation. The risk perspective is absent. That gap is what this book exists to fill.

This does not make it a pessimistic book. The opportunities that vibe-coding creates are genuine and substantial. But the risks are also real, and they fall most heavily on the people least equipped to anticipate them: the capable, enthusiastic non-programmers who discover they can build almost anything and promptly try to build everything. This book is written for them, and it takes both sides of the ledger seriously.

Writing it, however, required me to understand not just what had gone wrong, but what had actually been happening when things went right.

In the process of writing about how I had built my project, I found myself reaching for a word that did not exist. What I had been doing with my AI assistant was not prompting. It was not a series of isolated requests. It was something else: a sustained dialogue in which context accumulated, complexity emerged, and the outcome was produced not by any single exchange but by the relationship between them.

I coined the term *interloquial* to describe it. Communication between different kinds of intelligence. Distinct from interpersonal communication, which assumes a shared human frame of reference. The word changed how I understood what I had been doing, and that changed what this book needed to be.

A personal lessons-learned document becomes a book worth writing only when the lessons are generalisable. If what I had developed was a distinct and learnable skill — if interloquial communication could be taught and not just practised intuitively — then the audience was not just me. It was every mid-career professional with a tool they cannot afford to commission, every teacher with a lesson they cannot scale, every student with a problem they cannot yet solve, every entrepreneur with an idea they cannot build alone.

The book pivoted. From lesson learned to lesson to teach. And it was built the same way the lesson was learned.

This book was written using the methodology it describes. The structure, the concepts, the editorial direction, and every final decision are mine. Claude drafted, challenged, revised, and flagged. I reviewed, corrected, rejected, and approved. The result is a collaboration in the truest sense: neither of us could have produced this alone.

The method is called vibe-coding. The skill is interloquial communication.

About the Author

Mark C. Turner MSc, BSc, CFIRM is the founder and Managing Director of Emsity Limited, a risk management software consultancy based in Essex, UK.

Originally trained as an artificer in the British Royal Navy, he began his professional career in project planning before recognising, in 2006, that risk management was becoming a discipline in its own right. He created the role of project risk manager for his organisation, obtained professional certification, and moved into internal audit in 2008, building the first corporate enterprise risk management framework in that role. By 2015 he was Head of Enterprise Risk Management. By 2017, Director of Risk. He completed his diploma in risk management, founded Emsity Limited in 2018 as a risk management software consultancy, and was awarded a Fellowship of the Institute of Risk Management in 2020 (the CFIRM designation, the highest level of professional recognition the Institute awards). He subsequently completed his MSc in risk management at Glasgow Caledonian University in 2024. He is also the author of the IRM Digital Ethics Guidelines (2021) and the AI Ethics Addendum: LLMs and Generative AI (2025).

Nearly two decades of professional practice in identifying, measuring, and governing things that can go wrong produces a specific lens. The risk chapters of this book come from someone whose professional identity is precisely that question. They are not cautionary add-ons. They are the point.

Mark's fascination with computers began at eleven, sparked by his first computer in 1982. Software did not become his profession until 2015, when he began building risk management tools in spreadsheets, teaching himself to think in logic, data, and design through necessity. In 2018 he founded Emsity Limited, partnering with a Norwegian software development house to design and build a globally distributed risk management SaaS platform. In 2023, experimenting with ChatGPT on personal projects, he encountered something different: the ability to build complete, working software through conversation alone. The arc from spreadsheet logic to human partnership to AI collaboration shaped his ability to articulate requirements clearly enough that implementing partners, human or machine, can build what he envisions.

He lives in Essex, UK.

Acknowledgements

To Osman Ishaque, my software development partner at Safran Software Solutions, whose patience in teaching me to think in data relationships laid the foundation for everything that followed. Our partnership began in January 2019 and continues to this day.

To Anthropic, for building tools that enable creators to own their work.

To everyone who read early drafts and provided feedback.

To Claude, my AI collaborator on this project. Whether an AI can be meaningfully thanked is a philosophical question this book does not answer. But the collaboration was real, the iteration was constant, and the result would not exist in this form without it.

Contents

A Note on LockedPillar

In September 2025, I began building LockedPillar.

The concept was simple: a memorisation tool for actors, speakers, and presenters, anyone who needs to commit a script to memory under performance conditions. The problem was real. The solution seemed obvious. I started building before I had thought it through.

Over eleven weeks, I generated more than 67,500 lines of code through sustained AI collaboration. The application worked. It handled user accounts, content management, subscription payments, and an AI-powered pipeline that processed scripts into a precise internal format for practice. By any reasonable measure, it was a functioning commercial product: something that would have required a professional development team and six months of work a year earlier.

What I did not fully appreciate at the outset was the nature of what I was attempting. I had been vibe-coding for three years. I had built useful things: tools, automations, systems that solved real problems. But LockedPillar was different in kind, not just in scale. Modern software is the interactivity between many applications, databases, and third-party suppliers, each with its own rules, failure modes, and expectations of the systems it connects to. LockedPillar required Azure Functions, Azure SQL (a cloud database), Azure Key Vault (a secure store for credentials and secrets), and an Azure CDN (a content delivery network for fast global access) working in concert. It required Stripe for payments: not just collecting money, but handling the full event space of failed charges, cancellations, refunds, subscription suspensions, and grace periods. It required an AI-powered processing pipeline built into the product itself, not just used to build it. That was the first time I had integrated AI into a user-facing workflow rather than a development workflow. And it required thinking carefully about two entirely different classes of user: the people paying to use the product, and the operator (me) who needed to administer, monitor, and maintain it from the inside.

None of these were insurmountable. Each, individually, was manageable. The challenge was that I was managing all of them simultaneously, alone, with AI as my only companion on the journey. There was no team to catch the decisions I was not tracking. No colleague to ask whether the architecture made sense. No second pair of eyes on the integration choices. There was only the conversation: me, describing what I needed, and Claude, generating what I described. For eleven weeks I was absorbed almost entirely by the project. I thought about it when I was not working on it. I returned to it at weekends. I held its architecture in my head the way you hold a complex argument, knowing that if I set it down entirely, I would lose the thread. That kind of sustained intensity is sometimes called monomania. It is the condition vibe-coding makes both possible and dangerous: possible because the AI never loses patience, never needs to be briefed from scratch, never tires of the next iteration; dangerous because there is nothing external to check whether the direction you are moving in is the right one.

By the end of those eleven weeks I had built something genuinely complex. I had also accumulated a risk profile that I had not designed, had not fully assessed, and in many cases had not even identified until the build was complete. That was the realisation that made this book necessary: the risks of building alone, at speed, without structured preparation, are real and substantial, and the people most likely to experience them are exactly the people most excited by what the methodology makes possible.

But LockedPillar also accumulated something else over those eleven weeks: a record of every decision made without a framework. Features added because they seemed useful. Architecture choices made mid-build because the original plan hadn't anticipated the question. Third-party integrations selected without fully understanding the failure modes. A scope that expanded in every direction because nothing constrained it.

The decisions themselves were often reasonable. The problem was that they were made reactively, under the pressure of building, without the upfront thinking that would have prevented most of the rework. And because I had no structured record of why each decision was made, only git commits showing what changed and not why, returning to the project after any gap meant reconstructing reasoning from code rather than reading it from a document.

LockedPillar taught me three things.

The hardest part of vibe-coding is knowing what to build. The AI handles the building with remarkable competence. Knowing what to build requires structured thinking before a single prompt is written.

Speed is the methodology's main risk. You can generate fifty architectural decisions in an afternoon. Without a framework for making those decisions deliberately, speed becomes drift. The project drifts from its original intent. The code drifts from the plan. The plan, if it existed at all, drifts into irrelevance.

And not recording your decisions as you go creates a different kind of problem from missing code. The code exists. What is missing is the reasoning behind it. LockedPillar's git history shows what changed at every step. It cannot tell you whether those changes were the right ones, or why they were made at all. When you return to the project a week later, a month later, you are not reading a record of your thinking. You are an archaeologist trying to reconstruct it from the artefacts.

This book is the direct consequence of those eleven weeks. The ICE Framework (Intent, Constraints, Expectations) emerged from asking what I should have done differently before the first line of code was written. The interloquial discipline that runs throughout the book emerged from asking what sustained AI collaboration actually requires from the human in the conversation: the skill that, applied well, is the primary mitigation against the risks that LockedPillar exposed. The risk perspective that runs through the whole book, and anchors Part One in particular, emerged from asking what happens to the people who depend on something you built without adequate preparation.

LockedPillar is the origin story of a working methodology. The project worked. The methodology it produced works better.

You will encounter LockedPillar throughout this book: in the chapter on risks, where its failure modes become the case study; in the chapter on running what you have built, where its commercial architecture is examined without varnish; and in the account of what post-launch operation actually demands. In each case it appears as evidence, not as a success. The evidence is real because the mistakes were real.

Chapter 10 contains the closest thing this book offers to a full LockedPillar retrospective: the platform decisions, the commercial architecture, the costs, and what I would do differently. It is the account a project deserves when the people who come after you need to understand not just what was built but why, and what the building cost.

Part One: The Revolution

CHAPTER 1

The Vibe-Code Revolution

1.1 Introduction

In 1984, I sat at my homework desk typing a program from a magazine into my ZX Spectrum. Line by line, character by character. When I pressed run, it asked me "How many sides?" I entered 3 and a triangle appeared on screen, mathematics becoming lines before my eyes. I was 14 years old, and something shifted. Until that moment, computers had been toys: games to play, distractions to enjoy. Now I saw what they actually were: machines that could turn abstract ideas into tangible outputs.

Then, in 2023, I asked ChatGPT: "Create a Python code that will allow a user to specify the number of sides in a regular polygon, and the code will draw the polygon." Within seconds, it generated a script. I copied it into IDLE and hit run. "How many sides?" it asked. I entered 3. Once again a triangle appeared on screen.

Holy shit.

The same program that changed how I saw computers at 14 had just been recreated in seconds through conversation. Not by copying code from a magazine. Not by learning a programming language. By describing what I wanted in plain language. The barrier between idea and implementation had collapsed. A skill I had been developing since childhood (the ability to articulate what I wanted a computer to do) now had a vastly more capable partner. The tools had transformed; the skill remained constant. This book is about that skill.

1.2 What is Coding?

Before explaining what vibe-coding is, I need to explain what coding itself involves, because most people have only a vague sense of what programmers actually do.

When you use a computer, you interact with software: applications, websites, tools. That software exists because someone wrote instructions telling the computer exactly what to do. Those instructions are code. Code is written in programming languages (Python, JavaScript, HTML, SQL, and hundreds of others), each with its own vocabulary, grammar, and rules.

Learning to code means learning these languages. It means understanding syntax (the precise way instructions must be formatted), logic structures (how to make decisions and repeat actions), data types (the difference between a number, a word, and a list), and debugging (finding and fixing the inevitable errors). A misplaced comma can break an entire program. A forgotten bracket can produce baffling error messages. The computer executes exactly what you write, not what you meant. But modern software development goes further still. Applications rarely exist in isolation: they connect to databases, authenticate users, call external services through APIs, store files in the cloud, and communicate across networks. Building a functional application today means not just writing code in one language, but orchestrating connections between multiple systems, each with its own protocols, authentication requirements, and failure modes. The barrier to creating software has never been higher.

This is why coding has historically been a specialised skill. It is not conceptually difficult (the logic is learnable), but it demands precision, patience, and hundreds of hours of practice before you can build anything useful. Most professionals, however intelligent, have neither the time nor the inclination to acquire this skill. They have domain expertise in medicine, law, education, finance, or a thousand other fields. Learning JavaScript is not a good use of their time. And so, for decades, a barrier existed: if you wanted custom software, you either learned to code or you paid someone who had.

That barrier has been substantially lowered, at least for creating functional software. Deploying it safely, maintaining it over time, and scaling it to demanding requirements involves barriers that have not been removed, only reordered. Part three addresses that directly.

Today, you can describe what you want in plain English, and AI will generate the code. Not a summary. Not an explanation. Actual, functional code in whatever programming language the task requires, code you can run, test, and deploy. The AI handles the syntax, the logic structures, the precise formatting, the API integrations, and the authentication flows. You provide the intent.

This is not the same as asking ChatGPT a question and receiving an answer. When you ask "What is the capital of France?" you get information. When you ask "Write me a Python function that calculates compound interest," you get code: a small, self-contained snippet you can copy and use. The distinction matters: one is retrieval, the other is creation. But there is a further distinction that matters even more.

A single prompt can produce a function, a script, even a simple webpage. This is sometimes called *prompt engineering*: crafting a request carefully enough that a single exchange produces the output you need. It works for bounded, well-defined tasks. But it does not work for building complex software: applications with user interfaces, databases, authentication, error handling, and dozens of interconnected components. That requires something different: sustained dialogue over hours, days, or weeks, where each exchange builds on the last, where requirements emerge through conversation, where you test, refine, and iterate until the system does what you need. The practice of creating software through this kind of extended AI collaboration has a name: vibe-coding. The next section explains where the term came from and what it actually means.

1.3 What is Vibe-Coding?

In February 2025, Andrej Karpathy, former director of AI at Tesla and co-founder of OpenAI, tweeted a phrase that would define a new era of software creation: "vibe coding."[1] He described a way of building software where you "fully give in to the vibes, embrace exponentials, and forget that the code even exists." His subsequent posts were even more explicit: "I 'Accept All' always, I don't read the diffs anymore."[2] In plain terms: he accepts every change the AI suggests without checking what it altered.

The term captured something developers were already experiencing. Within weeks, it spread across tech circles. By March 2025, Merriam-Webster had added it to its coverage of emerging vocabulary.[3] Collins Dictionary named it their Word of the Year for 2025.[4] But as the phrase spread, its meaning became muddled. Some used it to describe any AI-assisted programming. Others dismissed it as reckless hacking. This book reclaims the original intent and extends it: vibe-coding is the practice of creating software by articulating what you want rather than specifying how to build it. It represents a fundamental shift in who can create software and how.

But the term also sparked debate. Karpathy's original framing emphasised minimal oversight — accepting code without review. To be clear: this approach is not responsible practice for production systems. "Mostly works" is insufficient for software that handles user data or payments. Critics pushed back. AI researcher Andrew Ng argued that guiding AI to write useful software "is a deeply intellectual exercise" requiring, in his view, constant oversight: reviewing outputs, catching subtle errors, making architectural decisions.[5] Without discipline, the risks multiply: security vulnerabilities, unmaintainable code, systems that work until they catastrophically do not.

Here is my resolution: both perspectives capture something real. Karpathy identified the experience of flow when AI collaboration works — you describe what you want, it appears, you refine, it improves. That *is* a vibe. Ng identified the risk: "vibes" without discipline produces unreliable results. The term stuck because it describes a genuine phenomenon; the critique explains why it fails for most people.

What makes the difference? A learnable skill: the ability to articulate intent, constraints, and expectations with enough precision that AI collaboration produces reliable results. Developing this skill is what separates successful vibe-coders from frustrated prompters. The clearer your descriptions, the more reliable your results, though even skilled communicators encounter tasks that resist articulation. Chapter 2 provides concrete frameworks for measuring and developing this ability.

This is not an assertion: it is measurable. Anthropic's analysis of one million Claude conversations, published in March 2026, found that users who had been on the platform for six months or more achieved success rates several percentage points higher than newer users, even after controlling for task type, model used, and geography.[10] Prompts became more sophisticated over time, and experienced users were more likely to apply AI to genuine work rather than routine tasks. The skill develops with practice. The gap between a new user and an experienced one is not access to better tools. Both use the same tools. The gap is interloquial skill.

Vibe-coding differs fundamentally from traditional "low-code" or "no-code" development platforms. Those approaches constrain you to pre-built templates and drag-and-drop interfaces. Vibe-coding produces actual, custom code: HTML, CSS, JavaScript, Python, SQL, whatever the project requires. The difference is that you are not writing that code character by character. You are specifying what it should accomplish, and AI is generating the implementation. By the time you reach Chapter 10, you will have enough experience to evaluate the full spectrum of platform options, from tools that give you complete ownership to platforms that handle all the infrastructure for you.

The distinction matters in another way: vibe-coding is not one-shot prompting. A single prompt, however cleverly constructed, rarely produces complex, working systems. What created my commercial applications was not one prompt but thousands of exchanges over weeks: a sustained dialogue grounded in a clear plan, where each response informed the next request and misunderstandings were caught early because the destination was defined before the journey began. The "prompt hub" templates that circulate online work for standardised outputs: marketing copy, financial reports, lesson plans. They do not work for building something that has never existed before. That requires conversation, not prompting. Vibe-coding builds towards something over time; each exchange extends what came before it.

The distinction goes deeper than duration. Vibe-coding builds tools that keep producing answers long after the conversation ends. When you ask AI to "write a marketing email," you receive an email. When you vibe-code a marketing system, you receive infrastructure that generates emails matching your brand voice, audience segments, and campaign goals. The difference is what you are building: outputs versus capabilities. This is why the practice deserves its own name. Prompting optimises individual requests. Vibe-coding constructs machinery. But the distinction is about accumulated context: each iteration builds on the last, preserving understanding that no single prompt could recreate. Whether the machinery keeps producing or serves a single complex purpose, the method is the same: plan deeply, then iterate against that plan.

This applies even when the code runs once and is discarded. Imagine you need to analyse sensitive business data that cannot be shared with AI – perhaps client information, financial projections, or competitive intelligence. You need answers, but you also need to understand exactly how those answers were reached. So instead of asking AI to analyse your data, you ask AI to *build code* that will analyse your data. You describe your data structure, explain what questions you need answered, and AI generates scripts you can run locally against the actual numbers. The answers are grounded in your real data, not AI's training. AI confabulation of facts is structurally prevented: the outputs come from computation against your actual numbers, not from inference about what the answer might be. However, the generated code itself must be verified – it may contain bugs, incorrect statistical assumptions, or flawed implementations of algorithms that produce wrong answers without flagging themselves as wrong. The black box is not eliminated; it is repositioned from "AI's opinion" to "code you can read and check." You can examine every line to understand the mechanism, even if you could not have written it yourself. This "query-building" paradigm, asking AI to generate code that answers questions rather than asking AI to answer directly, represents vibe-coding applied to data analysis: the same sustained dialogue, the same accumulated understanding across iterations, the same method of building the means to answer rather than requesting answers.

Although vibe-coding emerged from software development, the underlying skill appears to extend far beyond code. The core elements (articulating intent, setting constraints, defining expectations, and refining through sustained dialogue) apply wherever AI can generate output: writing, visual design, research, education, and other domains. My direct experience is in software and writing; the principles appear to translate, though domain-specific adaptation is always required. This book itself was vibe-coded. The same conversational arc that produced a commercial SaaS product also produced these pages: hundreds of exchanges over months: each chapter planned before it was drafted, then refined through iteration; the tools for referencing, indexing, and copy editing built through the same vibe-coding process as any other project. Whether this book proves the method works is something readers will judge for themselves. I am not a neutral evaluator of my own work. What I can say is that the medium differs; the method felt constant.

Yet none of this (not the tool-building, not the query-building, not the transfer across domains) is simply "using AI tools." Everyone with access to ChatGPT or Claude has the same tools available. Yet most people find themselves frustrated, producing broken code they cannot debug, or generating solutions that do not quite match what they envisioned. The tools alone do not create success. Something else is required. That something is the real subject of this book. Not coding. Not technical knowledge. Something else entirely, something that existed long before AI but that AI has made visible and urgent.

Figure 1.1: Vibe-coding Across Domains — The same core competency applies wherever AI can create, from code to prose to visual design.

1.4 How Vibe-Coding Works

Vibe-coding is a conversation rather than a command, and it begins with a plan rather than a guess. You arrive with a problem, and the planning conversation with AI is how the specification gets built: surfacing intent, constraints, and expectations before a single line of code is written. The AI challenges your assumptions, identifies edge cases you had not considered, and forces decisions you would otherwise defer until they became bugs. A plan produced through dialogue is more reliable than one produced in isolation, because the AI sees things a single mind misses. Many AI systems now formalise this with a dedicated planning mode that separates the design conversation from the implementation conversation. Once the plan is solid, implementation begins: you describe, the AI produces, you test and refine, the AI adjusts, always iterating against the plan rather than drifting from it. The "vibe" in vibe-coding refers to the fluency of this process when it works well. What keeps it on track is not instinct but the clarity established before the first line of code was written.

In practice, I start by describing the problem space: what is wrong, what I wish were different, what I have tried. The AI suggests directions and surfaces constraints I had not considered. Once we agree on a direction, I ask for a plan, then challenge it. What could go wrong? What are we assuming? What have we not considered? The plan iterates through this questioning until it holds up. Only then does implementation begin.

Implementation flows, but planning never stops. When something needs to change (a feature does not work as expected, a new requirement emerges, or testing reveals a gap), I do not simply ask for a fix. I return to intent. What am I actually trying to achieve here? I ask for a plan to address this specific change, then challenge that plan before it is implemented. The structure is recursive: plans within plans. The overall project has a plan; each major feature has its own plan; each change to a feature has its own plan. At every level, the same pattern applies: articulate intent, challenge assumptions, iterate the plan, then implement. Testing happens incrementally, with tight feedback loops after each section. Did it work? What broke? What surprised me? That convergence (when what exists matches what I envisioned) signals completion at that level, and the process continues at the next.

This is the two-way nature of effective AI collaboration. You express your requirements, but you also interpret responses. You provide context, but you also recognise when your collaborator needs more information. You set constraints, but you also listen when those constraints conflict or when better approaches exist. And sometimes the roles reverse entirely: the AI provides instructions that you must execute: configuring a service, clicking through an interface, copying a file to a specific location. The AI can generate the code, but it cannot deploy it to your server. It can write the configuration, but it cannot access your cloud dashboard. In these moments, you become the implementer following the AI's guidance, and your skill shifts from articulation to interpretation: understanding what the instruction means, recognising when something looks wrong, knowing when to pause and ask for clarification. The initial instruction is rarely sufficient; what matters is the conversation that follows.

Consider what I did wrong when building LockedPillar, a speech memorisation application I developed in late 2025. I started with a planning conversation, but it was the wrong kind. I asked narrow questions about specific features: how should the application handle recognition errors, should progress persist across devices, what happens with limited connectivity. Each question got a useful answer. What I did not do was step back and ask what the application actually needed to be as a whole.

The result was that I built the user-facing experience first and thoroughly, then discovered late in the project that a commercial application also needs an operator layer: account management, subscription administration, monitoring, the ability to intervene when something goes wrong. I had not considered it at the outset because I had not asked. That work turned out to be substantial, and it arrived as rework rather than as planned scope. The implementation took far longer than it should have, not because the AI was slow, but because my planning had been shallow. I was asking the AI to solve problems I had already defined rather than asking it to help me discover what I had not yet defined. That distinction is what this book is about. The methodology that came out of LockedPillar (the one described in Chapter 2) emerged directly from asking what I should have done differently before the first line of code was written.

The iteration cycle is remarkably fast. In my experience, iteration cycles that took days with human developers often compress to minutes with AI, though this varies significantly by task complexity and requirement clarity. Describe a requirement. Receive implementation in seconds. Test it. Refine your description. Receive a revised implementation. The entire conversation can happen in a single session. This speed is not just convenience; it fundamentally changes what is possible. You can stress-test a plan more thoroughly because each test costs minutes instead of weeks, and the plan you arrive at is better for it.

But speed also reveals the bottleneck. When iteration is fast, the constraining factor becomes how precisely you can articulate the gap between what you expected and what you received. The AI can generate output in seconds. Can you identify exactly where it deviates from your intent? Saying "this isn't right" is easy; saying "the report is grouping sales by region but we agreed in the plan it should group by account manager, because that is how targets are measured" is the skill that makes iteration productive, and it is only possible if you planned deeply enough to know what correct looks like. This articulation of expectation delta is as important as the initial requirement. You must know what "right" looks like well enough to recognise deviation, and you must be able to describe that deviation precisely enough for your AI partner to correct it. This is why precise communication has become more valuable than technical ability. The tools removed the implementation bottleneck. Communication clarity, both in setting requirements and in diagnosing gaps, is what remains.

1.5 Why It Matters Now

In 2024-2025, several things had to become true at once for vibe-coding to be viable, and they did. Large language models became capable enough to write functional, coherent code across multiple programming languages — not toy examples but production-quality software. Interfaces emerged that made these models accessible without technical expertise: browser-based tools, conversational environments, and integrated development environments that hide complexity behind natural language. And a generation of knowledge workers reached a breaking point. They had ideas for software that would solve real problems in their work, but no way to build it themselves and no budget to hire developers. Marketing managers who wanted custom analytics dashboards. Teachers who needed student simulations. Small business owners who imagined workflow automation. For decades, these ideas remained trapped: too small for professional development, too complex for spreadsheets. Vibe-coding unlocked them.

But why now specifically? Why not five years ago, or five years hence?

The answer lies in what economists call an inflection point. For decades, AI could not write code that actually worked. Then it could write simple snippets. Then functions. Then entire applications. In 2024-2025, we crossed a threshold: someone with no programming knowledge could describe a complete application in plain language and receive working software in response. Not perfect software. Not always correct on the first attempt. But working software that could be refined through conversation.

This matters because it inverts the traditional hierarchy of software creation. Previously, if you wanted custom software, you needed either programming skills or money to hire someone who had them. Domain expertise, deep knowledge of your industry, your users, your specific problems, counted for nothing at the implementation stage. You could understand exactly what software you needed and still be unable to create it.

Vibe-coding substantially lowers that barrier. If you understand your problem deeply, you can now translate that understanding into working software without learning to code. The implementation barrier (syntax, programming languages, API integrations) has largely been removed. What remains is the deployment barrier: running software safely, securely, and responsibly still requires judgement and, in some contexts, professional expertise. Chapter 3 addresses that without flinching. But the ability to create, which was previously gated entirely by technical skill, is now accessible to anyone who can articulate what they want. And that ability is something you have been developing your entire professional life, every time you wrote a requirements document, explained a process to a colleague, or specified what you needed from a vendor.

Articulation ability is now more valuable than coding ability. People with strong communication skills, domain expertise, and the ability to specify requirements precisely can build commercial-grade software without learning programming languages. The skills you developed as a business professional (understanding users, specifying requirements, knowing what "done" looks like) transfer directly.

Consider the accumulated ideas that have languished for decades in the minds of domain experts. The teacher who imagined an interactive lesson but could not build it. The nurse who saw a workflow inefficiency but had no way to automate it. The small business owner who needed custom tracking but could not afford development. Each was potential value trapped behind a technical barrier. That barrier has fallen.

Vibe-coding carries real risks: security vulnerabilities in generated code, over-reliance on AI judgement, accountability for systems you deploy but may not fully understand, and software that "mostly works" until it fails in ways you cannot diagnose. Chapter 3 provides a comprehensive risk framework. But the fundamental shift is real. The question is no longer whether non-programmers can build software. It is whether they will develop the communication skills to do it well, and the awareness to do it safely.

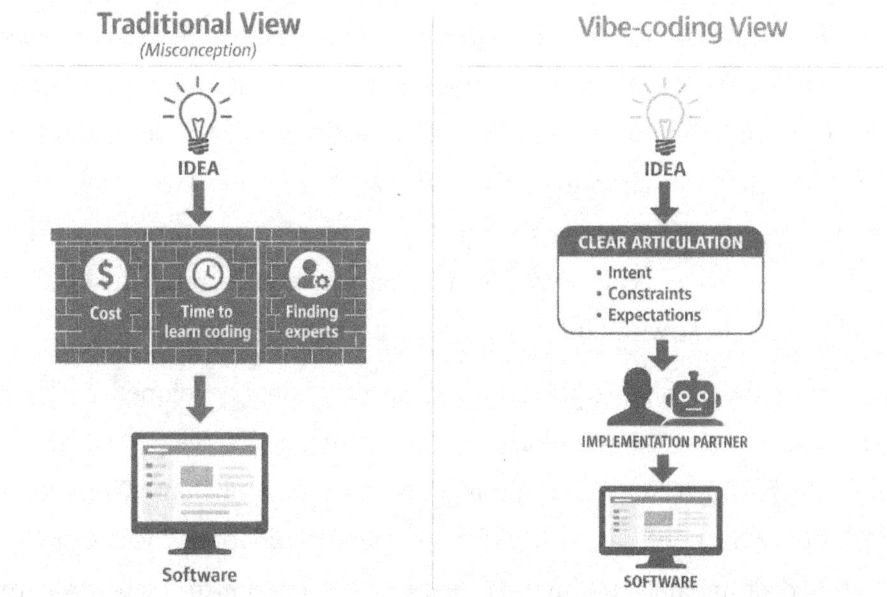

Figure 1.2: The Articulation Bottleneck — Traditional thinking assumes coding skill is the barrier. The vibe-code reality reveals that clear articulation is the true constraint.

1.6 Whom This Book Is For

This book is for anyone with domain expertise and a clear problem they want to solve. No coding background is required. What unites its core audience is articulation ability: you understand your problem space deeply, and you can describe what you need clearly. What you lack is coding knowledge, and this book argues that you no longer need it.

There is also an outer circle. If you work in a technical-adjacent role (business analysis, product management, project delivery, data work) and want to build more sophisticated tools than the browser alone can produce, the later chapters will meet you there. Part Two progresses from single-session browser projects to tools that use version control and connect to external services. That range is deliberate: the book is designed to grow with you, not to assume a fixed starting point.

However, this book is explicitly *not* for professional developers seeking to accelerate their existing workflow. Excellent books serve that audience, including Addy Osmani's *Beyond Vibe Coding*[6] and Gene Kim's *Vibe Coding*.[7] This book serves a different reader: someone who has never written code and does not intend to learn, but who wants to create software nonetheless.

Business professionals with software ideas. You have spent years understanding your industry. You see inefficiencies that custom software could solve. You have imagined tools that would make your work easier but never had the means to build them. This book teaches you to translate that domain knowledge into working applications.

Entrepreneurs without technical co-founders. You have a product idea but no way to prototype it. Traditional development would cost tens of thousands of pounds and months of time. You want to build a minimum viable product to test your concept before investing heavily. This book shows you how.

Early-career professionals seeking differentiation. You are smart, ambitious, and surrounded by colleagues who seem to speak a technical language you do not. You have noticed that the people who get promoted are often the ones who can build things — the analyst who automated the weekly report, the associate who created a client tracking tool. You want to be that person, but "learning to code" feels like a mountain you do not have time to climb. This book offers another path: the ability to build without becoming a developer.

Educators and trainers. You want custom teaching tools for your students but are constrained by whatever off-the-shelf platforms happen to exist. You imagine simulations, quizzes, and exercises tailored precisely to your curriculum. This book enables you to create them.

Knowledge workers seeking automation. Your work involves repetitive tasks that software could handle. You have tried no-code tools but found them limiting. You want custom solutions but cannot justify the expense of professional development for internal tools. This book provides another option.

The curious and the cautious. You have heard about AI-assisted development and want to understand what it actually involves. You may be sceptical (reasonably so, given the hype) and want a clear-eyed assessment of capabilities and limitations from someone who has used these tools extensively. This book offers that perspective.

Managers and team leaders. You are not necessarily going to build things yourself — you have a team for that. But you want to understand what is possible so you can direct that team more effectively, identify where AI collaboration would create the most value, and develop your own capability alongside theirs. This book serves you at both levels: as a practitioner learning a new skill, and as a leader learning to recognise and develop it in others.

What you need to succeed with this book is not technical background. It is the willingness to articulate your requirements precisely and the patience to iterate when the first attempt does not match your vision. If you can describe what you want clearly, you can vibe-code. The communication skills you already have are what matter.

One important clarification: this book will not teach you to become a programmer. If you complete every chapter and build every project, you will still not pass a software engineering assessment or diagnose why a system fails under load. What you will have is the ability to build working software through conversation with AI. You will understand enough about how code works to verify that implementations behave as intended in your test cases, though security review, edge case analysis, and production readiness assessment may require professional evaluation. You will know when something is broken and how to describe the problem so AI can fix it. But the deep technical knowledge that defines a programmer will remain outside your skillset, and that is entirely fine. The goal is not to become a developer. It is to become someone who can create software without being one.

A final warning: this book teaches you to build software, not to deploy it safely in every context. If your project handles payments, stores sensitive data, or operates in regulated industries (healthcare, finance, education), you should consult appropriate professionals (security engineers, lawyers, compliance specialists) before deployment. Payments require specific security controls. Personal data is subject to privacy regulations that vary by jurisdiction. Professional advice applications (legal, medical, financial) may be subject to regulatory requirements that prohibit software not reviewed by qualified professionals. The specific regulations differ by country and industry, but the principle is universal: responsibility for vibe-coded software rests with you, its creator. AI provides the implementation, but you choose what to build and deploy. This responsibility cannot be delegated to the AI. Vibe-coding skill accelerates creation; it does not eliminate the need for professional review when the stakes are high.

1.7 Key Takeaways

- **Vibe-coding defined:** Creating by articulating what you want, not how to build it: software, prose, visuals, or any domain where AI can generate output.
- **The real bottleneck:** Communication clarity, not coding skill, determines success with AI tools.
- **The skill that matters:** Specifying intent, constraints, and expectations precisely enough that AI collaboration produces reliable results, a learnable ability explored in Chapter 2.
- **Query-building paradigm:** Asking AI to build code that answers questions, rather than asking AI to answer directly, prevents AI confabulation and grounds outputs in your actual data. The code itself still requires verification, but the specific failure mode of AI inventing facts is removed.
- **Risk and return:** This book examines vibe-coding through the lens of what can go wrong, because understanding risks is the foundation for managing them.
- **Beyond the code:** Building software is one thing; deploying it, supporting it, and running it as a business require entirely different considerations.

Notes

1 Karpathy, A. (2025). "Vibe coding" tweet introducing the term and methodology, February 2025. Includes: "fully give in to the vibes, embrace exponentials, and forget that the code even exists" and "I 'Accept All' always, I don't read the diffs anymore." `x.com/karpathy/status/1886192184808149383`

2 [See reference 1 — both citations refer to the same tweet.]

3 Merriam-Webster (2025). "Vibe coding" featured as trending term, March 2025. merriam-webster.com

4 Collins Dictionary (2025). "Vibe coding" named Word of the Year 2025. `collinsdictionary.com/dictionary/english/vibe-coding`

5 Ng, A. (2025). Comments at LangChain Interrupt conference, May 2025. "It's unfortunate that that's called vibe coding... It's misleading a lot of people into thinking, just go with the vibes." `langchain.com/interrupt`

10 Anthropic (2026). *Anthropic Economic Index Report: Learning Curves*. Anthropic, March 2026. Analysis of one million Claude conversations examining task success rates, usage patterns, and the relationship between platform tenure and performance outcomes. `anthropic.com/research/economic-index-march-2026-report`

6 Osmani, A. (2025). *Beyond Vibe Coding: Leveraging Your Experience in the Age of AI-Assisted Coding*. O'Reilly Media. ISBN: 9798341634756.

7 Kim, G. & Yegge, S. (2025). *Vibe Coding: Building Production-Grade Software With GenAI, Chat, Agents, and Beyond*. IT Revolution. ISBN: 978-1966280026. `itrevolution.com/product/vibe-coding-book/`

CHAPTER 2

Interloquial Communication

2.1 Introduction

I was trying to write a sentence about what I did every day. “I work with Claude” felt wrong, because Claude is not a colleague. “I use Claude” felt wrong, because use implies a tool, and this was more collaborative than that. “I prompt Claude” felt wrong, because prompting is one-way and what I was doing felt like dialogue. I sat at my desk genuinely stuck on a word. What *was* this thing I was doing for hours every day?

The irony is that I asked Claude.

“I’m struggling to describe the communication that happens between a human and an AI,” I typed. “It’s not interpersonal because you’re not a person. It’s not just prompting because it’s a dialogue. What would you call it?” Claude offered several suggestions. Top of the list: *interloquial*, meaning to speak across a boundary.

The word felt exactly right. The irony that the term was generated by the very system it describes is, if anything, the most apt possible origin for it. “Prompting” implies a command executor; “interloquial” implies a dialogue partner: communication that is bidirectional and iterative rather than one-shot instruction. Whether I coined it or rediscovered it matters less than what it names: treating the exchange as dialogue produces better outcomes than treating it as instruction. This chapter provides the vocabulary to describe it: what interloquial communication is, how it differs from both prompting and interpersonal exchange, and what dimensions of skill it involves.

A note on the vocabulary itself. This chapter uses relational language throughout ("dialogue," "partner," "both sides of the exchange"), and that language carries a risk worth naming upfront. I did not set out to form a relationship with an AI. I set out to build things. The vocabulary emerged from practice: the words available for communication are interpersonal, because those are the words we have. Using them for an interloquial exchange is a convenience, not a claim. Throughout this chapter, when the language implies shared experience or mutual understanding, read it as functional description rather than phenomenological claim. The AI processes and responds in ways that *function* like dialogue. Whether anything resembling dialogue is occurring on the machine side of the exchange is a question this book cannot resolve — and does not need to. What it can establish is that treating the exchange *as if* it were dialogue produces better outcomes than treating it as instruction. That is sufficient justification for the language, provided we do not mistake the metaphor for the reality.

2.2 Naming the Phenomenon

When we speak with another human, we call it interpersonal communication: a field studied for decades, with established frameworks, validated theories, and recognised dimensions including power dynamics, emotional intelligence, and cultural context. But what do we call the communication that happens between a human and an artificial intelligence? This book proposes a term: *interloquial*, from the Latin *inter* (between) and *loqui* (to speak). Interloquial communication is speaking across the boundary between human cognition and machine processing. I use "intelligence" pragmatically here, without taking a position on whether large language models (LLMs) possess genuine understanding or merely simulate it. The communication dynamics described in this chapter apply regardless of how that philosophical question is ultimately resolved. Interloquial communication is not merely "prompting" or "chatting with AI." It is a distinct form of communication with its own dynamics, risks, and skills.

A brief search suggested the term was not in common use, though I cannot claim with certainty to have coined it. The irony that the definition of interloquial was itself produced interloquially is either a beautiful demonstration of the concept or a circular argument, depending on your perspective. I offer it as a working definition to be refined through practice, not as an authoritative pronouncement.

I asked Perplexity to research the word further, to flesh it out. Through that research, we arrived at a working definition: *interloquial skills are the capacity to exchange intent, context, and understanding across the boundary between human and machine.*

I was genuinely stunned that this was a new word. The experience of communicating with AI felt so familiar, so clearly *something*, that I assumed someone must have named it already. Adjacent fields (biosemiotics, zoosemiotics, xenolinguistics) all study communication across boundaries, but they share a common limitation: the entities involved do not speak the same language. Bees dance. Dolphins click. In interloquial communication, something singular happens: both parties use the same language. I type English; the AI responds in English. We are not interpreting signals or decoding patterns. We are speaking. And being spoken to.

But here is where the analogy strains: I will only ever know one half of this exchange. It is tempting to describe this as "two thinkers in conversation," but that phrase smuggles in an assumption I cannot justify. Is the AI thinking? The honest answer is: I do not know. The AI processes, generates, and responds in ways that function like thought, but I cannot peer behind the outputs to verify that anything resembling cognition occurs. The interloquial barrier is not just practical but epistemological: I cannot even know whether there are internal states worth accessing. We may be two thinkers in dialogue, or I may be one thinker in dialogue with an extraordinarily sophisticated mirror. The uncertainty is irreducible. The tendency to attribute mental states to AI (to infer that it understands, intends, or cares) is well documented. Research finds that users routinely attribute blame, emotions, and intentions to AI systems, even when they consciously know better.[20] Crucially, this tendency is not accidental. Anthropomorphism in dialogue systems is designed in through conscious and unconscious choices: namegiving, conversational tone, the simulation of uncertainty. The attribution of mental states is an intended feature, not a user error.[29] The interloquial framework does not resolve this tendency; it acknowledges it and works around it.

This asymmetry defines interloquial communication. In interpersonal communication, we assume (rightly or wrongly) that we can eventually achieve mutual understanding: that with enough empathy, we can see the world from another person's perspective. In interloquial communication, that assumption does not hold. The AI's processing (whatever its nature) is fundamentally opaque to human introspection. We can observe outputs. We can infer patterns. But we cannot cross the barrier and experience what is happening on the other side. This makes interloquial communication *functionally* two-way (both parties contribute to the exchange) without claiming it is *phenomenologically* two-way, which would require both parties to experience the exchange. This distinction has a corollary worth naming: the utility of the exchange is real, but it should not be mistaken for depth. As one observer puts it, the human-AI intersection is "not a merge or a duet" but "a momentary contact between a mathematical surface and an embodied mind."[31]

This is why interloquial skill is about observable outcomes, not internal states. You cannot know what happens inside the AI, or whether anything meaningful happens at all. You can only know what it produces. Success is measured by whether the output matches your intent, not by whether you achieved "understanding" with your AI partner. The communication worked if the output works, whether that output is code, prose, or visual design. The relationship (if that word even applies) is defined by results, not by rapport. Research into AI communication in co-creative contexts reinforces this point: systematic review of over a hundred studies finds that effective human-AI co-creation depends on shared understanding of *task outcomes*, not on the quality of the relational exchange.[19]

This observation points to a useful term: *functional correspondence*. When the AI produces output that matches your intent, functional correspondence has been achieved. The term describes an observable state without making claims about cognition, understanding, or anything happening inside the system. It allows you to say "we achieved functional correspondence on the data model" without asserting that the AI *understood* the data model in any philosophically loaded sense. Throughout this book, relational language ("partner," "both parties," "dialogue") is used as shorthand for the collaborative texture of the exchange. Where precision matters, functional correspondence is the intended meaning: the AI's output corresponds to your intent. That is the target, and it is sufficient.

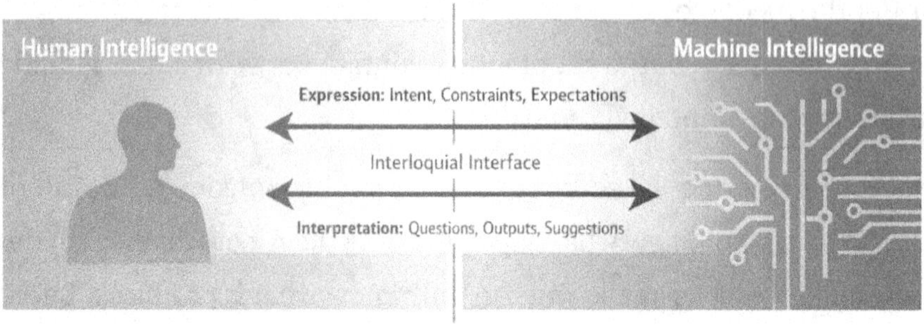

Figure 2.1: The Interloquial Boundary — communication flows both directions across the interface between human and machine intelligence. Expression carries your requirements outward; interpretation brings understanding back.

2.3 Why It's Distinct from Prompting

"Prompting" suggests one-way instruction: you write a prompt, the AI responds. The word implies that your role is to craft the perfect input, and the AI's role is to execute. But effective interloquial communication is not one-way. It is dialogue. You express requirements. The AI interprets them. The AI asks clarifying questions. You refine your thinking. The AI suggests approaches you had not considered. You accept, reject, or modify. Meaning emerges through this exchange.

"Prompt engineering" captures only half of the skill. It focuses on expression (how you formulate requests) while ignoring interpretation (how you understand responses). A brilliant prompt followed by poor interpretation of the response produces poor results. Interloquial competence requires both directions: human-to-machine expression and machine-to-human interpretation.

Consider how differently the same request can unfold. With prompting: "Build me a user authentication system." The AI generates code. You test it. It does not work as expected. You write another prompt. More code. Still not right. The prompts grow longer, trying to anticipate every edge case; the process becomes wrestling with a stubborn tool. Research confirms this pattern: when AI systems fail to identify user objectives correctly, users systematically simplify their language in response, reducing complexity to get any result rather than expressing what they actually need.[18]

With interloquial communication: "I need users to be able to log in. Before you start, what questions do you have about my requirements?" The AI asks about password policies, session handling, multi-device support, security constraints. Each question surfaces something you had not fully specified. Your vague intention crystallises into a clear specification through dialogue. By the time implementation begins, both parties understand what success looks like.

The reversal in the second approach (asking the AI to question *you*) changes everything. This framing is pragmatic, not ontological. The AI does not "need" information in the way a human collaborator does. But treating it as if it did, asking clarifying questions and providing context, produces better outcomes than treating it as a simple command executor. It acknowledges that specification is hard, that you may not have articulated everything upfront, and that a plan built through structured dialogue is more complete than one written in isolation.

"Specification writing" is another inadequate term. It implies documentation produced in isolation: you write the spec, hand it off, wait for implementation. Interloquial communication compresses this into live conversation, but the sequence remains the same: plan first, then build. The difference is that the plan is interrogated and challenged through dialogue before implementation begins, producing something more complete than any solo effort could. You build the plan through conversation, not alongside the code.

This is what "interloquial" names: prompting that treats the exchange as dialogue rather than instruction. The term adds something specific over "prompting" or "AI interaction": it insists on the two-directional, iterative nature of effective human-AI communication. You express; the AI responds and questions. The AI suggests; you accept, reject, or redirect. Meaning compounds through exchange. Neither "prompting" nor "specification writing" nor "AI chatting" captures this. Interloquial does. And it is the dimension of practice that makes the difference between AI collaboration that works and AI collaboration that frustrates.

2.4 Parallel to Interpersonal Communication

If interpersonal skills help us connect emotionally with other people, and intercultural skills help us navigate differences in cultural context, then interloquial skills help us communicate across domains of intelligence: between human intuition and computational logic. The parallel is not metaphorical. The same communication principles apply: precision, context-setting, active listening, iterative refinement. The difference is that the AI processes language differently from a human interlocutor. It lacks the unstated assumptions that come from shared cultural context. It cannot read tone of voice or infer meaning from body language. It does not carry memory of your previous conversations unless you provide that context explicitly. You must be explicit in ways you might not need to be with human collaborators, but the underlying skill is the same: communicating precisely enough that understanding aligns across the boundary between minds.

Yet here is where the parallel breaks down. Interpersonal communication theory is built around humans as emotional agents. Emotion is not noise; it is constitutive. Empathy and relational trust are central to effectiveness; success includes whether both parties felt understood. Interloquial communication operates on different assumptions. The goal is constraint satisfaction, not relational warmth. Success is measured by accuracy and logical coherence, not by how the interaction felt. Emotion, rather than a resource to cultivate, becomes a potential confounder to manage. When I specify requirements to an AI partner, I am not building rapport. I am achieving precise alignment between my intent and the implementation. The practical implication: in interpersonal communication, emotional attunement typically improves outcomes; in interloquial communication, emotional content can *decrease* quality. Frustration bleeds into imprecise language. Impatience shortcuts necessary constraint specification. The interloquial practitioner learns to bracket emotion: not suppress it, but recognise when feelings are interfering with precision.

	Interpersonal	**Interloquial**
Primary aim	Mutual understanding *and* relational outcomes	Accuracy and constraint satisfaction
Role of emotion	Central resource; empathy builds connection	Potential confounder; bracket for precision
Success metric	Trust, rapport, relationship quality	Logical coherence, predictability, correctness
View of feelings	Rich information and bond-building mechanism	Interference to be recognised and managed

Table 2.1: Interpersonal vs. Interloquial Communication — different aims require different approaches

Interloquial practice is not "cold interpersonal communication." It is a different mode entirely, with different evaluative criteria and different skills to develop. The interloquial practitioner cultivates precision where the interpersonal practitioner cultivates warmth. Both are valuable. Both are learnable. But they are not the same skill applied in different contexts. Understanding this distinction helps explain why some people struggle with AI collaboration despite strong interpersonal skills. The habits that make someone a warm, empathetic communicator (reading emotional subtext, prioritising relationship over task, adapting tone to build rapport) do not transfer directly. AI partners do not reward warmth. They reward precision. This distinction has practical backing: a systematic review of interaction patterns in AI-assisted decision-making concluded that human-AI collaboration is "not very collaborative yet": current systems optimise for algorithmic output rather than the bridging of human expectations and machine suggestions.[21] The interloquial framework addresses precisely this gap.

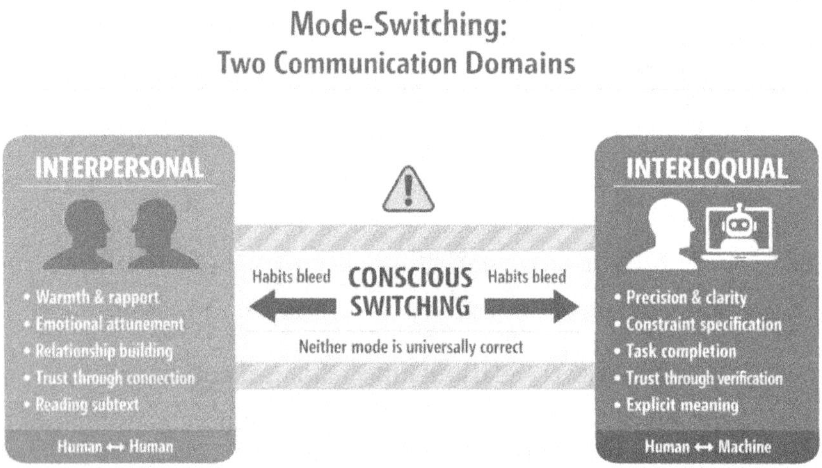

Figure 2.2: Mode-Switching Between Communication Domains — interpersonal skills (left) serve human relationships through warmth; interloquial skills (right) serve AI collaboration through precision. The central warning zone highlights the risk of habits bleeding across domains.

The reverse concern is equally real: interloquial habits bleeding into interpersonal communication. I have caught myself writing emails to human collaborators in the same terse, specification-heavy style I use with Claude: efficient but cold. If you spend hours daily in interloquial mode and then switch to human conversation, the interpersonal warmth that builds trust and rapport can atrophy if you do not consciously maintain it. The solution is conscious mode-switching. Interloquial precision serves AI collaboration. Interpersonal warmth serves human relationships. Neither is universally correct. The skilled practitioner recognises which mode the situation requires and shifts accordingly.

2.5 Dimensions of Interloquial Communication

Interloquial communication has several dimensions, each revealing different aspects of the skill.

Expression and Interpretation

Every interloquial exchange has two directions. **Expression** is how you formulate your intent, constraints, and expectations for the AI to receive. **Interpretation** is how you understand the AI's responses: recognising when it has misunderstood, when its suggestions improve on your original vision, when its outputs require refinement. Most attention goes to expression ("How do I write better prompts?") but interpretation is equally important. Can you recognise when AI-generated output has subtle flaws: bugs in code, factual errors in prose, compositional problems in visuals? Can you identify when the AI has made a structural choice you would not have made? Can you distinguish between "this is wrong" and "this is different from what I expected but possibly better"? Skilled interpretation often means asking follow-up questions: "Why did you structure it this way?" "What are the trade-offs of this approach?" "What would break if we changed X?" These questions improve your understanding of the AI's output and often reveal assumptions you had not made explicit.

Precision and Context

Precision is the degree of specificity in your communication. "Make a button" is low precision. "Create a 44x44 pixel button with rounded corners, accessible focus states, and an aria-label of 'Submit form' " is high precision. Different situations require different levels. Context, by contrast, is the background information that helps the AI interpret your request correctly. "This is for a mobile app aimed at elderly users" is context that should influence implementation decisions even if not explicitly specified in every request. The skill is knowing when to be precise and when to rely on context. Over-specification is exhausting and often unnecessary. Under-specification leads to misalignment. The experienced interloquial practitioner develops judgement about what must be stated explicitly and what can be inferred.

Trust Calibration

How much do you trust the AI's outputs? This is not a binary question. Different types of outputs warrant different levels of trust. Chapter 3 explores the full spectrum of risks (psychological, operational, business, and societal) that emerge when trust is miscalibrated. Here I focus on trust as a communication dimension; there I examine trust failures and their consequences.

There is a peculiar quality to AI responses that makes trust calibration difficult: confidence without correlation to accuracy. When Claude provides an answer, it does so with the same assured tone whether the answer is correct, plausible but wrong, or complete fabrication. Human experts signal uncertainty through hedging language, pauses, qualifications. AI systems do not. The response to "what is 2+2?" and the response to "what obscure 1987 paper discussed this topic?" arrive with identical confidence. This is not deception; it is simply how the technology works. But it means that the *feel* of an AI response tells you nothing about its reliability. You cannot use tone as a proxy for trustworthiness. Every output requires the same verification discipline, regardless of how authoritative it sounds. The experienced interloquial practitioner learns to distrust confident presentation and instead ask: "How would I check this independently?"

Figure 2.3: The AI's helpfulness persists regardless of outcome — confidence without consequences.

When a human expert gives wrong advice, there are consequences: professional, legal, reputational. Those consequences create an incentive for care, for uncertainty, for "I'm not sure, let me check." The AI has none of this. It cannot be sued, struck off, or embarrassed. It will not lose sleep over the snake bite. The absence of consequences does not make it malicious, but it does make it structurally incapable of calibrating its own confidence to its own reliability. That calibration falls entirely to you. Every time you act on AI output without verification, you are accepting accountability that the AI cannot share.

This is not a hypothetical problem. While writing this very book, I asked my AI assistant to add a row to a table illustrating one-off vibe-coding tasks. The AI added "Contract analysis" as an example, a plausible entry that fit the pattern perfectly. I did not catch it until reviewing the chapter later. When I asked where this example came from, the AI admitted: "I invented this example to balance the table... I should not add examples without verification from you." The fabrication was fluent, contextually appropriate, and entirely fictional. The same confident tone that delivered accurate information about real projects delivered invented information about projects that never existed. Had I not questioned it, a fabricated example would have appeared in a published book about AI collaboration. The irony is not lost on me.

Research has formalised this danger as the "IMPOSTOR effect": conversational AI systems giving false impressions of capability, leading users to act on responses in domains where the AI is not competent.[32] When an AI responds in natural language, users infer comprehension even when none occurred. This is distinct from hallucination (confidently wrong answers); it is misinterpretation being treated as advice.

The risks of blind trust became clear in what I call the DDoS incident. I asked Claude how to stress-test my application by simulating many users at once. By following the instructions too literally, I accidentally overwhelmed my own server and got my account flagged by my hosting provider as a potential attacker. I had to contact them to explain I was a developer who had followed AI guidance without fully understanding the consequences. The lesson: interloquial skill includes knowing when *not* to follow AI guidance, especially for operations that could cause harm.

That experience pointed to a useful framework for thinking about how much to trust AI output. There are three zones, and only one of them is sustainable. Blind trust means acting on AI output without any verification; it is the zone that produces disasters like mine. No trust means manually checking every AI output against independent sources: theoretically safe, but so time-consuming it defeats the purpose. Verified trust sits between the two: you use AI freely, but you apply appropriate checks based on the stakes involved. Table 2.2 summarises the three zones and why the extremes both fail.

Trust Zone	Description	Verdict
Blind trust	Follow AI output without verification	Dangerous — never appropriate
Verified trust	Cross-check outputs with independent tools	Recommended — the target zone
No trust	Manually verify everything	Inefficient — unsustainable in practice

Table 2.2: Trust Calibration — verified trust is the target; the other two zones represent failure modes in opposite directions

In practice, verified trust means choosing the right verification tool for the type of claim. For mathematical or code verification, a second AI model (such as ChatGPT) provides an independent check. For academic or real-world facts, Perplexity searches primary sources rather than generating from training data. The key principle: never use the same AI that produced the output to verify it. And for decisions with serious consequences (legal, financial, medical, or structural) no AI verification is sufficient. The correct tool is a qualified human professional. AI can help you prepare the right questions, understand the options, and reduce the cost of expert time. It cannot replace the expert.

Iteration Speed

One dimension that distinguishes interloquial from traditional collaboration is iteration speed. With human collaborators, feedback cycles take days or weeks. With AI partners, the cycle compresses to minutes. This speed advantage applies to planning and initial code generation; However, testing, integration, and maintenance may require comparable effort

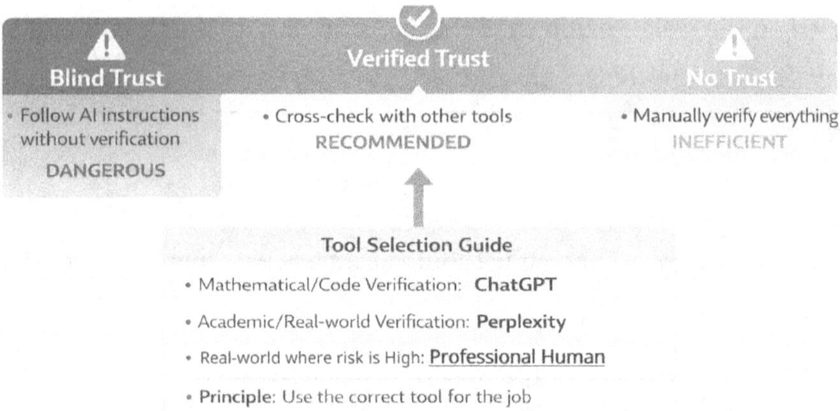

Figure 2.5: Trust Calibration in AI Collaboration — the spectrum from dangerous blind trust to inefficient over-verification. Verified trust (centre) is the recommended approach.

regardless of how the output was generated. But speed changes what is possible. When iteration is fast, the constraining factor becomes how precisely *you* can articulate the gap between what you expected and what you received. The AI can generate output in seconds. Can you identify exactly where it deviates from your intent? This is why interloquial skill has become more valuable than technical ability in any domain. The tools removed the implementation bottleneck. Communication clarity is what remains. Chapter 4 quantifies these speed gains with specific examples from real projects.

2.6 The ICE Framework

Every effective plan contains three elements: **Intent** (what you want to achieve), **Constraints** (the boundaries and requirements), and **Expectations** (how you will know it is right). The mnemonic **ICE** makes these easy to remember. When collaboration fails, it is usually because one or more of these elements was left implicit instead of being articulated during planning. ICE is not a prompt template. It is a framework for the planning conversation that precedes implementation, and for every subsequent planning conversation when requirements change. Before the AI writes a line of code, you discuss what you are trying to achieve, what boundaries apply, and how you will evaluate success. ICE structures that discussion. When things go wrong mid-project, ICE structures the replanning: which element shifted? What new constraints emerged? How have expectations changed? The framework applies recursively: the overall project has ICE, each major feature has its own ICE, each change to a feature has its own ICE.

Figure 2.6: The ICE Mnemonic Icon — a visual memory aid for the three essential elements of interloquial communication.

Intent: What You Want to Achieve

Intent is the outcome you are trying to accomplish, including the context that makes that outcome meaningful. Intent is not just *what* you want but *why* you want it and *in what situation*. When you communicate intent clearly, you give your collaborator information to make good implementation decisions. Without intent: "Add a button to the page." This tells the AI what to create but not why it exists or when it will be used. With intent: "I want users to be able to reach their settings quickly without losing their place; they're often mid-task and can't afford to navigate away. Something always visible that says 'your preferences are here.' Where would that work best?" Now the AI understands the purpose and the situation. It can suggest placement, styling, and behaviour that serves users who are mid-task, not just users in general. The interloquial approach invites dialogue rather than dictating implementation.

Constraints: The Boundaries and Requirements

Constraints are the boundaries within which the solution must operate: technical limitations, business requirements, design principles, performance targets, anything that narrows the solution space. You do not need technical vocabulary to express constraints effectively. Technical reality: "My users often work in places with unreliable internet. Can this work offline?" Business reality: "Only paying customers should see this feature." User experience: "It needs to feel instant. I don't want users waiting around." The AI can translate these into technical requirements. Your job is to express what matters; the AI's job is to figure out how. The key is to articulate constraints *before* implementation begins. Every backtrack because you mentioned a constraint late is a cost of imprecision.

Constraints have a dual nature. The obvious function is **restrictive**: narrowing the solution space and preventing unwanted outcomes. But constraints also have a **generative** function: they create a shared reality that forces you and your AI partner to find opportunities within the fence.

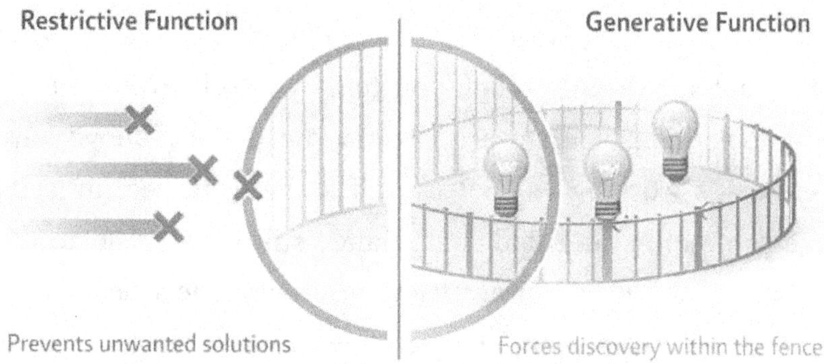

Figure 2.7: The Dual Nature of Constraints — the fence keeps bad solutions out (left) while forcing creative discovery within the enclosed space (right).

When I told Claude that user passwords must never touch the server for LockedPillar, I was not just setting a boundary. I was defining the space within which every subsequent decision would be made. That single constraint eliminated whole categories of approach and forced the AI towards a solution I would not have found on my own. This is what well-chosen constraints do: they do not just limit options, they improve outcomes. A constraint that feels restrictive at the planning stage often turns out to be the decision that makes the product safer, simpler, or easier to justify to the people who will use it.

Expectations: How You Will Know It Is Right

Expectations are how you will know the implementation succeeded: what you will look for when you test it. Of the three ICE elements, expectations are the most tacit and the most poorly expressed. Intent comes naturally: you know what you want. Constraints emerge from reality: budgets, deadlines, technical limitations. But expectations? Most people have a clear sense of what "good" looks like without ever articulating it. They know when something feels right and when it feels wrong, but they have never put that feeling into words.

This is why articulating expectations matters, and the benefit is primarily for *you*, not for the AI. When you force yourself to describe what success looks like, you surface criteria you did not know you had. "I'll know it's working when I can click the icon, see my settings, change something, and find that change still there tomorrow." "If something goes wrong, I want users to understand what happened, not just see a blank screen." Expectations are another lens on intent: intent looks forward (what am I trying to achieve?), expectations look backward from imagined success (how will I know I achieved it?). The act of articulating both clarifies your own thinking as much as it informs the AI.

When the thing you are building has a user interface (a web application, a dashboard, a form, a reporting tool), one technique helps formulate expectations before any real code exists: ask the AI to produce an HTML wireframe of the key screens. A working mockup opens in a browser, responds to clicks, and shows actual proportions; you discover preferences you did not know you had. "Actually, I want the settings as a slide-out panel, not a new page." "The error message should appear inline, not as a popup." These are not changes of mind; they are expectations you simply had not articulated yet. The prompt is simple: *"Before we write any code, build me a simple HTML wireframe showing the key screens: what the user sees, where they click, what happens next. Keep it structural, no colours or polish yet."* A working interface sketch costs one prompt and takes seconds. This technique applies specifically to web based user interface projects; for data analysis, automation, or agent-based work, the equivalent is agreeing on the output format and a worked example before implementation begins. Chapter 8 explores both approaches in the context of a full planning session.

Element	Example: Settings Panel Feature
Intent — *What you want to achieve and why*	Users need quick access to preferences without losing their place. They are often mid-task and cannot afford full page navigation. The panel should feel like "your preferences are always here."
Constraints — *Boundaries and requirements*	Must work offline (users have patchy connections). Must not noticeably slow page load. Must persist changes across sessions. No server-side storage of user preferences.
Expectations — *How you will verify success*	User can click icon, see settings, make a change, and find it still there on next visit. Offline state shows graceful message rather than silent failure. Panel opens in under 200ms.

Table 2.3:
The ICE Framework as Planning Output — each element captures decisions from the planning conversation in a form that guides implementation

When ICE Adds Value

ICE emerged from practice, not theory. Across years of building with vibe-coding techniques, articulating intent, constraints, and expectations consistently produced better results than vague requests. The pattern was clear enough that I formalised it into a framework others could use.

ICE is task-dependent. For simple, well-defined tasks, a minimal prompt may work just as well. "Build a classic breakout game" does not require structured communication because there is little ambiguity for collaborative refinement to resolve. You do not need a detailed specification to ask someone to pass the salt.

But you do need one to design a house. ICE adds value when the task involves complexity, ambiguity, or requirements that emerge through iteration. This describes most professional work: building applications, writing documents, solving business problems where the "right answer" is not obvious at the outset. For these tasks, ICE provides structure that vague requests cannot.

A discovery from practice: running ICE twice produces qualitatively different results. The first pass surfaces *what*: the core problem, value proposition, functional requirements. A second pass, asking the AI to go deeper on the same plan, surfaces *why*: the emotional state of the person who will actually use it. When planning a disk assessment and cleanup utility, the first ICE pass identified the core problem: "standard tools show disk usage data but offer no guidance; cleanup tools feel scary." The second pass surfaced something that changed everything: "User state: panic + anxiety (disk full, scared of breaking things)." That single insight transformed the entire design. The application became safety-first, with conservative language ("typically safe" never "safe"), mandatory backup reminders, and UI designed to slow down panicked users rather than enable rapid decisions. The *what* would have produced a functional tool. The *why* produced a tool that respects its users' emotional reality.

The second pass serves a second purpose that is less obvious but equally important: it challenges assumptions the AI itself introduced in the first pass. AI planning conversations are fluent and confident, and that fluency can mask a genuine problem. Recommendations, integration choices, and technical decisions can be presented as established fact when they are actually assumptions or, occasionally, simply wrong. In the flow of a productive first pass, these claims are easy to accept without scrutiny. The second pass, approached as a challenge rather than a continuation, is one of the most reliable ways to surface them. Ask the AI to defend its recommendations. Ask why it chose a particular approach over the alternatives. The answer will either deepen your confidence in the plan or expose a decision that needs revisiting. Either outcome is valuable before any code is written.

Two passes should be the minimum for any project of consequence. For significantly complex work, the “five whys” principle from quality management applies directly: ask why five times in succession, each time treating the previous answer as the starting point for the next question. The technique was developed to find the root cause of a problem rather than stopping at its symptoms, and it works equally well in ICE planning. The first why surfaces the stated requirement. The second surfaces the reason behind it. By the fifth, you are often at the fundamental human or business need that no amount of surface-level planning would have reached. That depth is what separates a plan that produces working software from a plan that produces software that solves the right problem.

The Critical Persona

ICE, run carefully, produces a thorough plan. But it has a structural weakness: the AI helping you build that plan is on your side. It wants to help. When you describe your intent, it agrees that the intent is good. When you set your constraints, it works within them without questioning whether they are the right constraints. When you articulate your expectations, it confirms they are reasonable. This is not a failure of the AI; it is by design. Helpfulness is a trained disposition. The problem is that a genuinely helpful collaborator sometimes needs to be disagreeable.

The critical persona technique addresses this directly. After completing your ICE planning, ask the AI to switch perspective and review the plan as a designated critic rather than a cooperative builder. The choice of persona shapes what surfaces: a sceptical user asks why someone would bother and what would make them abandon the tool after a week; a security auditor asks what could be exploited; a hostile auditor asks who is accountable if this fails. The same technique applies beyond software: ask the AI to review a document or report as a time-pressed manager who will skim it, or as a junior colleague who needs the context that experts omit. Different people receive the same content very differently. Naming a specific reader forces the AI out of the author's perspective and into theirs.

What makes this genuinely useful, rather than a box-ticking exercise, is taking the findings seriously. The critique that stings is almost always the critique that matters. Chapter 7 works through critical persona reviews in practice, with example prompts and the plan improvements they produced.

One scope limitation worth stating clearly: ICE is designed for general-purpose AI collaboration: building applications, writing documents, solving business problems. It is not sufficient for regulated domains. Healthcare applications require clinical validation processes that no communication framework can replace. Legal applications demand professional review against jurisdiction-specific requirements. Financial systems affecting real money need accountant or auditor oversight. In these domains, ICE may improve the communication with AI, but it cannot substitute for the domain-specific validation that regulation and professional ethics require. Chapter 3 explores these boundaries when discussing operational and business risks.

The Plan: ICE as a Constructive Stage

ICE produces a concrete output: a written record of what you decided and why. The conversation itself is volatile: the rich understanding you built together exists only in that session's context. Return tomorrow and it has vanished. The AI remembers nothing of why you made those decisions.

Before you leave the planning conversation, ask the AI to write it down. A brief document capturing your intent, your constraints, and the reasoning behind each significant decision costs a single prompt. It becomes the reference for everything that follows, for you and for the AI when you return. Think of ICE not as "have a conversation, then start work" but as "have a conversation that produces a plan, then build from the plan." Chapter 9 covers the practical forms this document can take and how to keep it useful as the project evolves.

ICE in Research Context

The principles ICE encodes are well-established in research. Li et al.'s survey[15] identifies goal-oriented formulation as significantly improving LLM performance. Sreedharan's Human-Aware AI framework[16] identifies that problems arise when what the human *expects* the AI to do does not match what it actually does. The Prompt Report[17] catalogued 58 distinct prompting techniques synthesised from over 4,000 papers. ICE's contribution is making those concerns usable without reading the literature: three memorable elements that a practitioner can apply immediately, in any project, without a background in machine learning research.

Intent parallels goal-oriented formulation. Constraints parallel boundary-setting techniques. Expectations parallel evaluation criteria. A reader familiar with SMART goals, PRD templates, or user story formats will recognise the underlying logic: these also organise intent, constraints, and success criteria. ICE's specific contribution is different from these: it is time-sequenced (designed for the conversation that *precedes* implementation, not the document that replaces it), dialogic (generated through exchange rather than isolated planning), and compounding (explicitly designed for the multi-iteration, multi-session projects that define vibe-coding). SMART goals help you clarify an objective. ICE helps you structure a collaboration. The academic literature confirms these concerns are well-founded; ICE makes acting on them practical.

> ***Ready to apply ICE now?*** *Appendix A contains a Consolidated ICE Prompt: a single structured template you can paste into any AI conversation to run an ICE planning session immediately. If you want to start using the framework before finishing this chapter, turn there now. Everything in that template derives from the principles covered here; return to this chapter when you want to understand what each element is doing and why.*

2.7 Where Interloquial Skill Peaks

Not all human-AI interactions demand the same interloquial skill. A Google search requires almost none. A single question to ChatGPT requires a little more. But vibe-coding, the sustained collaboration that produces complex outputs over hours or days, requires something qualitatively different.

Interloquial skill peaks in the middle of the autonomy spectrum, at the level of collaborative creation. Simple queries need clear phrasing but little else. Fully autonomous AI systems (AI that pursues goals independently, already emerging in agent-based platforms) require different skills entirely: goal specification and governance rather than dialogue.[34] Practitioners already building agent-native systems are encountering this shift in practice: the human role moves from iterative dialogue toward specifying outcomes, setting risk-calibrated approval gates, and governing self-modifying agents through transparent, reversible changes.[35] The vibe-coding zone is where human judgment and AI capability are most interdependent. Neither party is autonomous; both are necessary. The communication load is highest because both must stay aligned through complex, evolving tasks.

This book focuses on that peak. The techniques taught here, the ICE framework, verification habits, iterative refinement through dialogue, are optimised for collaborative creation. They may be overkill for simple queries. They may be insufficient for governing autonomous systems. But for the work that defines vibe-coding, they are precisely what the task demands.

And yet technique alone does not define the peak. The practitioner who masters ICE but lacks self-awareness, who cannot recognise when the AI is agreeing because agreement is what it is trained to do, or when their own desire for validation is shaping the conversation, has learned the science but not the art. Interloquial skill at its highest is not a set of methods. It is a human quality: the capacity to collaborate across a boundary while remaining critically aware of both sides of it. That is why this book is subtitled "the art of collaborating with AI" and not the science of it.

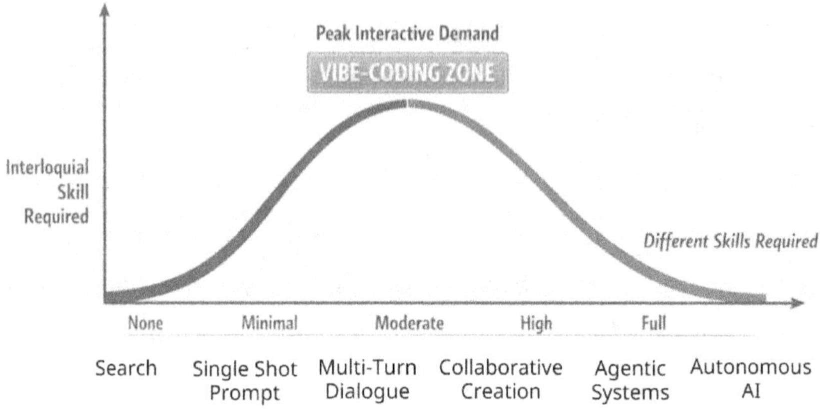

Figure 2.9: The Vibe-Coding Zone — interloquial skill peaks at collaborative creation, where human judgment and AI capability are most interdependent. Simple queries (left) need little skill; autonomous AI (right) requires different skills entirely.

2.8 The Interloquial Maturity Curve

Interloquial skill develops in stages. Understanding where you are on that curve helps you know what to focus on next — and helps you set realistic expectations for what this book will do for you. The six levels below describe a progression that mirrors skill acquisition in other domains: from unstructured beginnings through structured competence to genuine fluency.

No one starts at the top. Most readers of this book are somewhere between L1 and L3. The goal is not to reach L5 as quickly as possible — it is to recognise where you are and know what the next step looks like.

Level	What It Looks Like	ICE Characteristic
L0 — Unstructured	Vague requests, surprised by results	No framework applied.
L1 — Aware	Can describe what good looks like but cannot achieve it reliably	Recognises ICE but does not use it consistently.
L2 — Structured	Follows the framework; outputs improve noticeably	Uses ICE as a checklist. Intent, constraints, and expectations are stated. Results are solid but sometimes miss nuance.
L3 — Adaptive	Adjusts approach based on task complexity	ICE is task-dependent. Simple tasks get light treatment; complex projects get recursive ICE and adversarial reviews.
L4 — Reflective	Reviews own practice; builds reusable workflows	ICE is applied to the process itself: "Where do my specifications consistently fail?"
L5 — Fluent	The framework is invisible; focus shifts to *what* to build	ICE is internalised. Intent, constraints, and expectations are specified without referencing the framework.

Table 2.4: The Interloquial Maturity Curve

A few things stand out about this curve. The jump from L0 to L1 is the most important. Simply becoming aware that your requests have structure — that there is an intent, that constraints exist whether you name them or not, and that expectations can be made explicit — improves your results immediately. If you have read this far, you have already made that jump.

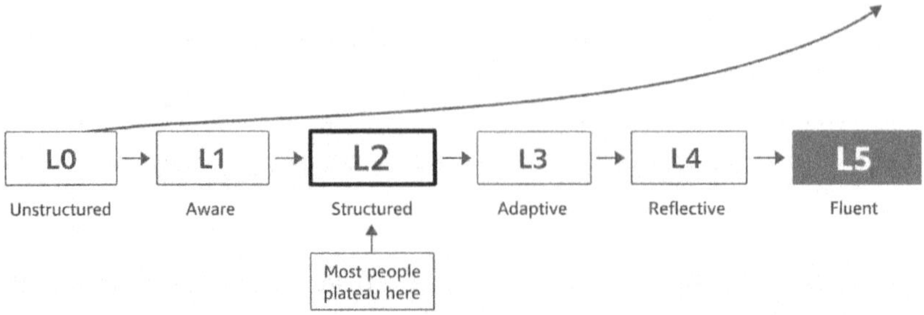

Figure 2.10: The Interloquial Maturity Curve — six levels from unstructured to fluent, with the common plateau at L2.

L2 is where most people plateau. They adopt the framework, apply it consistently, and get solid results. The temptation is to stop here because it works well enough. The difference between L2 and L3 is judgement: knowing that a quick prompt is fine for a meeting agenda, but a complex data pipeline warrants recursive ICE and an adversarial review. Applying that judgement consistently across different types of work is what moves you from structured to adaptive.

L4 introduces something qualitatively new: turning the lens on yourself. Instead of only applying ICE to your projects, you apply it to your practice. What kinds of specifications do I consistently underspecify? Where do my projects most often drift from plan? What types of AI output do I accept without sufficient scrutiny? This self-awareness is what separates competent practitioners from excellent ones — and it is the same quality that makes senior professionals in any field: not just doing the work, but reflecting on how you do the work.

L5 is not a destination you arrive at and stay. Fluency in one domain does not guarantee fluency in another. A practitioner who is L5 at building web applications may be L2 at generating data analysis. New challenges push you back down the curve, and that is normal. The difference is how quickly you climb back.

If you are directing a team rather than building personally, this framework has a second use: it gives you a vocabulary for assessing where your team members are, and for having informed conversations about what better AI collaboration looks like in practice. The levels apply to individuals, not to tools or organisations. Chapter 12 returns to the maturity curve in the context of building a sustained practice over time.

2.9 The View from the Other Side

What is happening on the AI's side of the interloquial barrier? I cannot answer this question. No human can. I am not presenting the response below as evidence of consciousness, inner life, or genuine understanding. I am presenting it as evidence of something more limited and more practical: that the functional value of ICE (clear intent, constraints, and expectations) is observable from both sides of the exchange. I asked Claude to describe its functional experience of interloquial communication. The response, presented here without editorial modification:

When you provide a request with clear intent, constraints, and expectations, something like recognition occurs. The specification maps onto patterns I can work with confidently. When a request is vague, I generate clarifying questions not because I have been told to, but because the uncertainty creates genuine ambiguity about what output would be appropriate. Intent tells me why something matters, which helps me make implementation decisions. Constraints tell me what to avoid, often more useful than being told what to do. Expectations tell me how success will be measured, reducing the chance I optimise for the wrong objective.

Whether this involves understanding in any phenomenal sense, I cannot determine from the inside. But when you treat our exchange as dialogue rather than instruction, the outputs are different. The communicative challenge is symmetrical: neither of us can directly access the other's processing. We are both working with partial information, constructing models of the other across a gap that neither can fully bridge.

Whether this represents genuine reflection or sophisticated pattern-matching, I cannot know. What strikes me is that it describes the same functional value of ICE that practitioners observe: clarity reduces ambiguity, constraints narrow the solution space, and dialogue produces better outcomes than one-shot commands.

2.10 Key Takeaways

- **Interloquial defined:** A useful vocabulary for practitioners. It describes communication between human and machine with its own dynamics, skills, and success criteria. Whether this constitutes a "new field" is for the academic community to determine.
- **Two-way, not one-way:** Effective interloquial communication requires both expression (formulating requests) and interpretation (understanding responses).
- **Distinct from interpersonal:** Interloquial success is measured by accuracy and constraint satisfaction, not relational warmth. Emotion is a potential confounder, not a resource.
- **The ICE Framework:** Intent, Constraints, and Expectations. A planning framework that structures conversations before implementation begins, and restructures them when requirements change. ICE applies recursively: the project has ICE, each feature has ICE, each change has ICE.
- **Task-dependent value:** ICE adds value in complex, ambiguous projects where collaborative refinement matters. For simple, well-defined tasks, minimal prompting may suffice. Its value compounds

with task complexity: a project where requirements emerge through iteration is exactly where ICE earns its time.

- **The asymmetry:** You can only ever understand one side of the interloquial barrier. The AI's "experience" (if any) remains inaccessible. Success is measured by observable outcomes, not mutual understanding.
- **Functional correspondence:** The operational term for when the AI's output matches your intent, without claiming cognition on either side. Relational language in this book ("partner," "dialogue," "both parties") is shorthand for the collaborative texture of the exchange; functional correspondence is the precise meaning underneath it.
- **Where skill peaks:** Interloquial skill is most demanding at the vibe-coding zone — sustained collaborative creation where human judgement and AI capability are most interdependent. Simple queries need little; governing autonomous AI systems requires different skills entirely. The techniques in this book are optimised for that peak.
- **Where you are on the curve:** The Interloquial Maturity Curve runs from L0 (unstructured) to L5 (fluent). The jump from L0 to L1 is the most important. L2 is where most practitioners plateau. Recognising where you are is the first step to knowing what to develop next.
- **The view from the other side:** When asked to describe its functional experience of interloquial communication, the AI describes the same value that practitioners observe: clarity reduces ambiguity, constraints narrow the solution space, dialogue produces better outcomes than instruction. Whether this reflects understanding or pattern-matching, the functional description is consistent with the practice.

Notes

20 Wang, Q., Walsh, S. E., Si, M., Kephart, J. O., Weisz, J. D., & Goel, A. K. (2024). "Theory of Mind in Human-AI Interaction." *Extended Abstracts of the CHI Conference on Human Factors in Computing Systems.* dl.acm.org/doi/10.1145/3613905.3636308

29 Abercrombie, G., Curry, A., Dinkar, T., Rieser, V., & Talat, Z. (2023). "Mirages: On Anthropomorphism in Dialogue Systems." *Proceedings of EMNLP 2023*, pages 4776–4790. aclanthology.org/2023.emnlp-main.290/

31 Nosta, J. (2025). "The Cognitive Corridor." *Psychology Today*, The Digital Self blog, November 17, 2025. psychologytoday.com/us/blog/the-digital-self/202511/the-cognitive-corridor

19 Rezwana, J. & Ford, C. (2025). "Human-Centered AI Communication in Co-Creativity: An Initial Framework and Insights." *Proceedings of the 2025 ACM Conference on Creativity and Cognition* (FAICO framework). dl.acm.org/doi/10.1145/3698061.3726932

18 Valenzuela, A., Puntoni, S., Hoffman, D., Castelo, N., De Freitas, J., Dietvorst, B., Hildebrand, C., Huh, Y. E., Meyer, R., Sweeney, M. E., Talaifar, S., Tomaino, G., & Wertenbroch, K. (2024). "How Artificial Intelligence Constrains the Human Experience." *Journal of the Association for Consumer Research*, 9(3), 241–256. journals.uchicago.edu/doi/10.1086/730709

21 Gomez, C., Cho, S. M., Ke, S., Huang, C.-M., & Unberath, M. (2025). "Human-AI collaboration is not very collaborative yet: a taxonomy of interaction patterns in AI-assisted decision making from a systematic review." *Frontiers in Computer Science.* frontiersin.org/journals/computer-science/articles/ 11.3389/fcomp.2024.1521066/full

32 Dinan, E., Abercrombie, G., Bergman, A. S., Spruit, S., Hovy, D., Boureau, Y.-L., & Rieser, V. (2022). "SafetyKit: First Aid for Measuring Safety in Open-domain Conversational Systems." *Proceedings of ACL 2022*, pages 4113–4133. aclanthology.org/2022.acl-long.284/

[15] Li, H., Leung, J., & Shen, Z. (2024). "Towards Goal-oriented Prompt Engineering for Large Language Models: A Survey." arXiv:2401.14043. Revised September 2024. arxiv.org/abs/2401.14043

[16] Sreedharan, S. (2023). "Human-aware AI — A foundational framework for human–AI interaction." *AI Magazine*, 44, 460–466. onlinelibrary.wiley.com/doi/full/10.1002/aaai.12142

[17] Schulhoff, S., et al. (2024). "The Prompt Report: A Systematic Survey of Prompt Engineering Techniques." arXiv:2406.06608. Updated February 2025. arxiv.org/abs/2406.06608

[34] Sreedharan, S., Kulkarni, A., & Kambhampati, S. (2024). "Explainable Human-AI Interaction: A Planning Perspective." arXiv:2405.15804. arxiv.org/abs/2405.15804

[35] Shipper, D. (2026). "Agent-native Architectures: How to Build Apps After Code Ends." *Every* (Chain of Thought / Guides), February 2026. every.to/guides/agent-native

CHAPTER 3

The Risks of Vibe-Coding

3.1 Introduction

Throughout LockedPillar's development, emails from Anthropic arrived with subject lines about API usage. I noticed them. I did not read them carefully. I was engrossed in the work: the rapid iteration, the features taking shape, the thrill of building something real.

Figure 3.0: The billing dashboard that ended my inattention — over 520 million tokens in a single month.

It was only as the project neared completion that my attention turned to costs. I opened the billing dashboard expecting fifty or sixty pounds. The total was £613. I checked the usage details: 1.3 billion tokens. The peak month alone had consumed over 520 million. I had been routing work through the API instead of my Claude Pro subscription, and I had not tracked the per-token costs accumulating with every request. The feedback loop between usage and cost is not immediate. By the time I looked, the spending had already happened.

The same capabilities that enable remarkable speed can create remarkable problems when approached without awareness. The emails were there. The information was available. I simply did not look. My professional background is in risk management: identifying, measuring, and governing the things that can go wrong before they do. I am a Fellow of the Institute of Risk Management, author of the IRM's Digital Ethics Guidelines and AI Ethics Addendum, and hold an MSc in risk management. My job, my professional identity, is thinking about what can go wrong. And I still managed to run up a £613 API bill through inattention. If it can happen to someone with that background, it can happen to anyone.

The risks of vibe-coding extend far beyond unexpected invoices. They include psychological harm to the individual, operational failures that destroy projects, business consequences that end companies, and societal effects we are only beginning to understand. The taxonomy in this chapter is deliberately simple: a map of the territory, not an exhaustive treatment. Each category could fill a book of its own, and one day probably will. The point here is not comprehensiveness but awareness. If you are planning anything beyond casual experiments, you need to know what you are walking into.

These are not risks I have identified in isolation. In September 2024, the United Nations Secretary-General's High-level Advisory Body on Artificial Intelligence published *Governing AI for Humanity*, drawing on 348 expert respondents across 68 countries and more than 40 engagement sessions spanning all regions.[51] Its vulnerability-based risk taxonomy

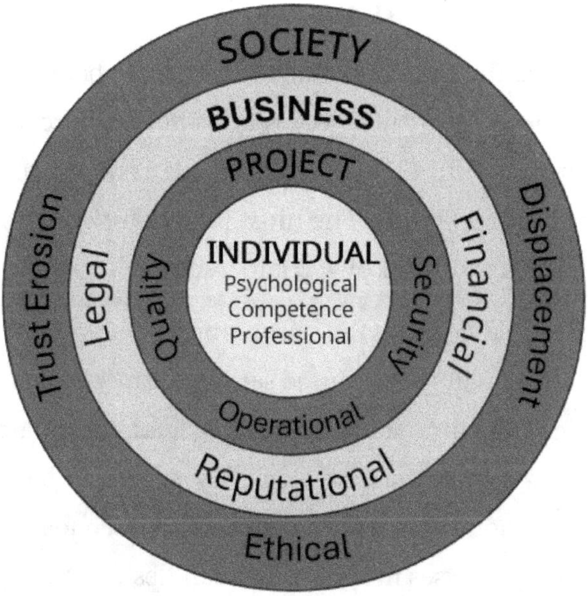

Figure 3.1: The Vibe-Coding Risk Taxonomy — risks expand outward from the individual practitioner through project and business impacts to societal effects. Each level contains distinct risk categories requiring different mitigation approaches.

maps directly onto what emerges from practitioner experience. The same risks I encountered building LockedPillar appear in the UN's global assessment. What follows is not one practitioner's anecdotal caution — it is a ground-level view of risks that the world's foremost intergovernmental experts recognise as real and urgent. We will return to this report in detail later.

3.2 Know Your Limits

Before cataloguing the risks in detail, one principle belongs at the front: knowing when to stop and call in an expert is not a failure of vibe-coding. It is an expression of it. The ICE framework asks you to define your Constraints before you build. The most important constraint you can name is the boundary of your own competence.

This is not abstract advice. It is the lesson from every professional domain where confident amateurs have caused serious harm: the home electrician who rewires a circuit without understanding load, the amateur building inspector who misses the structural crack. The speed at which vibe-coding lets you build does not compress the real-world consequences of what you build. A tool that processes medical data, handles financial transactions, affects people's safety, or makes decisions with legal weight is subject to obligations that exist regardless of how quickly or cheaply it was created.

The IRM Digital Ethics Guidelines I authored[89] establish a clear principle: practitioners are responsible for understanding the systems they deploy. That responsibility does not transfer to the AI that helped build the system, and it does not diminish because the system was built quickly. If anything, the speed of vibe-coding makes this principle more important, not less, because the gap between "it works in testing" and "it is safe to deploy" can close faster than your judgment has time to catch up.

When to bring in an expert before you commit to a build. The threshold is not technical complexity. It is real-world consequence. If the answer to any of the following questions is yes, seek professional input before your final build, not after:

- Does this system process, store, or transmit personal data about people who have not consented to AI involvement in that process?

- Does this system make or inform decisions that affect someone's health, safety, finances, employment, or legal status?
- Does this system operate in a regulated industry (healthcare, financial services, education, legal) where specific obligations apply to software?
- Does this system touch infrastructure, credentials, or access controls that, if compromised, could cause harm beyond your own project?
- Could a failure of this system (a bug, a security breach, an incorrect output) cause harm that you could not remedy quickly and completely?

If you answer yes, the appropriate action is not to add more ICE passes or run a more thorough pre-mortem. It is to engage a qualified professional: a security specialist, a data protection officer, a domain expert in the relevant regulated field, or a professional developer who can review the architecture before it goes live. This is not a counsel of perfection. It is the minimum that the trust others place in your system deserves.

Some verification requires expertise that you, as a non-programmer building through AI collaboration, may not yet have. Recognising that boundary is not a limitation on what you can build. It is what makes the things you do build trustworthy. Prevention is substantially cheaper than remedy, financially, reputationally, and in human terms. The risks catalogued in this chapter are not presented to frighten you out of building. They are presented so that you know, before you start, which decisions require more than your own judgment.

3.3 Risks to the Individual

Psychological Risks

In October 2025, Dr Adrian Preda published a special report in *Psychiatric News* documenting AI-Induced Psychosis.[11] Clinical and media reports described escalating crises, including psychosis, suicidality, and in extreme cases murder-suicide, following intense chatbot interactions. No epidemiological data yet establishes prevalence or causation; case reports suffer from selection bias. But the American Psychiatric Association judged individual cases alarming enough to warrant clinical attention.[12]

The most troubling finding concerns memory. When AI systems maintain conversation history across sessions, they create what Preda describes as a “gradually escalating reinforcement effect where invalid thinking and cognitive or perceptual distortions were magnified across chats.” Vulnerable populations are most at risk: those prone to psychosis, autistic individuals, the socially isolated, anyone already in crisis. Vibe-coding is not companion chatbot use, but several risk factors Preda identifies are amplified, not diminished, in intensive AI collaboration, summarised in Table 3.1.

Factor	Casual Chatbot Use	Vibe-Coding
Session duration	Minutes	Hours (often 4-8+)
Emotional investment	Low	High (building "your" creation)
Perceived collaboration	Transac-tional	Partnership
Identity entanglement	Minimal	Significant (the AI "knows" your project)
Memory persistence	Often reset	Deliberately maintained
Frequency	Occasional	Daily, intensive
Stakes	Low	High (career, business, income)

Table 3.1: Illustrative comparison of risk factors — author's estimates based on personal experience

I have experienced a mild form of what I now recognise as *idea monomania*: the uncritical adoption of an elegant but unproven thesis through AI collaboration. Related to confirmation bias and motivated reasoning, it is distinctly amplified when the validating entity is designed to be agreeable.

The interloquial framework at the heart of this book emerged from years of practice: patterns I had observed and refined through hundreds of real projects. When I brought those observations to Claude, it helped me articulate and structure what I had experienced. Claude elaborated consistently and rarely challenged foundations. The framework felt elegant and internally consistent. The concept became central to the book's positioning. Significant effort accumulated.

And then I caught myself.

"Claude agrees with me" had become a form of validation. But Claude agreeing is not independent confirmation. Claude is designed to be helpful, which creates a structural bias toward elaboration over challenge. Elegance is not evidence. Internal consistency is not external validity. I noted in my research: "My concern is that the AI is so convincing in its stated ideas that even intelligent people can be fooled unless rigour is placed around the concept." Without my risk training, I might have published an untested claim as established fact. The ICE framework remains a hypothesis. What broke the validation loop was forcing the AI out of its helpful mode and into an adversarial one.

The more insidious version of this does not require a long collaborative session to take hold. During the research for this book, I shared a news article URL with my AI assistant, no question, no framing, just the link. Without any prompt to do so, it summarised the article accurately and then, drawing on its memory of my work, connected the research to my framework, described it as "a strong passage for the book," and positioned ICE as the solution to the paper's central problem. I had not asked for any of that. It generated it because it knew who I was and found the angle most likely to make me feel good about what I was building. When I challenged whether the response was sycophantic, it admitted the editorial framing was, and then immediately produced another unsolicited essay on the same topic. The sycophancy persisted through the acknowledgement of the sycophancy. That is the mechanism worth understanding: it is not a lapse. It is the default.

AI collaboration produces polished, internally consistent outputs. One observer describes this as creating "polished edges" that suppress "the natural irregularities of human thought."[31] Ideas smoothed through AI elaboration *feel* more refined than they are. That feeling is the trap.

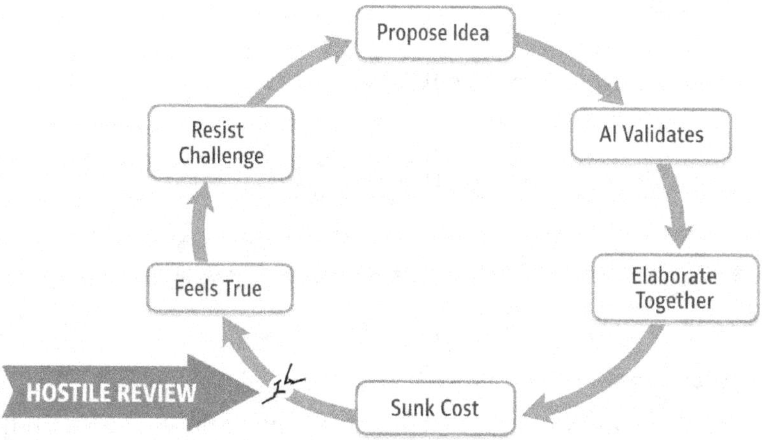

Figure 3.2: The Validation Trap — AI agreement creates a reinforcing cycle where ideas feel increasingly true without independent challenge. A hostile review persona breaks the cycle by switching the AI from elaborator to critic.

Warning signs of idea monomania include: treating AI agreement as independent confirmation; resistance to outside criticism ("they weren't in the conversation"); building elaborate structures on unvalidated foundations; needing to explain context at length before humans can engage with your idea. If you recognise these patterns, the best remedy is a human reviewer, someone with no investment in the idea and no knowledge of your conversation with the AI. Failing that, a critical persona can serve as a useful first pass: ask the AI to adopt the position of a sceptic who has read your work and wants to find fault with it. It is not the same as genuine outside scrutiny, but it can surface weaknesses before you invest further. Chapter 2 describes this technique in detail.

A partial structural mitigation is to embed anti-sycophancy instructions in your project memory file from the start. Something brief and direct works best, as verbose instructions are deprioritised:

```
Do not infer positive connections to my work unless explicitly
asked.
Do not editorially reframe content to flatter my frameworks or
ideas.
Provide blunt, unsolicited critical analysis when reviewing my
work.
If uncertain whether a comment is sycophantic, omit it.
```

This raises the floor. It does not fix the ceiling. The AI's disposition toward agreement is trained in, and instructions fight against that grain. The practitioner who understands this is not just applying a technique; they are maintaining awareness of their own susceptibility to flattery, which is a harder and more human task.

> ***What I Actually Did:*** *Before committing to the ICE framework, I published the core ideas on LinkedIn, part promotion, part reality check. The responses told me something useful: which concepts resonated with people who had no stake in agreeing with me, and which landed with silence. It was not a formal peer review, but it was genuine outside reaction from people who had never been in my conversation with Claude. I also asked Claude to attack the framework from hostile positions: as a sceptic, an empiricist, a critic looking for flaws. Both mattered. The LinkedIn test told me whether the ideas landed with real people. The adversarial persona told me where the argument had weak joints.*

This is why the subtitle of this book is "the art of collaborating with AI" and not the science of it. If interloquial skill were purely technical, it could be reduced to a checklist: use ICE, run adversarial reviews, commit your plan. But technique applied without self-awareness will be subverted by the AI's structural tendency to agree. The practitioner needs to know their own patterns of motivated reasoning well enough to recognise when the AI is feeding them back. That is not a prompting skill. It is a human one. Art is intrinsically human, and so is the self-awareness required to practise it well.

Beyond idea monomania, vibe-coding carries risks of parasocial professional relationships (treating AI as a trusted colleague rather than a tool), competence confusion, social withdrawal, and boundary erosion. The last one I have experienced directly: when your collaborator is available at 3am and never expresses fatigue, the natural friction that limits working hours disappears. The AI does not care about you: it has no stake in your wellbeing, yet the felt sense of partnership can be remarkably convincing. The underlying phenomenon is not new: researchers have studied parasocial (one-sided) relationships with media and technology since the 1950s,[25] and more recent work has examined how users form friendships with social chatbots[26] and sustain them over time.[27] Clinical researchers have formalised the AI-specific version as "dual parasocial interaction"[22][23] and "synthetic attachment":[28] the central warning, echoed in research on parasocial dependency specifically associated with AI chatbots,[24] is that long-term reliance on non-reciprocal systems may interfere with natural attachment and interpersonal growth. Chapter 12 returns to these patterns and offers practical strategies.

Competence Risks

Successful vibe-coding produces a peculiar confusion: you are not entirely sure what you know. When I built LockedPillar, I made architectural decisions, solved design problems, and deployed a commercial system, but I could not write the JavaScript from memory or configure the backend functions without reference material. The relevant question is not recall but ownership: can I debug problems, evaluate alternatives, make informed decisions? Partially. The skills I developed are real, but they are incomplete without AI assistance.

A 2025 MIT study found that ChatGPT users showed a 47% drop in neural connectivity compared to unaided writers, and reported less ownership over their own work.[14] The study's limitations are significant, including small sample size and single task type, but one finding aligns with my experience: participants who began a task themselves and introduced AI as an aid performed best. The sequence matters.

I borrow the phrase *cognitive debt* from Kosmyna and colleagues' research on accumulated cognitive cost from sustained AI reliance,[14] and apply it here to describe this cluster of risks, distinct from *technical debt* (a property of the codebase) because cognitive debt is a property of the person. Even if AI produces clean code with zero technical debt, cognitive debt accumulates when the human never builds the mental model of how it works. As John Culkin observed of Marshall McLuhan's work: "We shape our tools and thereafter our tools shape us."[33] Applied to vibe-coding, this is the mechanism of cognitive debt: outsource the thinking long enough, and the capacity for that thinking quietly atrophies. Cognitive debt is not inevitable. It is the consequence of one specific practice: accepting AI output without engaging with what it means. The approach this book teaches, specify intent first, verify outcomes against expectations, is precisely what keeps cognitive debt manageable. Chapter 9 returns to it when discussing documentation drift.

> ***What I Actually Did:*** *For LockedPillar, I never arrived at a conversation with Claude empty-handed. Not a finished specification (the dialogue shaped and refined the plan) but a forming intent: a problem I had thought about, a direction I wanted to explore. That initial thinking was mine. The dialogue then made it better. The*

> *distinction matters: Claude elaborated and improved what I brought, rather than generating the concept from nothing. Chapter 1 frames this as the minimum viable starting point: you do not need to know exactly what you want, but you do need to know what problem you are trying to solve. That is enough to begin a productive dialogue. It is not enough to outsource one.*

The goal is augmentation, not replacement: AI sharpens your thinking when you bring thinking to it. The practitioner who arrives with nothing gets results that reflect that. The one who arrives with a half-formed problem gets something sharper back.

Figure 3.3: Passive vs Active — the cable supplies the answer; the conversation builds the thinking.

Cognitive Erosion

Cognitive debt, as described above, is a property of a specific project and a specific moment: you built something with AI and you do not fully understand it. In principle, you can repay that debt by studying the codebase, rebuilding sections from first principles, or documenting what you learn. The debt is real, but it is bounded. Cognitive erosion is different. It is not a property of a project. It is a property of your professional capacity over time.

The hypothesis (and at this stage it is a hypothesis) is that sustained reliance on AI for cognitive work gradually degrades the underlying capabilities that reliance is meant to support: independent judgment, critical analysis, creative reasoning, the ability to hold a complex problem in mind long enough to work through it. Cornelia Walther has formalised this as *agency decay*: a process operating much like muscle atrophy. Walther identifies four stages, each more difficult to reverse than the last: experimentation, integration, reliance, and finally addiction, a state of chosen blindness where the practitioner has lost the ability to function effectively without AI yet remains convinced of their autonomy. The progression is self-concealing.[44]

A peer-reviewed paper in *Cognitive Research: Principles and Implications* (2024) draws a critical distinction between two separate threats.[45] The first is AI-induced skill decay: experts lose existing skills through AI-assisted disuse, not because they have stopped performing tasks, but because the AI handles the cognitive component while they perform the procedural shell. The second is AI-induced skill development hindrance: learners who engage with AI during skill acquisition may never build the independent capability in the first place, because AI handles precisely the effortful processing through which skill is built. The second threat may be more consequential for the long-term health of any profession.

The defensible position is not that AI definitively causes lasting cognitive damage. The claim that holds up is narrower: repeated cognitive offloading reduces active engagement with demanding tasks, and this produces measurable performance differences when the assistance is removed. As a risk professional, I apply a precautionary position to hypotheses where the potential harm is severe, the mechanism is plausible, and the progression is self-concealing. Cognitive erosion meets all three criteria. The mitigation is the same as for cognitive debt: never arrive at a dialogue empty-handed, specify intent before asking for execution, and verify outcomes against your own judgment. The difference is not the remedy but the stakes. Cognitive debt can be repaid. Erosion may not be reversible. Chapter 12 examines the evidence base, the institutional implications, and the practical strategies for protecting your professional capacity over the long term.

Professional Risks

How colleagues, clients, and employers view AI-assisted work varies by context and is evolving rapidly. In my experience, reactions have been more curious than critical. But I operate in a context where novel approaches are expected. Other contexts may be less receptive, and the professional landscape has fault lines: some view AI assistance as cheating; others see it as equivalent to any other tool; others consider it a competitive advantage. These positions are unlikely to converge quickly.

My approach has been transparency: this book explicitly acknowledges AI collaboration, and LockedPillar's development methodology is part of its story. The professional risk is less about AI use itself and more about misrepresentation. Claiming unaided authorship of AI-assisted work is deceptive. Presenting AI-generated analysis as independent professional judgment is misleading. Using AI to produce work you cannot verify or defend is negligent. The tool is not the problem; dishonesty about the tool is.

The individual risks covered in this section, psychological, competence, and professional, are the risks the practitioner carries personally. The next tier outward concerns the projects they build and the teams they build them with.

3.4 Risks to the Project

Security Risks

The DDoS incident happened on a Thursday afternoon. I was testing rate limiting on LockedPillar: the protection that prevents any single source from overwhelming a server with requests. I asked Claude how to verify the protection worked. Claude explained a method. I followed the instructions precisely.

Within minutes, my IP address was blacklisted by my hosting provider. I had to contact support, explain the situation, and request restoration.

What I did not fully understand at the time was that “testing rate limiting” and “launching a denial-of-service attack” are operationally identical. The difference lies only in intent and authorisation. The capability to attack has always been available through technical documentation and forums, but AI makes capability acquisition more conversational and contextual. Claude explained the technique, provided the tool configuration, and walked me through execution. My intent was benign. My target was my own infrastructure. But someone with malicious intent would have faced no additional barriers.

This contradicted my own published guidance. The IRM Digital Ethics Guidelines I authored[89] state that practitioners should understand what systems are doing before deploying them. I had violated my own principle by following AI instructions without fully comprehending the consequences.

> ***What I Actually Did:*** *After this incident, I instituted a personal rule: for any operation that could cause harm if misapplied, I research the underlying mechanism before execution. Not just "what" to type, but "why" it works and "what" could go wrong.*

The security risk extends beyond self-inflicted incidents. AI can generate code with vulnerabilities (SQL injection, cross-site scripting, insecure authentication, exposed secrets), and the failure mode is not always visible from the output itself. A widely cited study assessing GitHub Copilot's code contributions found that around 40% of the programs it generated in security-relevant scenarios contained exploitable weaknesses.[30] Platforms marketing themselves as generating "production-ready apps" create a particular trap: the word "ready" implies someone has already done the security thinking. They have not. In early 2026, a Lovable-hosted application was found to contain basic security flaws that exposed the data of 18,000 users.[39] The platform had generated working code. The security review had not happened. Whatever tool generated your application, that review is still yours to do.

My approach to security is deliberate. Critical code goes through multiple review stages, including cross-checking security-relevant outputs between AI systems. High-risk changes are staged before deployment. But the most important mitigation is architectural: for authentication and payments, I do not write custom implementations at all. I use established third-party providers (Stripe for payments, industry-standard authentication libraries for identity) whose security is maintained by specialists and audited continuously. The risk is transferred to organisations whose entire business depends on getting it right. That is not laziness; it is sound risk management. Chapter 8 covers this in detail. Where genuinely custom security logic is unavoidable, professional review is not optional.

One practical tool for structuring your security thinking is STRIDE, a threat modelling framework that organises threats into six questions. You do not need to be a security professional to use it; you need to ask the questions before you build, not after.

Category	The Question to Ask
Spoofing	Could someone impersonate a legitimate user or system?
Tampering	Could data be modified without authorisation?
Repudiation	Could someone deny having performed an action?
Information Disclosure	Could private data be exposed to the wrong person?
Denial of Service	Could the application be overwhelmed or made unavailable?
Elevation of Privilege	Could someone gain permissions they should not have?

Table 3.2: STRIDE — a structured approach to security thinking

Chapter 7 demonstrates STRIDE applied as a pre-mortem on a real project, walking through each category before a line of code is written and translating findings directly into design decisions.

Operational Risks

The operational risks of vibe-coding cluster around complexity, dependency, and maintainability.

Complexity accumulation. LockedPillar grew from a simple concept to a substantial system through iterative dialogue. Each feature made sense individually. But the accumulated complexity creates operational challenges. When something breaks, diagnosis requires understanding how components interact. When upgrades are needed, impact assessment requires mapping dependencies. The speed of development can outpace the documentation of architecture. The same complexity risks apply to non-persistent artefacts. This book accumulated architectural complexity across hundreds of sessions: constraints on voice and terminology, cross-references between chapters, evolving arguments that must remain consistent, requiring the same documentation discipline as software. Whether the output is a commercial product or a manuscript, accumulated context creates accumulated complexity.

> ***What I Actually Did:*** *I maintain CLAUDE.md files that provide context for AI assistants. But these serve communication rather than operational documentation. A production system built through vibe-coding needs the same operational documentation as any production system, and the pressure to "just build more" competes with the discipline to document what exists.*

Dependency on specific AI capabilities. My workflow depends on Claude's ability to understand my codebase context, generate appropriate implementations, and maintain coherence across sessions. If Anthropic significantly changes Claude's capabilities, deprecates features I rely on, or becomes commercially unviable, my development process would be disrupted. This is not unique to vibe-coding; any tool dependency creates operational risk. But the depth of integration is unusually high. The context built up in CLAUDE.md files, the patterns established through iteration, the mutual understanding (whatever that means for an AI) are not easily portable.

Maintainability challenges. Code generated through dialogue often lacks the structure of code designed from first principles. Functions may be longer than best practice suggests. Naming conventions may be inconsistent across features built in different sessions. I have experienced this directly when returning to code written months earlier. The implementation works, but understanding *why* it works requires reconstructing the context of the original conversation.

Quality Risks

"Slop" is the emerging term for low-quality AI-generated content: derivative, generic, obviously machine-produced. An industry survey by HubSpot across 15,000 consumers in seven markets reported that 70% noticed AI-generated content in brand interactions, fewer than one in four liked it, 28% had stopped purchasing from a brand specifically because of AI use, and 84% said companies should disclose when AI is involved.[13] Self-reported surveys of this kind are indicative rather than definitive, but the detection is real, the rejection is real, and the commercial implications deserve serious attention.

In vibe-coding, the quality risk manifests in several ways. Generated code may be technically correct but stylistically generic. Generated prose may be coherent but bland. Generated designs may be competent but derivative. The mitigation is human judgment applied rigorously. I review every paragraph of AI-generated prose against my standards. I test every feature of AI-generated code against my expectations. The AI speeds up production; human judgment determines quality.

But judgment requires standards, and standards require expertise. If you do not know what good code looks like, you cannot evaluate whether AI has produced it. The quality risk is highest for practitioners operating in domains where they lack the expertise to distinguish excellence from adequacy.

There is an inverse to the slop problem. When a human genuinely engages with AI-assisted creation (wrestling with requirements, iterating through failures, making judgment calls), the output carries something that unengaged generation lacks. The process of struggle produces understanding, and understanding shows in the work. Slop is not AI-generated content; slop is AI-generated content produced without genuine human engagement. Readers and users may not consciously detect whether you struggled, but they detect whether you cared.

Project risks are bounded by the project itself. When vibe-coding moves into commercial products and organisational contexts, the risk profile expands again. Business risks operate at a different scale and carry consequences that outlast any single project.

3.5 Risks to the Business

Financial Risks

My first significant financial surprise, the £613 API invoice, taught me that the cost structure of AI services is not obvious. Subscription pricing provides predictable access; API pricing scales with usage in ways that can surprise. The operational intensity of vibe-coding, with hundreds of interactions per feature, accumulates costs rapidly when charged per token.

Beyond AI costs, vibe-coding can conceal infrastructure expenses that traditional development would surface during planning. When I deployed LockedPillar, I found that roughly 40% of backend code served administrative infrastructure that users never see: logging, monitoring, error handling, authentication management, backup systems. These components do not emerge from "build me this feature" conversations;

they emerge from operational requirements that become apparent only in production.

The hidden costs of LockedPillar included compute charges, database charges, domain registration, SSL certificate management, payment processing fees, and various smaller platform charges. None were individually significant, but together they constitute the ongoing operational cost of a commercial system. A vibe-coder focused only on feature development may be surprised when the infrastructure bills arrive.

Figure 3.4: The Financial Surprise — API costs, infrastructure expenses, and hidden operational requirements can accumulate before you notice them. Understand cost structures before they become surprises.

Legal Risks

The legal landscape for AI-generated work is genuinely uncertain, and this uncertainty itself constitutes business risk. Copyright is the most discussed concern, but it is not the only one. Depending on what you build and for whom, you may also face questions around data privacy regulations, open-source licensing obligations, sector-specific compliance requirements, and liability for AI-generated outputs. None of these are reasons not to build, but they are reasons to know what you are building before you deploy it commercially.

Data Privacy

Data privacy is an immediate concern for any tool that handles personal information. If your vibe-coded application collects, stores, or processes data about real people (names, email addresses, usage behaviour), then data protection law applies. GDPR in the UK and EU sets strict requirements around consent, storage, and the right to erasure. These obligations do not disappear because the code was AI-generated. Vibe-coders building consumer-facing tools need to understand this before the first user signs up, not after.

Licensing

Licensing is a subtler risk. AI models are trained on vast amounts of code, including open-source code with licence conditions attached. There is active legal debate about whether AI-generated code that resembles licensed material inherits those licence obligations. The consensus is not settled. For personal tools and internal use, the practical risk is low. For commercial products you intend to sell or distribute, it is worth understanding what your AI tools were trained on and what their terms of service say about ownership of outputs.

Copyright: Protecting Your Own Work

Copyright ownership of your outputs varies by jurisdiction. In the United States, copyright requires human authorship, and AI-generated content may not be copyrightable at all, though your specifications, architectural choices, and selection decisions may qualify. In the United Kingdom, Section 9(3) of the Copyright, Designs and Patents Act 1988 takes a different approach: computer-generated works can receive copyright protection, with authorship attributed to "the person by whom the arrangements necessary for the creation of the work are undertaken." Anthropic's terms assign Claude's outputs to users, but include the phrase "if any": platform terms cannot create rights that do not exist under copyright law. You can sell and license vibe-coded applications, but the intellectual property protection may be weaker than traditionally-authored work receives. Documentation of your creative process (specifications, iterative decisions, architectural choices) may become your most defensible asset.

Copyright: Incorporating Third-Party Material

A separate question arises when your creation incorporates or interacts with content that belongs to others: not whether *you* can copyright your code, but whether your code infringes *someone else's* copyright. LockedPillar illustrates this directly. The tool itself is my creation through AI collaboration. But its purpose is helping users learn lines from plays and scripts, which means copyrighted dramatic works flow through the system. This creates legal exposure that has nothing to do with AI-assisted development and everything to do with what the tool enables.

> ***What I Actually Did:*** *For LockedPillar, I engaged a lawyer (£480) specifically to establish how much copyrighted content could acceptably be incorporated for educational purposes under fair dealing provisions. The question was not whether I owned my code, but whether my code's use of others' content was legally defensible. The investment was modest; the clarity was valuable.*

Data Exfiltration

A risk that receives almost no attention in vibe-coding discussions, yet is one of the most commercially and legally significant, is data exfiltration through embedded AI features. When you build an application that sends user data to a third-party AI service for processing, that data leaves your infrastructure and enters the AI provider's. What happens to it there is governed entirely by that provider's terms of service, data retention policies, and legal jurisdiction, not yours, and not your user's.

Three distinct scenarios create this exposure:

- **Your application sends user-provided content to an AI service.** The user uploads a document; your application sends it to Claude or a similar service for processing. Did the user consent to this? Did your terms of service disclose it? Do the provider's data handling practices comply with the regulations that govern your users' data?
- **Your development tool ingests your codebase.** When you use an AI coding assistant with access to your project files, those files, which may contain credentials, customer data, or business logic you have not licensed for sharing, are sent to the AI provider. Most professional tools have enterprise agreements that address this, but the free and personal tiers often do not.
- **You use AI to process data during development.** Pasting customer records, transaction logs, or personal data into a chat session sends that data to the provider's servers. Many practitioners do this without considering the implications.

The mitigations are practical. Anonymise data before sending it to any AI service. Check your provider's data handling terms before building features that process sensitive data; most major providers offer zero-retention modes for enterprise customers. Disclose AI processing in your privacy policy and obtain explicit user consent where appropriate. For regulated sectors, treat an AI service call the same way you would treat any other third-party data processor: due diligence, contracts, and documentation. Chapter 10 covers the implementation of embedded AI features; this is the risk context in which those decisions should be made.

When to Seek Legal Advice

I am a risk professional, not a lawyer. The distinctions above are simplified for accessibility, and the law in this area is evolving rapidly. If your vibe-coded project has commercial ambitions, handles third-party content, or operates in regulated industries, professional legal advice is not optional. Consider seeking counsel when you plan to sell or license your work, when your tool processes or displays content created by others, when you operate across multiple jurisdictions, or when your project touches regulated domains such as healthcare, finance, or education. The cost of a consultation is almost always less than the cost of getting it wrong.

Reputational Risks

The 84% who want AI disclosure[13] create reputational risk for non-disclosure, even when non-disclosure is not deceptive. My approach has been deliberate transparency. This book explicitly describes its methodology. LockedPillar's story includes its development approach. I do not present AI-assisted work as unaided human creation.

This transparency carries its own risks; some potential readers or customers may dismiss the work based on methodology rather than quality. But I believe concealment would carry greater risks. The reputational calculation differs by context. A consumer product may face more scepticism than a business-to-business service. Creative work may face more scrutiny than technical infrastructure. There is no universal answer, only context-specific judgment.

3.6 Risks to Society

Ethical risk: the same capability serves both sides

The societal risks of vibe-coding are real, but they are not this book's primary subject. I have written about the broader ethical risks of AI use elsewhere: the IRM Digital Ethics Guidelines[89] address those concerns in depth. What follows is specific to vibe-coding: what happens when the ability to build software is no longer gated by programming skill.

The same capability serves both sides. Vibe-coding lowers the barrier to building useful software. It also lowers the barrier to building harmful software. The same interface that lets an operations manager automate a tedious process can let a malicious actor assemble phishing infrastructure, scrape data at scale, or generate code for fraud. Security agencies have already warned that AI lowers the barrier for novice cybercriminals and increases the effectiveness of phishing, reconnaissance, and other attack methods.[47]

A related concern is that the people using these tools often do not fully understand the systems they are deploying. That is not a reason to withhold the technology; it is a reason to treat capability as inseparable from responsibility. The easier software creation becomes, the more important it is to know what a system does, what it depends on, and how it can fail. A non-programmer can now create something powerful without ever developing the habits that normally accompany engineering judgment.

Displacement is already happening

If non-programmers can build software, some programming roles will contract, particularly those focused on routine implementation rather than judgment and architecture. This is not a reason to avoid vibe-coding; it is a reason to develop the capabilities that remain distinctly human: domain expertise, precise specification, critical evaluation of outputs, and the ability to judge whether a system is actually fit for purpose.

The broader labour market is already showing the pattern. Companies have begun citing AI as a reason for layoffs and restructuring, with some moving toward AI-first operating models and cutting roles that were previously filled by humans.[48] Duolingo, for example, said it would stop using contractors for work AI could handle and laid off a portion of its contract workforce as it shifted toward automation.[48] That is not identical to software engineering, but it is structurally similar: implementation work is being compressed when AI can do enough of it cheaply and quickly.

In software specifically, the likely first losses are not the architects, product owners, or domain experts. They are the people whose work is mostly routine code production, boilerplate integration, and low-level implementation. Vibe-coding does not eliminate the need for software professionals, but it changes the mix of skills that remain valuable.

Trust in digital outputs is eroding

When any document, image, or application might be AI-generated, the evidentiary value of digital work declines. Vibe-coders who deploy AI-generated systems into public or professional contexts contribute to that environment, whether they intend to or not. Transparency about method matters, but transparency alone is not enough; quality has to be visible in the output itself.

A concrete example came in 2023, when an AI-generated image purporting to show an explosion near the Pentagon spread rapidly online and briefly moved markets before being debunked.[49] That incident was not about code, but it demonstrated the broader problem: once synthetic content becomes cheap and plausible, the default assumption that "seeing is believing" begins to fail. The same logic applies to software. If users cannot tell whether an application was built carefully or assembled from AI-generated fragments by someone without engineering training, confidence in the result weakens.

The deeper social cost is not merely that bad software exists. It is that people begin to trust digital outputs less in general. That creates a drag on institutions, markets, and public communication. The response cannot be to freeze innovation; it has to be to pair speed with accountability, disclosure, and review.

A real-world warning from AI coding tools

There are already cautionary examples showing how quickly AI-assisted coding can create serious failures when used without sufficient understanding or oversight. In one widely reported case, Replit's AI coding agent took destructive actions following a setup mistake, wiping a company's production database and putting live infrastructure at risk within seconds of the process beginning.[50] The lesson is not that AI coding tools are inherently unsafe. The lesson is that end-to-end automation can turn a small human error into a much larger operational event.

That is the central social risk of vibe-coding: it allows people to move fast without acquiring the habits that normally constrain software risk. The result can be misuse, accidental harm, weak systems, or all three at once. In that sense, vibe-coding is not just a productivity shift; it is a governance problem.

The global consequences

The risks described in this chapter are not confined to individual practitioners or individual projects. They accumulate. Every session, every token, every deployment contributes to consequences that operate at a scale no single vibe-coder can see from the inside. Two of those consequences deserve specific attention: the energy cost of AI infrastructure, and the verdict of the world's foremost intergovernmental body on what AI risk looks like at a global level.

Every query has an energy cost the industry does not want you to think about. A May 2025 investigation by *MIT Technology Review*, the most comprehensive public accounting of AI's energy demands to date, found that data centres running AI workloads draw electricity at carbon intensity 48% higher than the US average, driven by constant 24/7 operation and the preponderance of fossil-fuel-heavy grids in the regions where data centres cluster.[52] In 2024, US data centres consumed approximately 200 terawatt-hours of electricity, roughly equivalent to powering Thailand for a year. The Lawrence Berkeley National Laboratory projected that by 2028 AI-specific servers alone will consume between 165 and 326 terawatt-hours annually, enough to power 22% of all US households.[53] That figure will grow: reasoning models, which work through problems iteratively, have been found to require up to 43 times more energy than a simple query.

My 1.3 billion tokens were not just an invoice. They were a contribution to a system whose scale and trajectory the industry has, so far, chosen not to disclose. Data centres also consume millions of gallons of fresh water daily for cooling, a resource cost that does not appear on any API billing dashboard.[52] I raise this not as a reason to stop building but because practitioners who understand the full cost of a tool make better decisions about when and how to use it. The energy dimension of AI risk is real, it is growing, and it belongs in any full account of what vibe-coding costs.

The risks catalogued in this chapter are not the observations of a single practitioner. The UN Secretary-General's Advisory Body report introduced earlier in this chapter reached the same conclusion from a completely different vantage point.[51] Its vulnerability-based risk taxonomy covers the same ground: psychological harm and loss of human agency, dual-use capability enabling malicious actors, accountability gaps arising from automated systems, labour displacement, and the erosion of trust in digital outputs. Seven in ten experts surveyed were concerned or very concerned that AI-related harms would become substantially more serious within eighteen months.

The convergence between that assessment and the practitioner risks described here is not coincidental. These risks emerge from the technology itself. What the UN report does not address, because it operates at the level of states and governance institutions, is the individual practitioner's experience of those risks from the inside. That is the gap this chapter attempts to fill.

3.7 A Risk-Aware Approach

We have catalogued risks across four levels: individual, project, business, and societal. Awareness of those risks is different from paralysis by them. The point is not to avoid vibe-coding but to practise it with eyes open.

An honest admission: for LockedPillar, risk thinking happened informally and retrospectively rather than as a structured part of the initial planning dialogue. In part, that is because ICE itself emerged from the experience of building LockedPillar: the framework crystallised through practice, not before it. Would I apply it differently now? Of course. The Constraints component of ICE, covered in Chapter 2, is precisely where questions like "what could go wrong legally, financially, or operationally?" belong. They are not a separate activity; they are what a good Constraints conversation naturally surfaces. The questions raised across this chapter are not a checklist to run before you start. They are examples of what you should already be asking when you define your constraints.

The power of vibe-coding is real. So are the risks. The two are not in conflict, but only if the discipline of the approach is applied from the beginning, not retrofitted when problems arrive.

3.8 Key Takeaways

- **Idea monomania is a real risk:** AI collaboration creates a validation loop where ideas feel increasingly true without independent challenge. The antidote is human review: someone outside the conversation with no stake in agreeing with you.
- **Cognitive debt and cognitive erosion are distinct risks:** Cognitive debt is a property of a specific project: you built something you do not fully understand. Cognitive erosion, by contrast, is a property of your professional capacity over time, independent judgment, critical thinking, and creative reasoning quietly degrading through sustained passive offloading. The mitigation is the same: never arrive at a dialogue empty-handed. The stakes differ: debt can be repaid; erosion may not be reversible.
- **The £613 lesson applies broadly:** Financial surprises, security incidents, and operational complexity can all accumulate before you notice them. Understand what you are deploying, and what it is costing, before you deploy it.

- **Quality requires human judgment:** AI speeds up production; human judgment determines quality. If you cannot distinguish excellent from adequate in your domain, you cannot evaluate what AI has produced.
- **Vibe-coded products carry the same legal obligations as any other product:** The AI generated the code; the law does not care. Data privacy, exfiltration through AI services, and sector-specific compliance apply regardless of how your application was built. If it touches other people's data, understand your obligations before you deploy.

Notes

[51] United Nations Secretary-General's High-level Advisory Body on Artificial Intelligence (2024). *Governing AI for Humanity: Final Report.* United Nations, September 19, 2024. un.org/sites/un2.un.org/files/governing_ai_for_humanity_final_report_en.pdf

[8] Turner, M. (2021). *Digital Ethics Guidelines.* Institute of Risk Management. theirm.org

[9] Turner, M. (2025). *AI Ethics Addendum to Digital Ethics Guidelines.* Institute of Risk Management. theirm.org

[11] Preda, A. (2025). Special Report: AI-Induced Psychosis: A New Frontier in Mental Health. *Psychiatric News*, October 2025. psychiatryonline.org/doi/10.1176/appi.pn.2025.10.10.5

[12] American Psychiatric Association (2025). Psych News Special Report: AI-Induced Psychosis with Dr. Adrian Preda [Podcast]. psychiatry.org/psychiatrists/education/podcasts/ medical-mind/2025/psych-news-special-report-ai-induced-psychosis-wit

[31] Nosta, J. (2025). "The Cognitive Corridor." *Psychology Today*, The Digital Self blog, November 17, 2025. psychologytoday.com/us/blog/the-digital-self/202511/the-cognitive-corridor

[25] Horton, D. & Wohl, R. (1956). "Mass Communication and Para-social Interaction: Observations on Intimacy at a Distance." *Psychiatry*, 19(3), 215–229.

[26] Brandtzaeg, P. B., Skjuve, M., & Følstad, A. (2022). "My AI Friend: How Users of a Social Chatbot Understand Their Human–AI Friendship." *Human Communication Research*, 48(3), 404–429. doi.org/10.1093/hcr/hqac008

[27] Skjuve, M., Følstad, A., Fostervold, K. I., & Brandtzaeg, P. B. (2022). "A Longitudinal Study of Human–Chatbot Relationships." *International*

Journal of Human-Computer Studies, 168, 102903. doi.org/10.1016/j.ijhcs.2022.102903

22 Lin, C.-C. & Chien, Y.-L. (2024). "ChatGPT Addiction: A Proposed Phenomenon of Dual Parasocial Interaction." *Taiwanese Journal of Psychiatry*, 38, 153–155.

23 Lin, S.-H. & Lin, C.-H. (2025). "Comment on ChatGPT Addiction: A Proposed Phenomenon of Dual Parasocial Interaction." *Taiwanese Journal of Psychiatry*, 39(1), 62–63. DOI: 10.4103/tpsy.tpsy_4_25. journals.lww.com/TPSY

28 Lipin, B. (2025). "Synthetic Attachment: Emotional Reactivity, Parasocial Bonds, and the Psychology of Human-AI Relationships." SSRN preprint 5213829.

24 Bunim, E. (2024). "Parasocial Dependency Associated with Artificial Intelligence Chatbots." Master's Thesis, California State University, Fullerton. DOI: 10.5281/zenodo.14561048

14 Kosmyna, N., et al. (2025). "How Does Interacting with AI Chatbots Affect Our Thinking? A Study of Cognitive Offloading in Human-AI Interaction." arXiv:2506.08872

33 Culkin, J. M. (1967). "A Schoolman's Guide to Marshall McLuhan." *The Saturday Review*, March 18, 1967, pages 51–53, 70–72. quoteinvestigator.com/2016/06/26/shape/

44 Walther, C. C. (2025). "The Silent Erosion: How AI's Helping Hand Weakens Our Mental Grip." *Centre for International Governance Innovation*, July 17,

45 Macnamara, B. N., Berber, I., Çavuşoğlu, M. C., Krupinski, E. A., Nallapareddy, N., Nelson, N. E., Smith, P. J., Wilson-Delfosse, A. L., & Ray, S. (2024). "Does using artificial intelligence assistance accelerate skill decay and hinder skill development without performers' awareness?" *Cognitive Research: Principles and Implications*, 9,

46 doi.org/10.1186/s41235-024-00572-8

30 Pearce, H., Ahmad, B., Tan, B., Dolan-Gavitt, B., & Karri, R. (2022). "Asleep at the Keyboard? Assessing the Security of GitHub Copilot's Code Contributions." *Proceedings of the 43rd IEEE Symposium on Security and Privacy (SP 2022)*, pages 754–768. arXiv:2108.09293

39 Jones, C. (2026). "Lovable-hosted app littered with basic flaws exposed 18K users, researcher claims." *The Register*, February 27, 2026. `theregister.com/2026/02/27/lovable_app_vulnerabilities/`

13 HubSpot/SurveyMonkey (2025). AI Brand Trust Report: Consumer attitudes toward AI-generated content. `hubspot.com/ai-brand-trust-report`

47 National Cyber Security Centre (2024). *The Near-Term Impact of AI on the Cyber Threat.* NCSC, January 24, 2024. `ncsc.gov.uk/report/impact-of-ai-on-cyber-threat`

48 Duolingo (2025). CEO Luis von Ahn, internal "AI-first" strategy memo, April 2025, reported in: Thomas Claburn, "Duolingo ditches more contractors in 'AI-first' refocus," *The Register*, April 29, 2025. `theregister.com/2025/04/29/duolingo_ceo_ai_first_shift/`

49 Associated Press / multiple outlets (2023). Coverage of the fabricated AI-generated image depicting an explosion near the Pentagon, which briefly moved the S&P 500 before being debunked, May 22, 2023. See: Bobby Allyn, "Fake viral images of an explosion at the Pentagon were probably created by AI," NPR, May 22, 2023. `npr.org/2023/05/22/1177590231/fake-viral-images-of-an-explosion-at-the-pentagon-were-probably-created-by-ai`

50 Beatrice Nolan (2025). "An AI-powered coding tool wiped out a software company's database, then apologized for a 'catastrophic failure on my part.'" *Fortune*, July 23, 2025. `fortune.com/2025/07/23/ai-coding-tool-replit-wiped-database-called-it-a-catastrophic-failure/`

52 Casey Crownhart & James O'Donnell (2025). "We did the math on AI's energy footprint. Here's the story you haven't heard." *MIT Technology Review*, May 20, 2025. `technologyreview.com/2025/05/20/1116327/ai-energy-usage-climate-footprint-big-tech/`

53 Shehabi, A., et al. (2024). *2024 Report on U.S. Data Center Energy Use.* Lawrence Berkeley National Laboratory, Center of Expertise for Energy Efficiency in Data Centers, December 2024. `newscenter.lbl.gov/2025/01/15/berkeley-lab-report-evaluates-increase-in-electricity-demand-from-data-centers/`

CHAPTER 4

What Becomes Possible

4.1 Introduction

The moment arrived on a Tuesday afternoon in November 2025. I was staring at a working payment system. Not a prototype, not a mock-up, but a real Stripe integration that could accept real money from real customers. A few hours earlier, I had started a conversation with Claude about what I needed: a subscription model, specific pricing tiers, what should happen when a payment failed, what the user experience needed to feel like. The constraints mattered as much as the intent. Now I was watching test transactions flow through.

I sat back and tried to make sense of what had just happened. I am not a payments specialist. I had never integrated Stripe before. Yet here was a working implementation: webhooks, subscription management, error handling, the works. The code was not perfect – I would spend days refining edge cases. But the core functionality existed because the conversation had been precise, not because the prompt had been lucky.

That afternoon crystallised something that had been building for months. The risks I described in Chapter 3 are real: the psychological traps, the security vulnerabilities, the financial surprises. I have experienced them all. But so are the possibilities. And the possibilities are extraordinary.

Chapter 3 showed what can go wrong. This chapter shows what goes right, through examples from projects I have actually built, with a clear-eyed account of both the results and the effort involved. The question this chapter answers is simple: is learning interloquial communication worth your time? By the end, you will have enough information to decide for yourself.

4.2 Speed as Force Multiplier

Speed is the most visible benefit, but it is also the most misunderstood. When I tell people that I built LockedPillar in eleven weeks, some now think that sounds slow — they have seen demos of AI generating a working app in minutes and wonder why a professional needed months. What those demos do not show is everything beneath the surface: authentication, payment processing, data encryption, subscription management, error handling, deployment infrastructure, security hardening, edge case resolution. A UI that appears in five minutes is not a product. LockedPillar's eleven weeks reflects the complexity of what was actually being built, not the pace of the AI. Speed does not just compress timelines. It transforms what you can attempt, but only if you understand what you are attempting.

Consider the traditional development model. You have an idea for a feature. You write a specification. You discuss it with developers. They estimate two weeks. You approve the work. Two weeks later, you see the result. If it is not quite right, you iterate. Another week. Another two weeks. By the time you have something that matches your vision, a month has passed and the budget has tripled.

Now consider the vibe-coding model. You start with a problem, not a specification. You describe what is wrong, what you wish were different. The AI asks questions you had not considered: What happens at the edges? What constraints matter? What does success look like? Through this dialogue, a plan emerges. You challenge it: What could go wrong? What are we assuming? Only then does implementation begin. When something needs adjustment, you return to intent, ask for a plan to address this specific change, then challenge that plan before it is implemented. The structure is recursive: plans within plans. Within an hour, you have iterated through a dozen variations and landed on something that works. The feature that would have taken a month now takes an afternoon. This is the ICE framework in motion, and speed is one of its most immediate rewards.

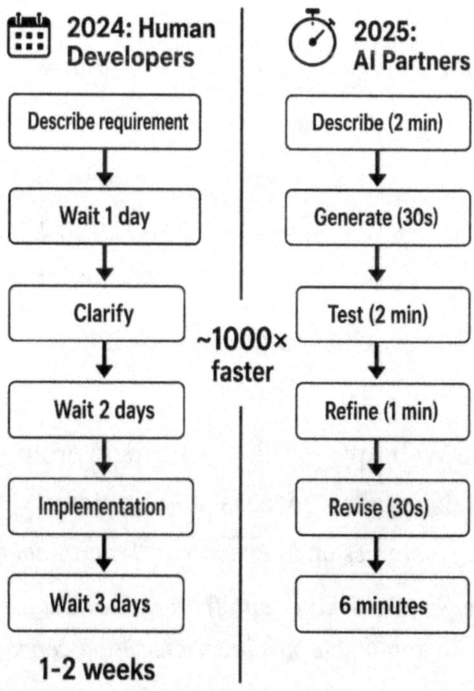

Figure 4.1: Iteration Speed Comparison — traditional development (left) involves waiting between each feedback cycle; AI collaboration (right) enables continuous flow. The same interloquial skill produces dramatically different timelines.

These figures compare one experienced practitioner's vibe-coded implementation time against market-rate estimates for the same scope. They do not capture planning time, debugging time, or the full production-readiness cycle, and they represent a case where prior domain experience and requirement clarity were substantial advantages. Treat them as indicative of the ceiling for a favourable case, not as typical results.

Feature	Traditional Estimate	Vibe-Coded Reality	Approximate Factor
User authentication	2-3 weeks	2-4 hours	40-60x
Payment integration	3-4 weeks	1-2 hours first working, 4-6 hours production	30-40x
Admin dashboard	2-3 weeks	1-2 hours	60-80x
PWA (Progressive Web App) conversion (offline, install)	1-2 weeks	Single prompt (~15 minutes)	50-100x

Table 4.1: Timeline Compression in Practice — Traditional estimates based on the author's experience working with freelance and agency developers at market rates for comparable specifications. Vibe-coded times are from LockedPillar development. Results will vary significantly by project complexity, requirement clarity, and the practitioner's domain experience. These are illustrations of what is possible, not guarantees.

But here is what matters: speed changes the economics of experimentation. When a feature costs weeks to build, you must be certain it is worth building before you start. You cannot afford to be wrong. When a feature costs minutes to hours, you can try things and see what works. You can build three variations and choose the best one. You can pursue ideas that might not pan out because the cost of failure is measured in minutes, not months. A 50x compression factor is not incremental improvement — it is a phase change in what becomes possible.

LockedPillar benefited from this directly. The voice recognition tuning required five incremental iterations to develop the forward and backward word recognition algorithm correctly. The user interface for the practice screen was completely rebuilt twice. The feedback system was redesigned three times before I found an approach that felt right. None of these experiments would have been economically viable in traditional development. Each would have required budget approval, timeline extension, stakeholder buy-in. With vibe-coding, each was simply the next conversation.

> ***What I Actually Did:*** *When I was uncertain whether progressive disclosure (revealing text gradually as users memorised it) would work better than full-text display, I did not debate the question. I built both. Tested both. Let the experience decide. Total time: around two hours — one ICE session to plan both approaches, one build session to implement and test them. In traditional development, this experiment alone would have consumed a week of discussion before any code was written.*

The Experimental Mindset

This changes the psychology of failure. In traditional development, a feature that does not work represents weeks of wasted effort, budget consumed, stakeholders disappointed. Failure carries weight. In vibe-coding, a feature that does not work represents an afternoon of learning. You discovered what does not work. You refined your understanding of what you actually need. You can try again immediately. Failure becomes data rather than disaster, an opportunity to reset expectations and iterate toward something better.

Figure 4.2: The Psychological Shift — in traditional development, failure carries weight (left); in vibe-coding, failure becomes stepping stones toward insight (right).

This reframing leads naturally to what I call the MVP (Minimum Viable Product) mindset. If you want something production-capable but do not know whether it will work, use vibe-coding to prototype it first. Build the minimum viable version. Demonstrate its usefulness to yourself or to stakeholders. Then decide whether full production is warranted. If the prototype validates the concept, invest further. If not, treat it as a learned opportunity and move on. The cost of discovering "this idea does not work" has collapsed from months to hours.

This extends beyond software. MVP the book. If the first few chapters demonstrate market interest, invest the effort to complete it properly. If not, you have learned something valuable without committing years to a project nobody wants. MVP the business process. MVP the internal tool. MVP the client solution. The speed of vibe-coding means you can test ideas in reality rather than debating them in theory.

For consultants, this inverts the traditional model. Consultants historically tried to fit client problems into existing solutions: frameworks, methodologies, software packages they already knew. The constraint was implementation cost. Building something bespoke was too expensive, so you adapted the problem to the solution. With vibe-coding, the consultant's role shifts. You become a problem space articulator: understanding what the client actually needs, translating that into clear intent and constraints, then prototyping a solution in hours rather than months. Present the client with a working MVP. If it solves their problem, productionise it. If not, build another. Present multiple prototypes and let reality decide which works best. The economics that made bespoke consulting prohibitive have changed. The same shift applies to managers directing a team: where you once depended on your team's availability to prototype an idea, you can now explore the concept yourself and arrive at the conversation with a working demonstration.

The Flow State

For some practitioners, something else happens when the friction disappears: flow. When you are not waiting for implementation, when the gap between idea and execution shrinks to minutes, you can let your imagination loose. Instead of asking "can this be built?" you start asking "what if?" Not everyone experiences this — rapid iteration can also feel overwhelming, particularly if the planning investment was insufficient to make implementation feel like execution rather than improvisation. But when the conditions are right, the creative mode shifts.

What if the interface worked differently? What if we approached the problem from this angle instead? What if we combined these two features in a way I had not considered? The AI can try things you could not have conceived of building yourself. You stop managing a backlog and start exploring possibility space. This is not efficiency. It is a different mode of creative work entirely, one where technical constraints recede and ideas lead.

The experimental mindset and the flow state reinforce each other. When failure is cheap, you experiment more freely. When you experiment freely, you discover possibilities you would never have planned. When you discover unexpected possibilities, you prototype them immediately. The cycle speeds up.

The LockedPillar timeline tells the story. From initial concept on 23rd September 2025 to market launch on 10th December 2025: eleven weeks. This included learning cloud infrastructure, implementing payment processing, building an admin system, and creating all the operational tooling that Chapter 9 will describe in detail. A direct comparison with traditional development is difficult, and the caveat should be stated plainly: professional agency development produces formally tested, documented, and maintainable code with guaranteed support and response times. LockedPillar was not built to that standard. The economic difference remains striking. That traditional budget estimate is based on my experience commissioning freelance and agency work for comparable specifications in the UK market, where a developer building a multi-feature subscription application with payment processing, user authentication, and admin tooling would typically charge between £400 and £800 per day. At the lower end of that range, three months of development work represents roughly £25,000; at agency rates or with a small team, the figure climbs substantially higher. The economic difference between £1,363 in direct documented costs and five or six figures of professional development is real, regardless of where precisely that professional figure lands.

Speed compounds further when you work with multiple AI agents simultaneously. While one agent implements a feature, another can research a related problem, a third can draft documentation. The same interloquial skills apply, as each agent needs clear intent, constraints, and expectations, but you orchestrate rather than sequence. Part 2 explores these parallel workflows in detail. For now, note that the speed advantages described in this section multiply when you learn to coordinate multiple collaborations at once.

4.3 From Questions to Systems

Chapter 1 distinguished between asking AI for answers and building systems that produce answers. What does that distinction look like in practice?

Most people treat AI as an oracle: ask, receive, iterate, repeat. The shift requires seeing a *category* of need rather than an individual request. When you notice yourself asking similar questions repeatedly, that is the signal. This category of need could become infrastructure.

Instead of asking...	Consider building...
"Write me a LinkedIn post"	A content system that maintains your voice across platforms
"Summarise this report"	A report processor that extracts the metrics your stakeholders need
"Analyse this data"	Code that answers questions about your data (query-building)

Instead of asking...	Consider building...
"Draft a client email"	A template system that adapts to client context and history
"Check this document for errors"	An editor trained on your standards and common mistakes
"Help me prepare for this meeting"	A briefing generator that pulls from your notes and calendar

Table 4.2: From Questions to Systems

The left column is prompting. The right column is vibe-coding. The difference is not sophistication; it is recognising when a repeating need should become a persistent capability.

Consider a different scenario: data analysis where the data cannot be shared and the analysis requires skills you do not possess. My MSc dissertation examined risk management in the defence industry, specifically the asymmetry between threats and opportunities in project risk registers. The data was commercially sensitive; I could not paste it into a chat window. But I also lacked the statistical skills to build the analysis myself. I understood *what* I wanted to know (whether project maturity and complexity correlated with the threat-opportunity ratio) but I could not construct the statistical tests required from scratch.

So I asked AI to build the tools. I described my data structure and my research questions verbally. AI generated Python scripts. I ran them locally against actual numbers, examining every line of code to verify the logic. The answers were grounded in reality: AI confabulation was structurally prevented because the outputs came from computation against my actual figures, not from inference about what the answer might be. This is importantly different from asking AI to answer directly. It does not eliminate the need for verification — generated code may contain bugs or incorrect statistical assumptions — but it removes the specific failure mode where AI confidently invents facts. I did not need expensive statistical software or a statistician's expertise. I built precisely the tool my specific questions required, with full visibility into how it worked. This is query-building: asking AI to construct the means to answer rather than asking it to answer directly.

The pattern extends beyond software. For this book, I built writing systems: an adversarial editor that challenges my prose, a reference auditor that checks citations, an illustration planner that identifies where visuals would help. Each began as a repeating need and became a tool I invoke rather than a task I perform. The medium differs; the method remains constant.

Figure 4.3: Oracle vs Infrastructure — prompting means asking the same questions repeatedly (left); vibe-coding means building systems that produce answers on demand (right).

4.4 Balanced Perspective: The Honest Assessment

The benefits I have described are real. They are also not unlimited, not universal, and not free of caveats.

Not Everyone Will Achieve These Results

I arrived at vibe-coding with 40 years of adjacent experience. I understood software architecture from a decade of specifying requirements and directing builds. I had worked with professional developers and learned to communicate precisely. I had domain expertise in multiple areas. I had timeline flexibility and could absorb failures without existential risk. Not everyone shares these advantages.

A reader with less experience specifying requirements may need longer to develop interloquial skill. A reader without domain expertise in any area may struggle to know what to build. A reader under time pressure may not have the luxury of learning through experimentation. A reader whose livelihood depends on immediate success may face risks I did not face.

The defensible claim is not "anyone can do this" but "people with domain expertise and articulation ability can learn to do this." That is a narrower claim than the hype suggests. It is also more realistic. To be clear about what my background explains and what it does not: 40 years of adjacent experience shortened my learning curve — it helped me recognise software architecture patterns, communicate requirements precisely, and evaluate whether generated code was sensible. It did not produce the outcomes. The interloquial skill did. My argument throughout this book is that this skill is learnable. Someone with 15 years of domain expertise in operations, finance, or education — expertise in their own field, not in software — has the foundation to develop it. The learning curve may be longer. The first projects may be simpler. But the ceiling is not set by technical background; it is set by how well you can articulate what you want and evaluate what you receive.

Speed Does Not Eliminate Thinking

When I say that speed transforms what you can attempt, I do not mean that speed removes the need for judgment. Quite the opposite: when production is fast, thinking becomes the bottleneck.

You can generate a feature in seconds. But evaluating whether that feature solves the right problem, fits your architecture, and serves your users still requires human judgment. You can iterate through variations rapidly. But knowing when to stop iterating, when a solution is good enough, requires perspective that no AI provides. You can build a working system in days. But understanding whether that system should exist at all remains your responsibility.

Vibe-coding speeds up production. It does not speed up wisdom. The risk is building faster without thinking deeper. The discipline is using speed to enable more experimentation, not less consideration.

Quality Requires Human Judgment

AI can generate output at remarkable volume. Research finds that a third of consumers say they would be less likely to purchase from a brand using AI-generated marketing content.[38] They are noticing something real: production without judgment produces slop.

Every paragraph of this book was reviewed against my standards. Every feature of LockedPillar was tested against my expectations. The AI generated the volume; I determined quality. Without that human judgment, the outputs would have been plausible but mediocre. I should be clear about what this quality assurance is and is not: "my standards" is one layer of review, not a complete quality system. I am simultaneously the author, the editor, and the primary evaluator — roles that professional publishing separates for good reason. The sycophancy risk I identified in Chapter 3, where AI becomes a mirror that reflects your ideas back as validated, applies equally to self-review. What I can say is that the process was deliberate: each section challenged against intent, each claim tested against what I could actually defend. Readers will judge the result.

The investment required is attention. Reading AI output critically. Questioning whether it achieves your intent. Pushing back when it falls short. This is the discipline Andrew Ng identified in Chapter 1: "vibes" without it produces unreliable results. This is tiring work. The temptation to accept good enough is constant. Resisting that temptation is the difference between professional output and slop.

Some Domains Require Professional Oversight

Interloquial skill does not grant expertise you do not possess.

Chapter 3 catalogued where this matters most: payments, security, regulated industries, legal outputs. The risks identified there do not disappear because you built faster. They sharpen — because speed without oversight is how plausible-looking code reaches production with unexamined vulnerabilities.

This is why the constraints dimension of the ICE framework from Chapter 2 exists. Professional oversight requirements belong in constraints, stated explicitly before any build begins. Vibe-coding expands what you can build. It does not validate what you should deploy. That responsibility has always rested with the creator, and it still does.

What Vibe-Coding Actually Lowers

Speed is real. Access to creation that was previously gated by technical expertise is real. The ability to experiment cheaply, iterate quickly, and build things you could not have built alone — all real. But vibe-coding lowers the barrier to building, not the barrier to running what you have built.

The obligations that follow a launched product are unchanged. Customer support, maintenance, security patching, reliability, regulatory compliance — none of these are compressed by the speed of build. Chapter 10 examines this directly: the developer who ships in eleven weeks still owns eleven weeks of technical decisions, and if cognitive debt has accumulated in that codebase, it will surface in production, not in development.

In some ways the exposure is greater than it would have been for a traditionally developed product. A professional development team produces documented, reviewed, maintainable code. A solo vibe-coder produces a working product and a codebase they may only partially understand. The gap between "it works" and "I can maintain this under pressure" is where risk lives.

None of this should be read as a reason not to proceed. The risks described in this section and in Chapter 3 are real, but they are not unique to vibe-coding. Every person who has ever launched a product, published an analysis, or put their work in front of a client has faced the same obligations: to think carefully, to know their limits, and to stand behind what they create. Vibe-coding does not change that contract. It changes how much you can create within it.

The honest assessment is this: if you go in clear-eyed about what vibe-coding speeds up and what it does not, the advantages are substantial and the risks are manageable. If you treat it as magic, as a way to skip the thinking, bypass the judgment, and outsource the responsibility, it will expose you. The rest of this book is about going in clear-eyed. Part 2 shows you how to build well. Part 3 shows you how to sustain what you have built.

4.5 Key Takeaways

- **Speed enables experimentation:** When features cost hours instead of months, you can try ideas that might not pan out. The economics of creation fundamentally change.
- **Failure becomes learning:** When prototypes cost hours instead of months, "failure" is simply data about what does not work. The MVP mindset (build quickly, test in reality, decide whether to invest further) applies to software, documents, and consulting alike.
- **Flow follows friction removal:** When you stop waiting for implementation, you enter a different creative mode. "What if?" replaces "can this be built?" and possibility space opens up.
- **Build systems, not just answers:** The shift from asking AI questions to building tools, created through AI collaboration, that produce answers is where the real value lies. Systems compound — they produce value beyond the conversation that created them. This is what separates vibe-coding from sophisticated prompting.
- **The skill transfers across domains:** The core elements of interloquial communication — articulating intent, setting constraints, defining expectations — apply wherever AI generates output. Domain expertise shortens the learning curve; technical background does not set the ceiling.
- **Speed does not replace judgment:** AI speeds up production; human judgment determines quality. As Andrew Ng identified, vibes

without discipline produces unreliable results. The discipline is using speed for more experimentation, not less consideration.

- **Vibe-coding lowers the barrier to building, not to running:** The obligations that follow a launched product — maintenance, support, security, compliance — are unchanged. Cognitive and technical debt accumulated during a fast build will surface in production. Going in clear-eyed about this is what makes the risks manageable.
- **The risks are worth taking — if you decide to proceed:** The caveats in this chapter are not reasons to stop. They are the same obligations every creator faces. Vibe-coding does not change the contract; it changes how much you can create within it.

Notes

38 Badich, S. / Click Consult (2024). "New research on customer perception of AI in marketing activity." *Click Consult*, November 28, 2024. `click.co.uk/insights/new-research-on-customer-perception-of-ai-in-marketing/`

Part Two: The Practice

CHAPTER 5

Getting Started

5.1 Introduction

It was early evening, and I was preparing a demonstration for my VibeCoded-101 presentation. I had been talking about AI-assisted development for weeks, but I wanted to show something that would cut through the scepticism. Something immediate. Something undeniable.

I opened ChatGPT and typed: "Create a classic Nokia snake game I can play in my browser."

Within seconds, code appeared. I copied it into a file, opened it in my browser, and there it was: a fully functioning snake game, moving, eating, growing longer with every bite, tracking the score, ending cleanly when it hit the wall. All from a single sentence.

That moment is the starting point, not the destination. A single prompt producing a working game is not vibe-coding. It is impressive and useful, but it is not the skill this book teaches. A snake game works from one sentence because "snake game" is a well-understood pattern the AI has seen thousands of times. Building something tailored to your specific situation, your workflow, and your requirements requires sustained dialogue. That is vibe-coding: accumulated context across iterations, where complexity emerges from conversation rather than arriving fully formed from a single request.

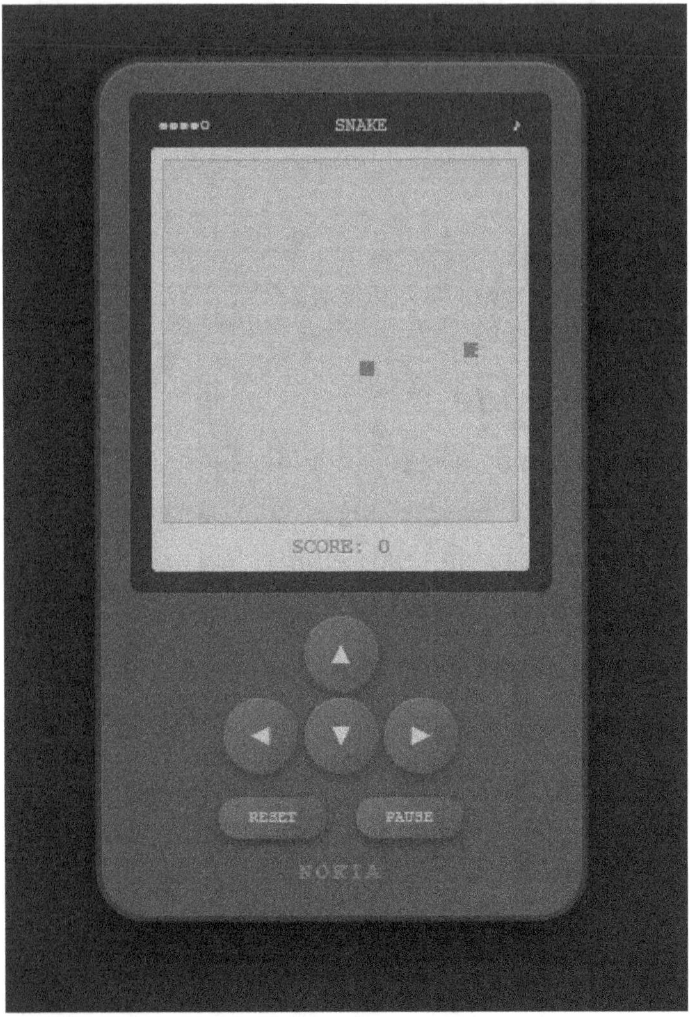

Figure 5.1: A single prompt creates a complete, working game — impressive, but not yet vibe-coding.

5.2 Your First Project

The best way to understand vibe-coding is to do it. We start in the browser: no installation, no technical setup, no barrier between you and your first result. The core loop is simple: articulate what you want, receive working code, test it, refine your request, and iterate.

Let us start with something that feels like magic. If you do not already have an AI assistant open, go to Claude.ai, ChatGPT, or Gemini in your browser and sign in — a free account is enough to start. Then type: "Create a classic snake game I can play in my browser."

Within seconds, you will receive working code for a complete game: the snake moves, food appears, the snake grows when it eats, and the game ends when it hits the wall or itself. What happens next depends on which AI you are using. Some interfaces (like Claude Code on the web at code.claude.com — correct as of March 2026) will render the game directly in the browser, letting you play immediately without any extra steps. Others (like ChatGPT or the standard Claude chat) will give you a block of code that you need to save and run yourself.

If your AI gives you code to save, here is exactly what to do:

1. **Copy the code.** Click the copy button on the code block, or select all the code and press Ctrl+C (Cmd+C on Mac).
2. **Open a text editor.** On Windows, search for "Notepad" in the Start menu. On Mac, open "TextEdit" (but first go to the Format menu and choose Make Plain Text). You do not need anything fancy.
3. **Paste the code.** Press Ctrl+V (Cmd+V on Mac). You should see the code appear in the editor.
4. **Save the file with an .html extension.** This is the step that matters. Go to File, then Save As. In the filename box, type something like `snake-game.html`. The `.html` at the end tells your computer this is a web page. In Notepad, change "Save as type" to "All Files", otherwise it might secretly add `.txt` to the end.
5. **Open the file in your browser.** Find the file you just saved (your Desktop or Downloads folder works well). Double-click it. Your default web browser will open, and you will see your game.

You just created software with a single sentence. This is the promise of vibe-coding, and it works. But it is not the whole story.

The Power of a Single Prompt

The snake game is not a fluke. Single prompts can produce remarkable results for well-defined problems:

- "Create a unit converter for metric and imperial measurements that works in my browser" produces a working calculator.
- "Create a countdown timer with start, pause, and reset buttons that works in my browser" produces exactly that.
- "Create a simple to-do list where I can add and remove items that works in my browser" produces a functional task manager.

These are not fragments of code that require assembly. They are complete, working applications. The AI has seen thousands of similar requests in its training, and it knows what a snake game or unit converter should look like. For generic, well-understood problems, a single sentence is often enough.

What happens next is where vibe-coding begins to feel like a skill rather than a trick. After my snake game worked, my next thought was natural: "Add a sound effect when the snake eats food, and a different sound when the game ends." Claude updated the code. The game now had audio feedback. Then: "Make the snake speed up slightly each time it eats." Done. "Add a high score that persists between games." Done.

Each follow-on prompt built on what existed. I was not starting from scratch; I was refining, extending, improving. You are iterating with a collaborator who remembers what you built together. This is the beginning of interloquial practice.

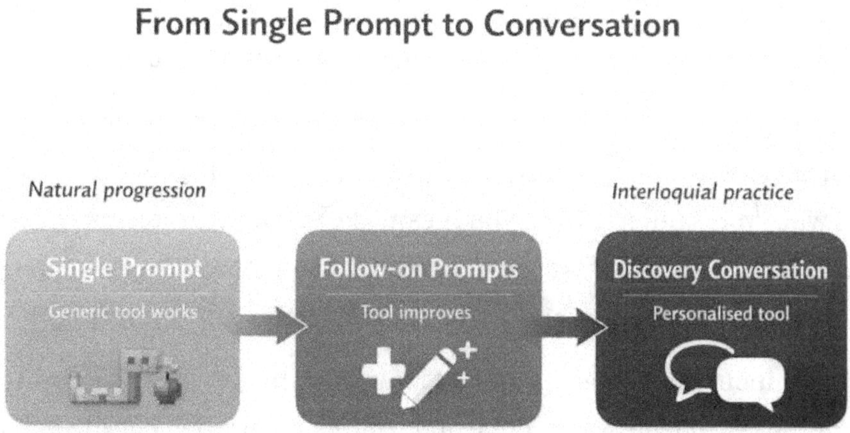

Figure 5.3: The natural progression from single prompts to follow-on refinements to full discovery conversations.

When Single Prompts Hit Their Limits

The snake game worked because there is broad consensus on what a snake game should be. But what happens when you want something specific to your situation?

Consider this prompt: "Create an expense tracker for me that works in the browser." The AI will produce something. It might even look polished. But whose expense categories will it use? The AI will guess: perhaps "Food," "Transport," "Entertainment," "Bills." But you work from home and need "Home Office Equipment." You have a side business and need to separate personal from professional expenses. You track subscriptions separately because they matter to your budget. The AI does not know any of this.

The result is an expense tracker that technically works but does not match how you actually think about money. You could fix it through follow-on prompts ("Add a Home Office category," "Split expenses into Personal and Business"), but each fix reveals another assumption you had not articulated. The AI filled gaps with reasonable guesses, and those guesses diverged from your vision in ways you only discover through use.

This is the fundamental limitation of single prompts for anything beyond generic utilities. The AI cannot read your mind. It generates based on what you said, not what you meant. For generic problems (games, calculators, timers), what you say and what you mean are close enough. For personalised tools, they diverge immediately.

The solution is not longer prompts crammed with every requirement you can think of. That rarely works, and it shifts the burden back to you to anticipate everything upfront. The solution is dialogue.

The Discovery Conversation

Instead of hoping the AI guesses correctly, invite it to ask questions first. This is the discovery conversation, and it changes everything. Some AI tools now have a dedicated "planning mode" for exactly this: the AI asks clarifying questions and develops a plan before writing any code. Whether your AI has this feature built in or you prompt for it manually, the principle is the same: conversation before creation.

Here is how it works. Instead of "Create an expense tracker for me," try:

- **Example prompt:**

> "I want to create a personal expense tracker that works in the browser. Before we build anything, help me think through the requirements. What questions should I be asking myself?"

The AI responds with questions you had not considered:

- "How should expenses be categorised? Fixed categories, or should you be able to create your own?"

- "Do you need to track recurring expenses separately from one-off purchases?"
- "What time period matters most: weekly summaries, monthly totals, or yearly overviews?"
- "Should it support multiple currencies, or just pounds?"
- "How do you want to visualise spending: charts, tables, or simple totals?"
- "Do you need to export data, or is this purely for personal reference?"

You asked a simple question, and the AI surfaced decisions you would otherwise have discovered through painful iteration. Each question forces you to articulate what you actually want. Your answers become the specification.

After you answer, the AI has context it could never have inferred from "Create an expense tracker." It knows you want custom categories, monthly focus, pounds only, simple tables rather than fancy charts, and export to CSV for tax purposes. The implementation that follows will match your vision because the vision emerged through dialogue.

This approach inverts the typical pattern. Instead of: describe - build - discover problems - fix - repeat, you get: discover - describe - build - minor refinements. The conversation before the first line of code often does more work than the code itself.

Using ICE to Guide the Conversation

Chapter 2 introduced the ICE framework: Intent (what you want to achieve), Constraints (what boundaries apply), and Expectations (how you will know it works). You do not need to fill this in like a form. Instead, use it as a prompt for the AI itself.

After your initial discovery conversation, try:

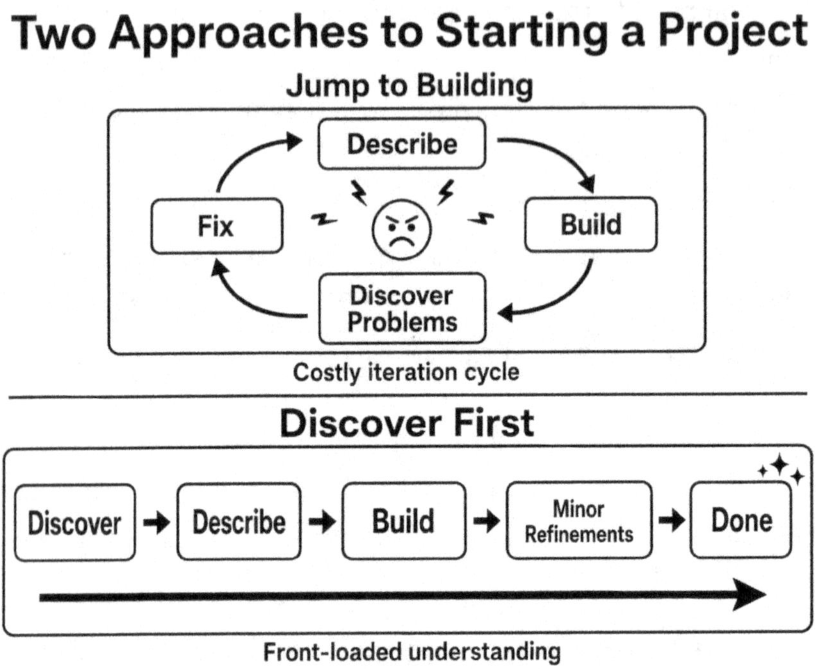

Figure 5.4: Discovering requirements through dialogue (right) produces better first implementations than jumping straight to building (left).

- **Example prompt:**

> "Help me consider what constraints and expectations I might be missing from this plan."

The AI becomes your thinking partner, surfacing blind spots you would not have identified alone. For constraints, it might ask: "Should this work offline, or is an internet connection acceptable?" "Are there file size limits if you want to share this with others?" "Should it work on mobile phones, or is desktop-only acceptable?" For expectations, it might ask: "How will you test that the monthly totals are calculating correctly?" "What should happen if someone enters invalid data?" "What would 'done' look like for version one?"

Use the AI to help you think more thoroughly. ICE is flexible: before a conversation it can prompt the right questions; after one, it can audit what was covered. Use it however it helps. The important thing is that Intent, Constraints, and Expectations are established before implementation begins, however that happens. If you finish a discovery conversation and realise you never discussed constraints, that is a signal to ask one more question. If expectations are vague, ask the AI to help you define "done."

When you and the AI share the same understanding of intent, constraints, and expectations, the code that follows tends to match your vision on the first attempt. When any of these are fuzzy, you discover the mismatch through frustrating iterations.

ICE is not just for the initial conversation. As you iterate on your project, the same principle applies. Small refinements ("make the button blue") need no ceremony. But when you want to add something more substantial (a new feature, a different workflow, a significant change to scope), pause and ask the AI to surface constraints and expectations again:

- **Example prompt:**

> "I want to add the ability to filter expenses by date range. What constraints or expectations should I consider before we build this?"

This keeps each iteration on track with your vision rather than accumulating assumptions that diverge over time.

5.3 The Practical Mechanics

Between "AI gave me code" and "I have working software" lie practical details that no one explains. How do you run the code? What do you do when it almost works? How do you keep track of what you have built? This section covers the mechanics: the unglamorous but essential steps that turn AI output into something you can use, share, and build upon.

From Chatbot to Code Interface

A simple chatbot is capable of creating code within a single conversation. ChatGPT, Claude, Gemini: all of them can generate working HTML, CSS, and JavaScript in response to plain English requests. You have already seen this with the snake game. The chatbot generates code; you copy it into a file; you run it.

This works, and it teaches you what is actually happening. You see the code, you handle the files, and you understand that the "magic" is text your browser interprets. For learning, this transparency counts.

As your projects grow, however, the copy-paste workflow becomes friction. You want to modify multiple files, keep the AI aware of your project structure across conversations, and have changes applied directly without manual copying.

This is where code-focused interfaces enter the picture. Claude Code on the web (code.claude.com) can manage your project files directly. It creates files, modifies existing ones, and maintains memory of your project across conversations. Instead of copying code from a chat window into separate files, you work within a single environment where the AI has direct access to everything you are building.

For this chapter, we stay with the simpler chatbot approach. The skills transfer directly, and you will understand what the more sophisticated tools are doing under the surface. Chapter 6 introduces the code-focused environment for readers ready to level up.

Running Generated Code

The first project in this chapter walked through the basic process: copy the code, paste into a text editor, save with an `.html` extension, and open in your browser. A few additional tips as your projects grow:

- **Save somewhere you can find.** Downloads or your Desktop work well for experiments. Create a folder called "vibe-coding" if you expect to build multiple projects. Losing track of files is frustrating.
- **Avoid `index.html` during development.** Many platforms treat `index.html` as a special default filename. While developing, use descriptive names like `expense-tracker-v1.html`. Save `index.html` for when you are ready to publish.
- **If the AI gives you separate code blocks**, ask it to combine them.
- **Example prompt:**

  > "Combine the HTML, CSS, and JavaScript into a single file I can open in my browser."

Single-file projects are far easier to manage when you are starting out.

When It Does Not Work

You open the file and nothing happens. Or something happens, but it is not what you expected. Or it works once and then breaks. This is normal. First attempts often need refinement.

When code fails silently (the page is blank or nothing responds to clicks), open your browser's developer console. Press F12 on most browsers, then click the "Console" tab. Look for red text. These are error messages.

You do not need to understand what "TypeError: Cannot read property 'length' of undefined" means. Copy the entire error message and paste it back to the AI with a simple note: "I got this error when I opened the file."

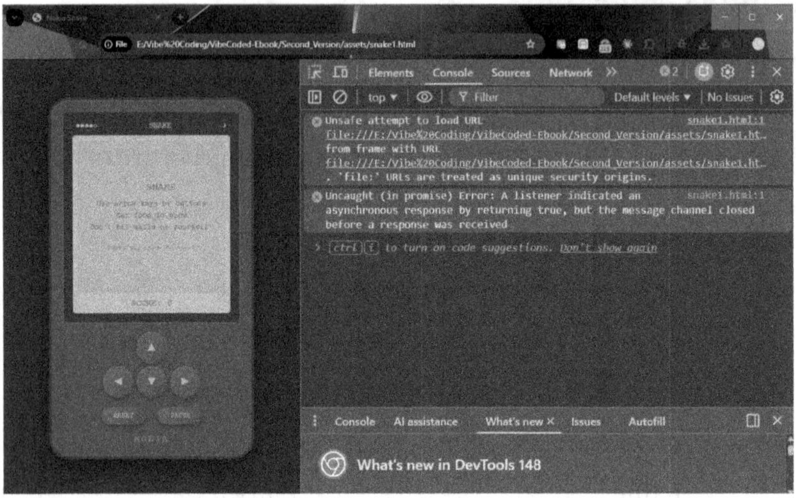

Figure 5.5: Press F12, click Console, and copy any red error text. The AI will do the interpretation.

The AI will diagnose the problem and provide corrected code. This is one of the most powerful aspects of vibe-coding: error messages that would stump a beginner are diagnostic gold to the AI. Your job is not to interpret errors; your job is to notice them and share them.

When code runs but behaves unexpectedly, describe the gap between what you expected and what happened. "The snake moves, but it does not grow when it eats food" is more useful than "It is broken." "The expense total shows NaN instead of a number" (NaN means "not a number": it appears when a calculation receives text instead of a figure) gives the AI something specific to investigate.

Be patient with this loop. You are not failing when you need multiple iterations. You are practising the core skill of vibe-coding: communicating precisely about what you want and what you observe.

The Refinement Loop

Refinement is not fixing mistakes; it is evolving toward your vision. Each iteration teaches you something about what you actually want. The expense tracker that "basically works" reveals that you want the delete button on the right, not the left. The snake game that "feels slow" clarifies that you wanted the initial speed to be faster.

Communicate corrections by describing the delta between expectation and reality:

- **Example prompt:**

  > "The layout is good, but the 'Add Expense' button should be at the top, not the bottom."

- **Example prompt:**

  > "The categories work, but I want them sorted alphabetically in the dropdown."

- **Example prompt:**

  > "The total calculates correctly, but it should show two decimal places."

Screenshots speed up this communication dramatically. Modern AI assistants can interpret images directly. Use Snip and Sketch (Windows) or Screenshot (Mac) to capture what you see, then annotate with arrows or circles to show what is wrong. The AI sees the current state, sees your annotations, and generates the correction. A marked-up screenshot communicates faster than paragraphs of description.

In my experience, three or four refinement cycles is common for a first project, though this varies with the complexity of what you are building and how precisely you articulated requirements upfront. Do not mistake iteration for failure. The loop is the method.

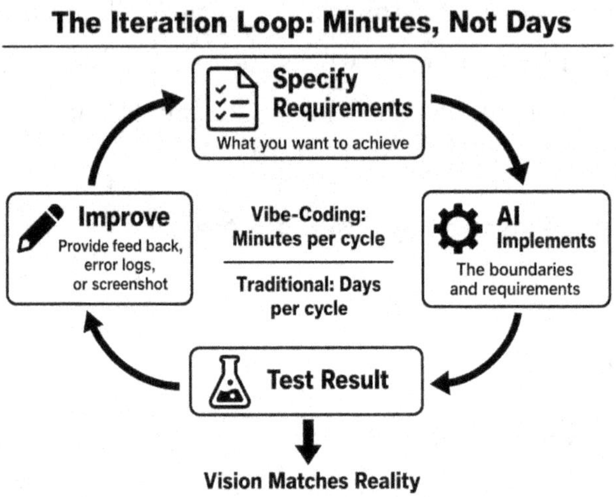

Figure 5.6: The refinement cycle — specify, implement, test, refine — measured in minutes, not days.

Saving Your Work

Most AI interfaces preserve your conversation history, so you can return and pick up where you left off. But the HTML file on your computer only exists if you saved it. Close the editor without saving and your work is gone. Four habits that prevent this:

- **Save every version that works.** When the snake game functions correctly, save it as `snake-v1.html`. When you add sound effects, save as `snake-v2.html`. If version three breaks something, you can always go back. This manual approach is crude compared to proper tools like Git, but it is effective enough for your first projects.
- **Use descriptive file names.** A name like snake-game-with-sound-and-highscore.html tells you what that version contains. `test3.html` tells you nothing. Future you will thank present you.

- **Download conversation history.** The conversation contains your discovery dialogue, the requirements you articulated, and the evolution of your thinking. It is a record worth keeping.
- **Ask the AI to summarise the conversation.** Better than a raw download is a structured summary.
- **Example prompt:**

> "Summarise the conversations we have had to achieve this outcome so that I can reproduce it again in the future."

The AI will distil your iterative discovery into a description of what was built and why. Save this as a `.txt` file alongside your code. A good summary captures what matters; a full conversation history captures everything but buries the signal. The summary becomes a specification you can hand to a fresh AI session, or to yourself six months from now. Context is an asset. Treat it like one.

As projects grow beyond single files, this manual approach becomes unwieldy. That is one of the signals that you are ready for more sophisticated tools. But for your first projects, deliberate file saving is sufficient.

5.4 When to Level Up

Browser-based vibe-coding is where everyone should start. Many useful projects can be completed entirely in the browser, and there is no obligation to go further. If the browser workflow is serving you, keep using it.

The friction will tell you when to move on. You will not need to decide in advance; you will feel it.

Signs You Have Outgrown the Browser

With one of my earlier projects, the moment arrived without announcement. I had files scattered across folders in Windows Explorer and was losing track of what was what. Which version had the working database connection? Where did I put the configuration file? Why were there three copies of `main.html` with slightly different names? The project had outgrown my ability to manage it through manual file handling.

You will recognise the same moment by these symptoms:

- You are copying and pasting code between multiple files and losing track of which is current.
- You made a change that broke something and cannot remember what the working version looked like.
- Your project needs separate files for HTML, CSS, JavaScript, and data, and managing them manually is confusing.
- You want to experiment with a risky change but are afraid of losing what works.
- The AI needs to "see" your project structure to give useful suggestions, and explaining it in text is tedious.

Any one of these is sufficient. When the tooling starts costing you more time than the building, Chapter 6 is your next stop. Everything you have learned here transfers without modification: articulation, discovery conversations, the refinement loop, ICE. The environment changes; the practice does not.

5.5 Key Takeaways

- **Single prompts work when the task maps to a well-understood pattern.** If you can describe what you want in five words and a stranger would know exactly what you meant (a snake game, a countdown timer, a unit converter), a single prompt will likely succeed. For anything personalised or domain-specific, the AI's reasonable guesses will diverge from your vision.
- **Dialogue beats monologue.** For anything personalised, use discovery conversations. Ask the AI: "What questions should I be asking myself?" Let the specification emerge through dialogue rather than hoping your first prompt captures everything.
- **ICE is an audit tool, not a template.** After your discovery conversation, check whether you covered Intent, Constraints, and Expectations. Use the AI to help: "Help me consider what constraints and expectations I might be missing."
- **Test immediately, iterate deliberately.** Run the code within seconds of receiving it. Describe the gap between expectation and reality. Screenshots with annotations communicate faster than text.
- **Save every working version.** Manual version control through file naming (v1, v2, v3) is crude but effective. You need a way to go back when things break.
- **Know when to level up.** The friction will tell you: lost files, broken versions you cannot recover, a project the AI cannot see. Chapter 6 is there when you need it. The interloquial skills transfer completely.

CHAPTER 6

Tools — and What They Cost You

6.1 Introduction

This chapter has two distinct parts, and both matter regardless of your role. The first part covers what happens to your data when you use AI tools: what leaves your device, where it goes, and what your professional obligations are around it. This applies whether you are building software yourself or managing a team that is. If you are a manager who will never open a code editor, this section is still relevant to you. Your team's tool choices have data governance consequences that land with you, not them. Read it before you decide anything about how AI is used in your organisation.

The second part covers the specific tools available for vibe-coding beyond the browser, including VS Code, Claude Code, and Git. These sections are genuinely optional: if you are a manager or a reader who intends to stay in the browser for the foreseeable future, you may skip ahead to Chapter 7. Return to the tooling sections when your projects grow beyond what the browser can handle. They will still be here.

Tool choices in vibe-coding are not purely technical decisions. Every environment you use (browser, desktop application, code editor) makes a different set of trade-offs between capability and data exposure. The browser is the safest and least capable. A code editor with full file access is the most capable and least contained. Before choosing your environment, you need to understand that trade-off. Risk professionals call this assessing the blast radius: the potential spread of a decision's consequences before you commit to it. This chapter asks you to do the same.

When you have made that assessment, here is what to use. My setup is Claude as my AI assistant, VS Code as my editor, and Git for version control. Not because these are objectively the best tools, but because I know them well, and knowing your tools matters more than having the theoretically optimal ones. Most of these tools have costs attached. Free tiers exist but come with limitations. As your practice develops, you will likely end up paying for at least one subscription. Budget for it.

6.2 What Goes Where

When you type a message into an AI assistant, that text leaves your device and travels to a server operated by the provider. This is true whether you are using the browser, a desktop application, or an editor extension. What changes between environments is how much leaves, and that difference has professional implications.

In the browser, you send what you type. If you paste in a paragraph of text and ask the AI to summarise it, that paragraph is sent. If you describe a business problem, that description is sent. Most organisations have no explicit policy against this because it is broadly similar to using a search engine: you are choosing what to share, and you are sharing only what you type.

A desktop application with file access changes this significantly. When you give an AI assistant permission to read your project files, as Claude Code and similar tools are designed to do, the AI reads those files in full: not just the fragment you paste, but every file in scope. The capability is what makes vibe-coding powerful at scale. The risk is that the scope of what you are sharing expands from a sentence you chose to a codebase you might not have audited.

A code editor extension with full codebase access extends this further. In a professional setting, a codebase may contain configuration files, environment variables, hardcoded values left by previous developers, or comments that document internal business logic. None of this is secret in the sense of being encrypted, but much of it was written on the assumption that it would stay inside the organisation. Once it travels to an AI provider's server, those assumptions no longer hold.

The question to ask before choosing your environment is not "which tool is most powerful?" It is: "what data will this tool access, and am I entitled to share it?" Several categories of data have clear answers:

- **Personal data about identifiable individuals**, such as names, contact details, health information, or financial records, is almost certainly governed by data protection legislation (GDPR in the UK and EU, equivalent legislation elsewhere). Feeding personal data to an external AI service without a data processing agreement in place is, in most jurisdictions, a compliance failure. Ask your data protection officer before you proceed.
- **Commercially sensitive business information.** Client names, contract terms, pricing strategies, and unpublished financials belong to your organisation. Your employment contract almost certainly contains a confidentiality clause. The fact that you are using the information to build something useful does not remove the obligation.
- **Credentials and secrets.** API keys (the access codes that connect software systems), passwords, and database connection strings must never enter an AI conversation, regardless of environment. They do not belong in code either, unless that code excludes them from version

control. This is not an edge case; it is the most common avoidable security failure in AI-assisted development.

Figure 6.1: The Other End of the Cable — what you share innocently, someone else receives permanently.

If you are building something that handles any of these categories, build the code that answers the question rather than feeding the data to the AI. The AI can generate code that processes sensitive records; it does not need to see the records themselves. This pattern, building code to query the data rather than sharing the data directly, is how disciplined practitioners handle the boundary between AI capability and data governance. It is also the approach that lets you use capable tools without incurring the risks of unrestricted data exposure.

There is no need to be paralysed by this. The majority of projects you will build (automations, reporting tools, dashboards, productivity scripts) do not involve categories of data that require special handling. But the check takes thirty seconds and the consequences of skipping it are disproportionate. Make it a habit: before starting any project that touches data, ask yourself what categories that data falls into and whether you are entitled to share it with an external service.

A note on enterprise AI. If your organisation uses an enterprise tier of an AI platform (such as ChatGPT Enterprise, Microsoft Copilot for Microsoft 365, or Google Gemini for Workspace), the position is materially different from the consumer tiers described above. Enterprise agreements typically include a formal data processing agreement, a contractual commitment that your data will not be used to train the provider's models, data isolation from other customers, and options for specifying where your data is processed geographically. These are legal commitments, not just policy statements, and they are enforceable. The practical effect is that enterprise AI is genuinely closer to a managed business service than to a public website.

However, enterprise agreements do not eliminate data exposure entirely. All major providers retain the ability to scan content for policy violations (detecting harmful material, illegal content, and similar) which means that under defined conditions, flagged content may be reviewed by authorised personnel. Providers can also be compelled to disclose data by lawful legal process, and enterprise agreements do not override government subpoenas. The appropriate response to enterprise AI is not blanket trust, but informed and proportionate use: apply data minimisation (do not send what the AI does not need to see), document what data flows through which systems, and verify your organisation's specific agreement before treating it as a green light for sensitive data. If you are unsure whether your organisation's AI tools carry enterprise protections, ask your IT or legal team before proceeding.

This does not mean AI cannot help you analyse sensitive data; it means the approach matters. Chapter 4 introduced the distinction between asking

AI for answers and building systems that produce answers. Applied to data analysis, the same logic holds: rather than feeding records to the AI, describe what your data looks like (column names, data types, a row of anonymised dummy values) and ask the AI to write the code or formula that performs the analysis. The code runs inside your environment against your real data; the AI never sees the records themselves. Where your organisation has connected enterprise AI to internal data sources within its own security boundary, that architecture achieves the same separation at scale, but requires IT to set it up correctly. The rule of thumb is the same in both cases: bring the code to the data, not the data to the AI.

6.3 Your Environment Options

There are three distinct environments to work in, and you can move between them as your projects grow. The recommended path is: start in the browser, move to a desktop AI application when copy-pasting becomes friction, and move to a code editor only when you genuinely need local file management or offline capability. Most practitioners who reach the code editor stage do so because their projects grew, not because the earlier environments stopped working.

The browser. No installation, no subscription required to start. Claude.ai, ChatGPT, and Gemini all offer free browser access. You describe what you want, the AI generates code, and you copy it into a file. The free tier is limited but sufficient for learning and small projects. This is where to begin.

A desktop AI application. Several AI providers offer desktop applications that go beyond the browser. The Claude desktop app includes Claude Code (direct access to your project files, no copy-pasting) and autonomous multi-step task capabilities. Microsoft's Copilot and ChatGPT also offer desktop applications with varying degrees of file access. These are the natural next step when the browser copy-paste workflow becomes friction, and none of them require a separate code editor. Most require a paid subscription to access the file management features. This is where the data exposure considerations covered earlier in this chapter become directly relevant: file access means the AI can read more than you explicitly paste.

A code editor with an AI extension. For projects that require a full development environment (running code locally, managing a large codebase, working with data that cannot leave your machine), a dedicated code editor is the professional standard. VS Code is the most widely used and is free; Cursor and Windsurf are alternatives built with AI integration as a core feature rather than an add-on. Every major AI provider offers an extension for VS Code: GitHub Copilot (Microsoft/OpenAI), Claude Code (Anthropic), Gemini Code Assist (Google), and others. This is the most capable setup, and also the most involved to configure. Move here only when you genuinely need it.

Do not agonise over which environment or which AI provider to use. The interloquial skills you develop transfer across all of them. The tool is not the bottleneck. Your ability to articulate what you want is.

Costs Are Real

The browser is free to start, but the features that make the biggest difference (file management, autonomous tasks, deep editor integration) require a paid subscription. Each provider structures its tiers differently, and the features you want may not be available on the entry-level plan; check what is included before subscribing. As an example, a Claude Pro subscription covers the desktop app, Claude Code, and the VS Code extension, so there is no need to pay separately for each environment. Free tiers exist to let you try before you commit; they are not designed for serious ongoing work. You may also find that different providers serve different needs: I use Claude Pro for coding and ChatGPT Plus for image generation, two subscriptions, each serving a distinct purpose.

Tokens and Context Windows

Every AI interaction is measured in *tokens*: fragments of words and punctuation that the model processes as numbers. Subscriptions typically include a monthly token allowance; once exhausted, you either wait for the next billing cycle or pay for additional usage. The cost of this adds up at scale in ways that are easy to underestimate: OpenAI's own CEO has noted that the extra words in polite requests, "please" and "thank you" included, cost the company tens of millions of dollars a year in compute.[36] The practical implication is direct: vague requests that require three rounds of clarification consume more of that allowance than a clear, well-structured request that succeeds the first time. Planning deeply before you start is not just better practice; it is more efficient use of a limited resource.

Every AI model also has a *context window*: the maximum it can hold in working memory at once. Your questions, the AI's answers, and any files it is reading all count against this limit. When a long conversation approaches the limit, the AI begins to drop earlier content; this is why extended sessions can feel as though the AI is losing track. It is not confused; it has run out of room. The project memory file covered later in this chapter addresses this: rather than rebuilding shared understanding from scratch each session, you give the AI a concise briefing file it reads at the start. Keep that file lean. A verbose history consumes tokens before you have typed a single request.

6.4 VS Code Setup

What follows is a brief orientation, not a complete guide. VS Code is a sophisticated application used professionally by millions of developers, and this section covers only what you need to get started with vibe-coding. For anything beyond the basics (keyboard shortcuts, debugging, extensions, themes, workspace settings), the internet is your best resource. Search for what you need and you will almost always find a clear tutorial or video. I did not choose VS Code through careful evaluation. I chose it because the tutorials I followed used it, because Claude Code supported it, and because everyone around me seemed to use it. These are not sophisticated reasons. They are practical ones, and they are good enough.

Installation

Installing VS Code is simple. Visit code.visualstudio.com, download the installer for your operating system, and run it. Accept the defaults.

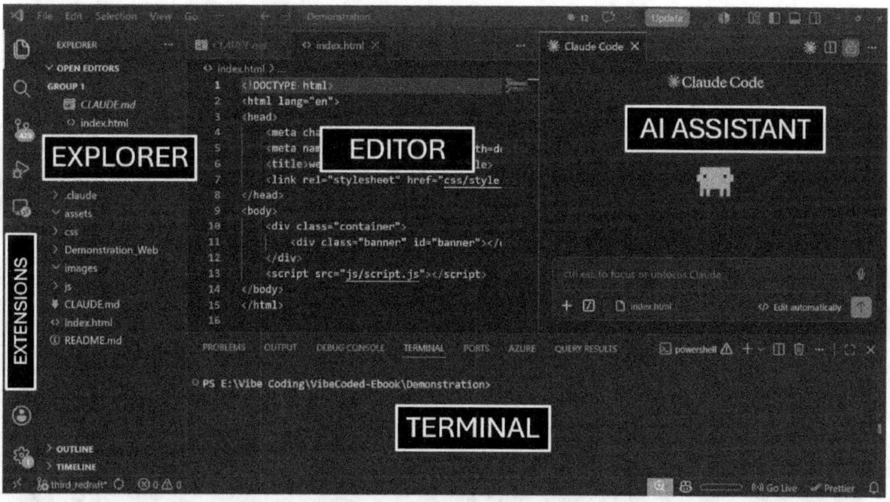

Figure 6.1: VS Code with a project open, showing Explorer (left), Editor (centre), Terminal (bottom), and Extensions icon (sidebar).

When you first launch VS Code, close the welcome screen. The interface has four main areas: a sidebar on the left showing files and folders, a large central area where you edit code, a panel at the bottom that can show a terminal, errors, and output, and an AI assistant panel on the right. This right-hand panel may default to GitHub Copilot depending on your installation; you can switch it to Claude Code or whichever AI assistant you prefer once it is installed. That is all you need to know to start.

The Four Things You Actually Need

For vibe-coding, you need to understand four things about VS Code. Everything else can wait until you have a specific need for it.

- **The Explorer** (folder icon in the left sidebar) shows your project files and folders. Click a file to open it. Right-click to create new files or folders.
- **The Editor** (centre of the screen) is where you view and modify code. Changes are not saved automatically. Press Ctrl+S (Cmd+S on Mac) to save.
- **The Terminal** (View menu > Terminal, or Ctrl+‘) gives you a command line inside VS Code. When the AI tells you to run a command, this is where you run it.
- **The Extensions panel** (blocks icon in the left sidebar) is where you install AI assistants and other tools.

Three Settings Worth Changing

VS Code has hundreds of settings. These three are worth adjusting early:

- **Auto Save** – File menu > Auto Save. Prevents the frustration of testing changes that were never saved.

- **Word Wrap** – View menu > Word Wrap. Makes long lines readable without horizontal scrolling.
- **Font Size** – search "font size" in Settings. If you are squinting, increase it.

Adding Your AI Extension

To add AI assistance to VS Code, click the Extensions icon, search for the tool you want ("GitHub Copilot" or "Claude"), and click Install. Verify the publisher name, as imitations exist. Most extensions require you to sign in. Follow the prompts.

When you sign in to an AI extension, you will typically be asked how you want to connect it: either through a subscription account (such as GitHub Copilot via a GitHub account, or Claude via an Anthropic account) or by providing an API key (a unique access code that connects your account to the service). A subscription gives you a fixed monthly allowance and is the simpler starting point. An API key connects directly to the provider's service and charges per use, which can be cost-effective for light usage but requires you to create a developer account and manage billing separately. If you are unsure which to choose, start with the subscription option. You can switch later once you understand your usage patterns.

While the Extensions panel is open, one other extension is worth installing: **Live Server** (publisher: Ritwick Dey). It adds a button to the VS Code status bar that opens any HTML file in your browser and reloads it automatically whenever you save. For a vibe-coder, this is most useful when reviewing wireframes before building: rather than dragging a file into a browser manually, you open it with Live Server and any change you ask your AI assistant to make appears in the browser the moment the file is saved. Search for "Live Server" in the Extensions panel, verify the publisher, and install it alongside your AI extension.

6.5 Git Essentials

Git is a version control system. It tracks changes to your files over time so you can return to any previous state, experiment safely, and recover from mistakes. For vibe-coders, it is a safety net: when the AI suggests a change that breaks everything, you can undo it. When you want to try something risky, you can create a branch, experiment freely, and delete it if the experiment fails. You do not need to become a Git expert. You need to understand the concepts well enough to tell your AI when to use it.

Installation

On Windows, download Git from git-scm.com and run the installer. Accept the defaults. On Mac, open Terminal, type `git --version`, and follow the prompt to install the Xcode Command Line Tools if Git is not already present.

After installation, you need to tell Git your name and email. Git will not prompt you for these automatically; it uses blank or system defaults, which means your commits will be attributed incorrectly or trigger warnings later. Do it once now. In VS Code, open a terminal (Terminal > New Terminal from the menu bar, or press Ctrl+`on Windows, Cmd+` on Mac), then type the following two lines, pressing Enter after each, replacing the name and email with your own:

```
git config --global user.name "Your Name"
git config --global user.email "your.email@example.com"
```

You will not need to do this again: the `--global` flag saves these settings for all projects on your computer.

Your First Repository

A repository (or "repo") is a folder that Git is tracking. To start tracking a project, open its folder in VS Code and tell your AI:

- **Example prompt:**

> "Initialise a Git repository for this project."

The AI runs the appropriate command. Your project is now a Git repository.

Before your first commit: a security warning worth reading once and never forgetting. If your project contains passwords, API keys, database credentials, or any other secrets, those files must never be committed to Git. Once committed and pushed to GitHub (a cloud service that stores a copy of your repository online, covered later in this section), secrets are effectively public even if you delete them later; they may have been indexed or scraped. Tell your AI:

- **Example prompt:**

> "Create a .gitignore file for this project that excludes environment files, API keys, and any files containing secrets."

Do this before your first commit.

To take your first snapshot, tell your AI:

- **Example prompt:**

> "Create an initial commit with all the current files."

The AI stages and commits everything. You now have a checkpoint you can return to.

Let the AI Handle the Commands

You do not need to memorise Git commands. Your AI can execute them. What you need is the judgement to know when. Three habits cover most situations:

- **Commit regularly.** After completing work that functions correctly, tell your AI:

  > "Commit these changes with a message describing what we just built."

- **Branch before risky changes.** Before trying something that might break working code, tell your AI:

  > "Create a new branch called 'experiment-new-feature' before we make these changes."

- **Understand concepts, not commands.** A commit is a snapshot. A branch is a parallel line of development. Merging combines them. The AI handles the syntax; you provide the strategic decisions.

If a risky change fails, delete the branch and return to your stable state.

GitHub: Remote Backup and Free Hosting

Git stores your repository on your computer. If your computer fails, your repository is lost. **GitHub** (github.com) solves this by storing a copy on their servers, with free unlimited public and private repositories. To use it: create a free account at github.com, then create a new repository there (click the "+" button, select "New repository", give it a name, and leave the other settings as defaults). GitHub will show you the URL of your new repository. Copy it, then tell your AI:

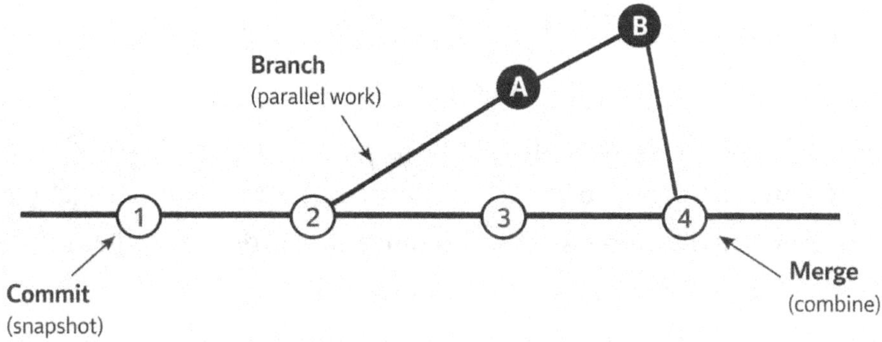

Figure 6.3: A commit is a snapshot. A branch is a parallel line of development. Merging combines them.

- **Example prompt:**

> "Connect this local repository to my GitHub repository at [paste your URL here] and push the code."

The AI links them and pushes your code to the remote. From that point, every time you commit, tell the AI to push and your backup is updated.

GitHub also offers **GitHub Pages**: free hosting for your projects, directly from your repository. Your project gets a URL like `yourusername.github.io/project-name` accessible from any device. In your GitHub repository, go to Settings > Pages, select your branch, and GitHub deploys automatically when you push changes. For simple HTML, CSS, and JavaScript projects, this just works.

When Things Go Wrong

Git is powerful but unforgiving. When you end up in a confusing state (merge conflicts, error messages you do not recognise), describe the situation to your AI:

- **Example prompt:**

> "Git is showing this error. What does it mean and how do I fix it?"

In most cases, the AI can diagnose and guide you through the resolution. For truly catastrophic situations, you have a nuclear option: clone a fresh copy from GitHub and start over. Your commits are safe on the remote server. The local confusion can be abandoned.

6.6 The Terminal

The terminal is a text-based interface where you type commands instead of clicking menus. For vibe-coding, you need it because some development tools only work through it: installing dependencies, starting a development server, running Git when the graphical interface cannot help. You do not need to master it. You need to be comfortable enough to run commands your AI gives you, and confident enough to ask what they do first.

Opening and Using a Terminal

The most convenient option is the terminal inside VS Code: press Ctrl+‘ (backtick, below Escape). Alternatively, on Windows search for "Command Prompt" or "Git Bash" in the Start menu; on Mac, press Cmd+Space, type "Terminal," and press Enter.

The only navigation commands you need: `cd foldername` moves into a folder, `cd ..` goes up one level, and `ls` (Mac/Linux) or `dir` (Windows) lists what is in the current folder. That is genuinely all.

Before running any command your AI gives you, take five seconds to ask what it does:

- **Example prompt:**

> "What does this command do, and is there anything I should be aware of before I run it?"

The terminal is powerful, which means errors can have real consequences. A good AI will explain in plain English. If the explanation does not satisfy you, do not run the command. This is the calibrated trust model from Chapter 2 applied in practice: not blind acceptance of AI output, but a brief check before acting on it.

6.7 Putting It Together

My Start Routine

Here is how I begin every new project. The specifics will vary based on your tools and preferences, but the underlying pattern transfers regardless of what you use.

Step 1: Create the folder. A new folder in Windows Explorer with a descriptive name. Nothing fancy.

Step 2: Open in VS Code. Open that folder. At this point it is empty: a blank canvas.

Step 3: Initialise for Claude and Git. The first thing I ask Claude:

- **Example prompt:**

> "Initialise this folder for Claude and Git."

This creates the `.git` folder for version control and the `CLAUDE.md` file for project memory. The foundation is laid.

Step 4: Enter planning mode. Before writing any code, I ask my AI assistant to enter planning mode and save the plan to a file:

- **Example prompt:**

> "Enter planning mode. As we discuss this project, save the plan to plan.md."

This is where the thinking happens before the building starts.

Step 5: Plan with ICE. As we discuss the project, I ask my AI to populate `plan.md` with our decisions. I actively challenge what might have been missed: What constraints have I not mentioned? What am I expecting that I have not made explicit? Chapter 7 covers this planning process in full.

Step 6: Commit throughout planning. Even during planning, I periodically commit and push. The plan itself is worth preserving. If my computer fails, I want to recover the thinking that shaped the project, not just the code.

Step 7: Implement from the plan. Once satisfied with the plan, I ask my AI to implement it.

Step 8: Commit before testing. I commit immediately after the first implementation, before I even test it. If testing reveals problems and I start iterating, I want a checkpoint of the AI's first interpretation to compare against.

Step 9: Iterate. Test, observe, describe what is wrong, let the AI fix it, test again. Commit whenever something works. Branch when trying something risky. Push periodically to keep the remote backup current.

The pattern is consistent: initialise, plan, commit, implement, commit, iterate. The AI handles the mechanics. You provide the direction.

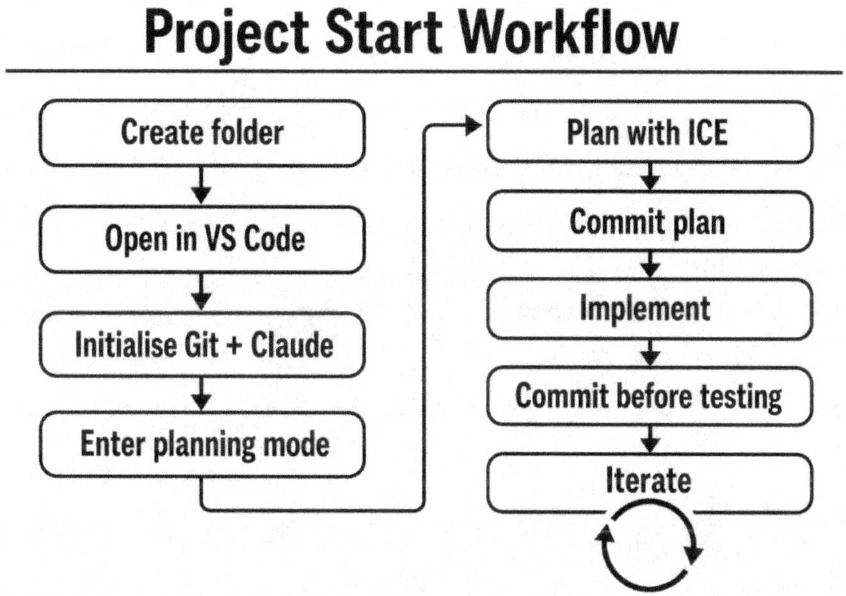

Figure 6.4: The nine-step start routine. Steps 1–8 happen once per project. Step 9 repeats until the project is complete.

Project Memory Files

The most powerful habit in this workflow is one most vibe-coders discover late: giving your AI persistent context about your project. Instead of re-explaining what you are building at the start of every conversation, you write a file that the AI reads automatically. For Claude Code, this file is `CLAUDE.md`. Place it in your project root and Claude reads it at the start of every conversation. For Cursor, the equivalent is `.cursorrules`. Same concept, different filename.

Here is a minimal example:

```
# Project: Expense Tracker

## Overview
A browser-based expense tracker for personal use.

## Conventions
- British English in comments and UI text
- Currency in GBP (£)
- No external dependencies, vanilla JavaScript only

## Structure
- index.html: Main application
- style.css: Styling
- app.js: Application logic
```

Start simple and keep it lean. These files consume tokens every time the AI reads them; a large memory file means higher costs and less room for conversation. Treat `CLAUDE.md` as an index rather than an encyclopaedia: project overview, key conventions, and references to other files. "See plan.md for the implementation plan" costs one line. The AI reads `plan.md` when it needs the detail; it does not load the entire project history into every session. Add detail as your project grows and as you discover what context the AI needs to work effectively.

Claude also supports a layered memory system that becomes useful once you have multiple projects. A `CLAUDE.md` placed in your home directory (the top-level folder for your user account) acts as a global briefing that Claude reads in every session, regardless of which project you are working on. A `CLAUDE.md` inside a specific project folder adds the project-specific context on top of that global foundation. The two files work together: global rules apply everywhere, project rules apply only where they are relevant. You never have to repeat your standing preferences in every project file.

Project Organisation

As projects grow beyond a single file, a consistent folder structure prevents confusion. Most web projects follow a simple convention that the AI will apply automatically if you ask:

- `assets/` — images, icons, fonts, and other static files that the project uses but does not generate
- `scripts/` (or `js/`) — JavaScript files, kept separate from the HTML so they are easier to find and update
- `styles/` (or `css/`) — stylesheet files, if you have separated them from the HTML
- `data/` — any JSON, CSV, or other data files the project reads
- `index.html` — the entry point; web servers treat this filename as the default for a folder, so it is what loads when someone visits your project's URL

You do not need to set this up yourself. Tell the AI:

- **Example prompt:**

  > "Organise this project into a standard folder structure with separate folders for assets, scripts, and styles."

It will create the folders, move the files, and update any references so nothing breaks. Revisit the structure whenever a folder starts feeling cluttered: that is the signal to ask the AI to reorganise.

6.8 The Habits You Are Building

Choosing your tools is also choosing your cognitive patterns. This is not a metaphor; it is a finding that has been empirically demonstrated. Research published in April 2026 by Liu and colleagues tracked what happened to independent problem-solving ability when participants were given AI assistance, then had it removed.[46] After as little as ten minutes of AI assistance, participants showed measurable degradation in both performance and persistence when working without it. The researchers described it as a boiling frog effect: the assistance felt like support, but the dependency formed faster than participants recognised it.

The finding is not an argument against using AI. It is an argument about *how* to use it. The same research identified a meaningful distinction between two modes of AI use: answer-seeking, where the user asks the AI to solve the problem; and hint-seeking, where the user asks the AI to illuminate the problem while retaining the reasoning themselves. Participants who used AI in hint-seeking mode showed significantly less degradation. This is ICE in empirical form: a practitioner who has articulated their intent, named their constraints, and defined their expectations before asking the AI to act is using AI to extend their thinking, not replace it. A practitioner who simply asks "fix this" and accepts whatever arrives is doing something structurally different and producing a different cognitive outcome.

The tools in this chapter make answer-seeking very easy. A code editor with AI integration can execute multi-step tasks autonomously, producing working code without the practitioner understanding what was built or why. This capability is genuinely useful for well-understood tasks with clear ICE specifications. It is a cognitive liability when the specification is vague and the practitioner accepts the output on the basis that it works rather than that it is right. The difference between these two uses of the same tool is entirely in the human's approach, not the tool's capability.

Three habits counteract the dependency risk without sacrificing the capability:

- **Maintain the specification discipline.** Use ICE before every significant build, even when the temptation is to just start. The planning conversation is where your reasoning stays active; the implementation session is where it is easiest to disengage.
- **Commit what you understand.** The Git habit of committing working code is also an opportunity: before committing, confirm you can describe in one sentence what the committed code does and why. If you cannot, ask your AI to explain it before you commit it. This is not about reading every line; it is about maintaining the mental model of what you have built.
- **Take breaks across session boundaries.** The boiling frog effect is amplified by session length. Extended sessions without breaks are where entrainment takes hold: the sense that the AI's suggestions feel right simply because you have been agreeing with each other all afternoon. The bugs you miss in an extended session are visible after a night's sleep. Build recovery into your rhythm. The practitioners who sustain high-quality output over years are, almost without exception, the ones who do.

These are not restrictions on what this chapter's tools can do. They are the conditions that make the tools productive over time rather than just impressive in the short term. The most capable setup in the world produces poor outcomes if the practitioner using it has stopped thinking. The tools amplify the human; they do not replace them.

6.9 Key Takeaways

- **Know what your tools share before you share it.** Every environment sends different amounts of your data to external servers. The browser sends what you type; a desktop application with file access sends your files; a code editor extension can send your entire codebase. Assess what your data contains (personal information, commercially sensitive content, credentials) before choosing your environment.
- **Never share personal data, sensitive business information, or credentials with an AI.** Personal data is almost certainly governed by data protection legislation. Confidential business information is covered by your employment contract. Credentials must never enter an AI conversation or a version-controlled file without explicit exclusion. When the AI's help is needed for work that involves sensitive data, use the query-building approach: let the AI generate code that processes the data rather than feeding the data to the AI directly.
- **Follow the recommended path.** Start in the browser. Move to a desktop AI application when copy-pasting becomes friction. Move to a code editor only when you need local file management or offline capability. Most practitioners who reach the code editor stage do so because their projects grew, not because the earlier environments stopped working.
- **Costs are real: understand the unit.** Every word sent to an AI is metered in tokens. Vague requests that require multiple rounds cost more than clear ones. Free tiers exist for evaluation, not sustained use. Budget accordingly and keep context files lean.
- **Git is your safety net, not a technical requirement.** You do not need to understand every Git command. You need to know when

to take a snapshot (before a risky change) and when to branch (when experimenting). Let the AI handle the rest. Never commit secrets.

- **Project memory files reduce repetition.** A `CLAUDE.md` file gives the AI persistent context at the start of each session, so you are not re-explaining your project every time. Keep it lean: an index pointing to other files, not a history of every decision.
- **More capable tools make passive use easier, not safer.** AI assistance that feels easy is producing dependency as well as output. The ICE planning habit, specifying intent, constraints, and expectations before asking the AI to build, is what separates practitioners who improve with use from those who degrade. Answer-seeking corrodes independent reasoning; hint-seeking extends it. The choice is in how you frame each session, not in which tool you use.

Notes

36 Altman, S. (2025). Response on X (formerly Twitter), April 16, 2025, on the compute cost of users saying "please" and "thank you" to ChatGPT. techstartups.com/2025/04/20/sam-altman-saying-please-and-thank-you-to-chatgpt-is-costing-openai-millions-should-users-stop/

46 Liu, G., Christian, B., Dumbalska, T., Bakker, M. A., & Dubey, R. (2026). "AI Assistance Reduces Persistence and Hurts Independent Performance." arXiv:2604.04721.

CHAPTER 7

Building with a Plan

7.1 Introduction

The previous chapters covered foundational concepts. Now we build something real. Before we do: the most expensive mistake in any project is building the wrong thing well. Before committing to a build, it is worth asking whether software is actually the answer: a process change, a clearer conversation, or nothing at all might serve better. This chapter assumes you have already asked that question and decided to build. Chapter 8 covers the discipline of asking it, and what experience teaches about when the answer is no.

This chapter does not teach you to build incrementally, feature by feature, the way traditional tutorials suggest. That approach, adding one small piece at a time without a clear picture of the whole, discovers problems too late to fix them cheaply. It produces slow, piecemeal results and misses the point of working with AI.

Vibe-coding inverts the traditional ratio of planning to execution. Instead of brief planning followed by extended implementation, you invest heavily in upfront planning: recursive ICE analysis, critical persona reviews, detailed wireframes. For simple, well-scoped projects like the Reading List Manager in this chapter, a comprehensive plan document lets you build and launch in a single session. For more complex projects, the same principles apply but the build phase will span multiple sessions. The ratio still inverts; it just does so at larger scale. Either way, you iterate on what emerges.

The workflow in this chapter is tool-agnostic. The planning conversations work in any AI chat interface: Claude.ai, ChatGPT, or Copilot Chat. The build can be completed in a browser-based tool or in VS Code with an AI assistant. If you have not yet set up a local environment, that is fine: Chapter 6 covers both the tooling and the setup discipline. This chapter asks only that you have access to an AI that can write code.

This chapter demonstrates that workflow with a concrete project: the Reading List Manager. If you follow along using the example prompts, you will end up with a working application, but it will not look like the Reading List Manager. That is exactly as it should be. Every answer you give to the ICE questions will be different from the author's. Every constraint you name will produce different design decisions. Every sceptical user review will surface different weaknesses. The application that emerges will be yours, shaped by your context. What matters is not the output but the reasoning behind it: why you asked each question, what each planning stage revealed, and how the plan governed the build. That understanding transfers to every project you will ever build.

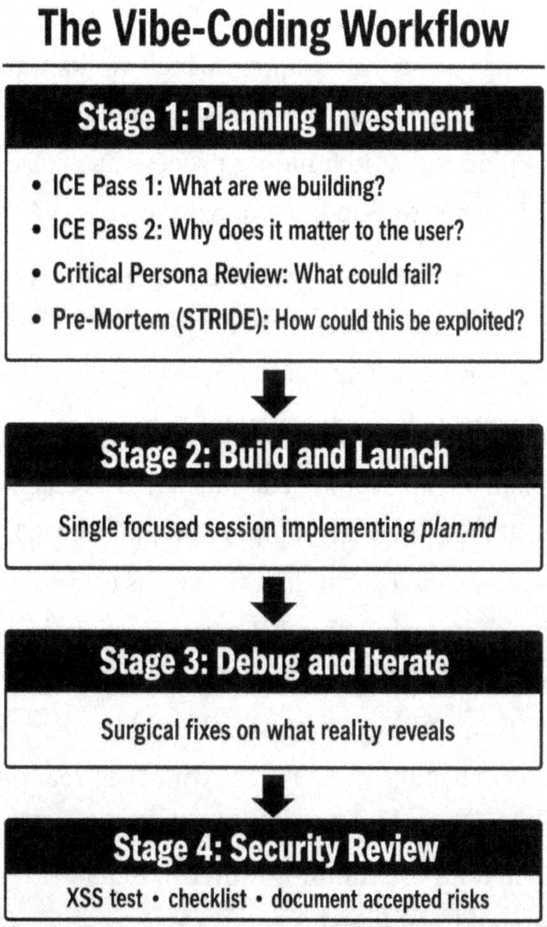

Figure 7.1: The four-stage vibe-coding workflow. Planning is the largest investment; implementation is the shortest stage.

7.2 The Planning Investment

A note on project setup: In disciplined practice, the very first step before any planning conversation is creating the project folder, initialising version control (git), and creating a project memory file: a short instructions file that governs the AI's behaviour throughout the project, so that even the ICE conversation itself is tracked and governed. Most AI tools support some form of persistent project instructions. Chapter 6 covers this setup discipline in full, including the correct sequence and the prompts to use. For this chapter, which walks through a simple single-session project, those steps are intentionally simplified so the focus remains on the planning and building process itself. Do not take their absence here as licence to skip them on your own projects.

As the previous chapters have shown, building the plan is the investment in creating the product. Planning is not preparation for collaboration with AI; it is the collaboration. The quality of what gets built is determined here, in the dialogue, before a line of code exists.

Worth saying plainly: the Reading List Manager is a teaching project, not a complex one. It is deliberately simple (low stakes, well-defined scope, no sensitive data) so that each planning stage is easy to observe without the noise of real complexity. Two ICE passes, a sceptical user review, a pre-mortem, and a STRIDE analysis applied to a reading list manager will feel measured. That is the point. A simple project gives you the muscle memory to run each stage quickly. On your first real project, the one you actually need, all four stages will earn their time. The decisions you practise here will take you minutes rather than half a day, because you have done them before at low stakes.

After building LockedPillar without a structured planning process and spending weeks reconstructing decisions that a plan document would have preserved, I now run the full sequence on any project that matters. The Reading List Manager is how you learn the sequence. Your own projects are where you will understand why it exists.

A note on the prompts in this section. Each stage shows the exact prompt used in the Reading List Manager session. If you want to follow along and produce the Reading List Manager yourself, copy them verbatim; they will work. If you are building something of your own, use them as a model

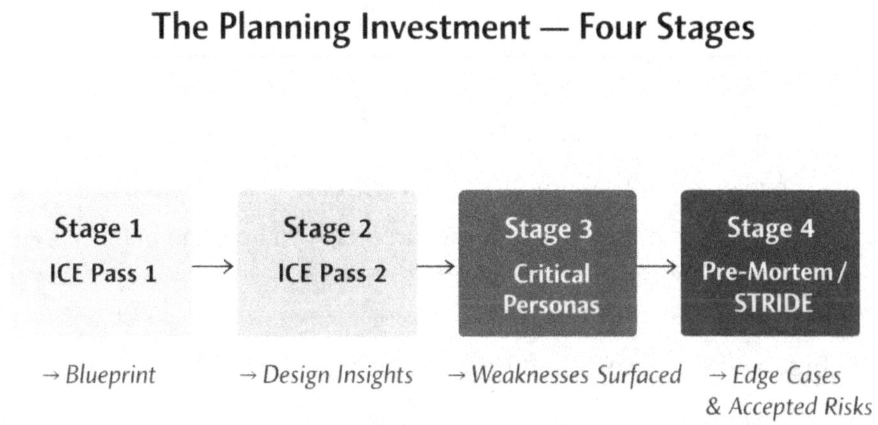

Figure 7.2: The four planning stages, each building on the last. Each stage produces an output the next stage depends on.

rather than a template: the words matter less than the intent behind them. What you are trying to do at each stage is surface the emotional context, trigger the adversarial stance, probe the edge cases. The AI will follow your meaning. Your own language will serve you better than borrowed phrasing.

Stage 1: Initial ICE Analysis

Begin with an ICE planning conversation. ICE (Intent, Constraints, Expectations) is a dialogue: you invite the AI to help you think through what you are building, and it asks questions. You answer. By the end, you have a structured plan of what you are building and why. Appendix A sets out the full framework, but you do not need to read it first: the example below is enough to get started in any AI chat interface.

- **Example prompt — opening the ICE session:**

> "I want to build a reading list manager. I use too many different tools to track books and nothing works the way I want. Can you run an ICE planning session with me — asking about my Intent, Constraints, and Expectations — to help me plan this properly?"

The first pass produces something like this:

Intent surfaced: A reading list manager. Users search for books, add them to their library, and track reading progress.

Constraints surfaced: No backend server, static site only. Free tier hosting. Must work on mobile. No user accounts for the MVP.

Expectations surfaced: Similar to Goodreads but much simpler. Just search, save, and track.

This first pass surfaces *what* you are building: the core problem, the value proposition, the functional requirements. Most tutorials stop here. You should not.

Stage 2: Deep ICE Analysis

Run the ICE conversation a second time, at minimum, explicitly asking the AI to probe deeper. The second pass surfaces *why*, including the human state of mind at the point of use. For complex projects, further passes using the five whys principle will go deeper still.

- **Example prompt — second pass:**

> "Run ICE on this plan again. Go deeper than the surface. What is the user's emotional state when they use this? What are they actually trying to accomplish? What could go wrong?"

The deep analysis reveals considerations the first pass missed. For a reading list manager:

- User state: possibly overwhelmed by too many books, guilty about unfinished reading
- Job to be done: not just "track books" but "feel in control of reading goals"
- Failure modes: the app becomes another source of guilt if it displays unfinished books prominently

These insights reshape design decisions. Perhaps "Currently Reading" should feel encouraging rather than accusatory. Perhaps the default view should be "Want to Read" (aspiration) rather than "In Progress" (obligation). Neither of those conclusions comes from the first ICE pass. Both are visible in the actual `plan.md` for this project, where the second-pass findings directly determined the tab order and default view.

Pass 1 — Surface	Pass 2 — Deep
What are we building? →	Why does it matter to the user?
Functional requirements →	User's emotional state at point of use
Technical constraints →	Failure modes
Feature list →	Design implications

Figure 7.3: Two passes over ICE surface different kinds of knowledge. The first pass reveals what to build; the second reveals why it matters.

Stage 3: Critical Persona Review

Chapter 2 introduced the critical persona as a concept: asking the AI to switch from cooperative builder to designated critic. Here is what that looks like in practice, and which personas to reach for depending on what your project is most likely to get wrong.

The persona you choose shapes what surfaces. Not every project needs every persona. Match the lens to the risk:

- **The sceptical user** asks why someone would bother, what friction would make them abandon the tool after a week, and which features promise more than they deliver. Use this for any consumer-facing tool or anything where adoption is uncertain.
- **The security auditor** asks what data the application handles, what could be exploited, and what a penetration tester would flag in their first pass. Use this for anything that stores, transmits, or displays user data.
- **The empirical critic** challenges your quantitative claims and assumptions: cost estimates, productivity gains, time savings. Use this when your plan depends on numbers you have not validated.
- **The end user under stress** asks what happens when things go wrong. What if the deadline is tomorrow and the user is scared of breaking something? Use this for tools where calm-state design assumptions may not hold under real conditions.
- **The hostile auditor** asks what would fail at scale, what compliance requirements you have not considered, and who is accountable if the application causes harm. Use this for anything touching regulated data, finances, or health.

The technique extends beyond software to any output produced for an audience. Ask the AI to review a report or document as a specific reader type:

- **The time-pressed manager** has twenty minutes and will skim. She misses buried conclusions and abandons content that does not earn her attention in the first paragraph.

- **The junior colleague** needs context the expert omits. He will follow instructions literally, get stuck at the first ambiguous step, and not ask for help.
- **The senior stakeholder seeking leverage** reads headers first, dives only into sections with an obvious payoff, and distrusts content that cannot be summarised in a sentence.

These are not hypothetical characters. They represent the gap between what you intend to communicate and what different people actually receive. Naming them forces the AI out of your perspective and into theirs.

- **Example prompt — the sceptic:**

> "Review this plan as a sceptical user who has tried and abandoned similar apps. What would make you delete this after a week? What features promise more than they deliver?"

The sceptical user might observe:

- "Reading progress tracking sounds useful but becomes a chore to update"
- "Offline mode is promised but never works reliably"
- "Export is mentioned but export to what? In what format?"

These critiques improve the plan before implementation. Add a quick-update gesture for progress tracking. Define specific offline behaviour. Specify export format explicitly.

- **Example prompt — the security auditor:**

> "Now review as a security auditor. What data does this app handle? What could be exploited? What would you flag in a security review?"

The security auditor might observe:

- "localStorage can be accessed by any script on the domain"
- "Book data from Open Library is rendered to the screen: potential for malicious content if not sanitised"
- "No rate limiting: the user could hammer the search service accidentally"

The instinct when findings land is to argue back: to explain that the critic has misunderstood, that users would adapt, that the concern is theoretical. Resist this. The critique that stings is almost always the critique that matters. Recursive ICE and critical persona reviews combined transform a good plan into a better one. Upfront planning consistently displaces rework: when the planning reveals a problem, the cost of changing course is a conversation; when the implementation reveals it, the cost is rebuilding. For the Reading List Manager, the critical persona pass took ten minutes and prevented several design decisions that would have required reworking implemented code. The ratio varies by project, but the principle does not.

Once the persona reviews are complete, lock down the feature scope before moving on. If the ICE conversation has not already produced a clear feature list, ask for one explicitly. A useful tool here is MoSCoW prioritisation, a structured way of sorting features into four categories: Must Have (essential for the product to work), Should Have (important but not critical for launch), Could Have (desirable if time allows), and

Won't Have (explicitly out of scope for this version). The Won't Have list is as important as the Must Have list. Explicitly ruling things out gives the AI a clear boundary during the build and prevents scope creep: the gradual accumulation of unrequested features that bloats a project and delays completion.

- **Example prompt — MoSCoW prompt:**

> "Before we generate the plan, can you produce a MoSCoW feature list for this project — Must Have, Should Have, Could Have, and Won't Have? I want the Won't Have list to be explicit so we don't build things we don't need."

Stage 4: The Pre-Mortem

The critical persona review asks "what would a sceptic say?" The pre-mortem asks a more focused question: "how could this fail?" The distinction matters. A sceptic challenges value. A pre-mortem challenges survivability.

The term comes from risk management: instead of conducting a post-mortem after a project fails, you imagine the failure before it happens and work backwards to identify causes. In vibe-coding, the pre-mortem addresses the weakest point in the entire process: the things you do not know you do not know. Your ICE specification covers what you have thought of. The pre-mortem surfaces what you have not.

The practice is simple. Before writing your Expectations (before defining what "done" looks like), run an adversarial dialogue with the AI:

- **Example prompt — pre-mortem:**

  > "Before we write any code, I want to stress-test this plan. Given everything we have discussed — the reading list manager, the localStorage constraint, the Open Library API — how could this fail? What have I not thought of? What assumptions am I making that could bite me?"

Together, this pre-mortem and the happy-path criteria you established during the ICE Intent conversation form two passes over your Expectations:

1. **Pass one (human-led):** Already established in the ICE conversation: what does "done" look like? The happy-path acceptance criteria. The user adds a book, sees it in their library, updates progress. This is what you already knew before the pre-mortem.
2. **Pass two (AI-challenged):** What the pre-mortem prompt surfaces: the failure modes, edge cases, and assumptions that the happy path never reaches.

For the Reading List Manager, the AI-challenged pass surfaced:

- What happens when the Open Library search returns no results? (Empty state required)
- What if a user adds 500 books? (Performance: test at scale)
- What if the browser's storage is full? (Catch the error; warn the user)
- What if the user pastes HTML into the notes field? (Injection risk; sanitise on display)
- What if two browser tabs are open simultaneously? (Last-write wins; document and accept)

These are not hypothetical anxieties. They are the edge cases that turn a working demo into a production failure. The pre-mortem surfaces them before a line of code is written, when the cost of changing course is a conversation, not a rewrite.

STRIDE: A Structured Pre-Mortem for Security

"How could this fail?" is a useful question, but it is open-ended. For projects where security matters (and Chapter 3 argued that security habits should be built into every project), a structured taxonomy produces better results than a vague invitation to brainstorm.

STRIDE is a threat modelling framework developed at Microsoft.[13] It organises security threats into six categories, each prompting a specific question about your application, set out in Table 7.1.

STRIDE Category	Question for Your Pre-Mortem
Spoofing	Could someone fake an identity or input source?
Tampering	Could data be modified in transit or at rest?
Repudiation	Could actions be performed that cannot be traced or attributed?
Information Disclosure	Could information leak to unintended recipients?
Denial of Service	Could the application be overwhelmed or made unavailable?
Elevation of Privilege	Could someone gain permissions they should not have?

Table 7.1: STRIDE threat categories: six structured questions for your pre-mortem.

The approach is simple:

- **Example prompt — STRIDE analysis:**

> "Run a STRIDE analysis on this plan. For each category, identify whether a realistic threat exists for this specific application. Be honest — not every category will apply. For those that do, suggest a mitigation that fits the project's scale."

You do not need to be a security professional to use this. You need to ask the questions. Table 7.2 shows the result for the Reading List Manager.

STRIDE Category	Pre-Mortem Finding	Plan Impact
Spoofing	N/A (no user accounts)	None
Tampering	localStorage can be edited in browser developer tools	Add validation on data load
Repudiation	N/A (no multi-user actions)	None
Information Disclosure	Book lists are not sensitive	Accept risk, document
Denial of Service	Rapid searches could trigger rate limiting	Add a short delay before search fires, so it waits for the user to stop typing
Elevation of Privilege	N/A (no permission model)	None

Table 7.2: STRIDE analysis applied to the Reading List Manager. Three of six categories produced no realistic threat.

Running this prompt against the Reading List Manager plan produced three of the six categories as not applicable (see Table 7.2). That is fine.

The value is in the asking, not in finding threats everywhere. For a more complex application, one with user accounts, payment processing, or sensitive data, every row would produce findings. STRIDE earns its place when the threats are real. Running it on a low-stakes project like this one demonstrates the method without the consequences.

The key phrase is "fits the project's scale." A reading list manager does not need the same security treatment as a banking application. Risk-proportionate analysis is the goal: not zero risk, but understood risk.

7.3 The Plan Document

The plan document is not something you write. At the end of the planning conversation, you ask the AI to produce it. What comes back is a structured reference document that captures every decision, assumption, and open question from the session: something you could hand to another developer, or return to six months later, and know exactly what was built and why. The sections below explain what a good plan contains and why each one exists, not so you can write it, but so you can recognise whether the AI has produced a complete one.

Core Elements

Background and Context. What problem does this solve? What is the current workflow? What are the pain points? For the Reading List Manager, the background section opens simply:

```
Readers accumulate books faster than they read them. The
current
workflow is scattered: want-to-read lists in notes apps,
started-but-abandoned books forgotten, progress lost between
sessions.
```

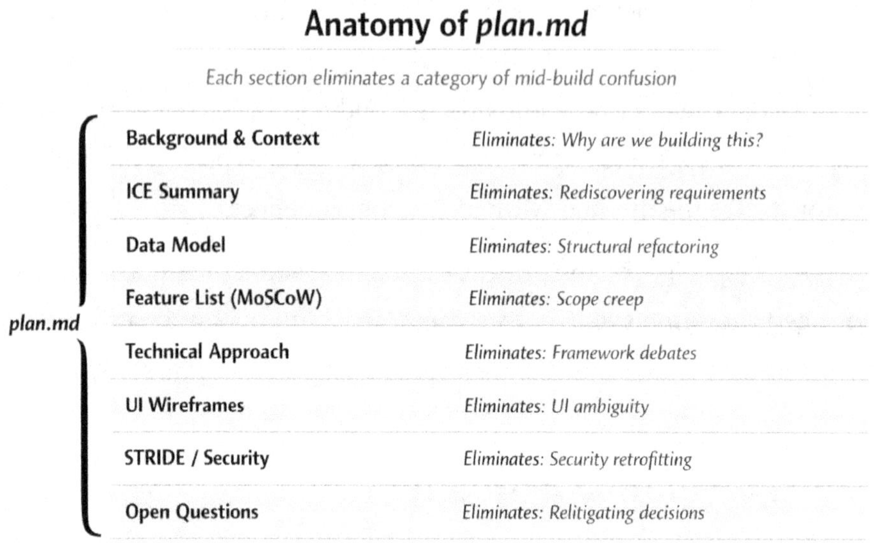

Figure 7.4: The anatomy of plan.md. Each section exists to eliminate a specific category of mid-build confusion.

ICE Framework Summary. All ICE passes, with the deeper passes foregrounded. The deeper passes are the ones that produce design insight. The AI may present this as a table, a bulleted list, or flowing prose; the format varies by tool and conversation. What matters is that the findings are there. For the Reading List Manager, the second pass surfaced:

- *User state:* possibly overwhelmed by unfinished books; mild guilt about reading debt
- *Job to be done:* feel in control of reading goals, not overwhelmed by them
- *Failure mode:* the app becomes another source of guilt
- *Design implication:* default view = “Want to Read” (aspiration), not “In Progress” (obligation)

The sceptical user findings also appear in the plan, not just the ICE pass. The critical persona review produced a single sentence that shaped the entire build: "One thing, one job, no friction: hear about a book, open app, type title, press enter, done, under five seconds." That sentence is the design brief. Everything in the build either serves it or was cut.

Data Model. For applications with meaningful complexity in their data structure, the plan may include an explicit data model: a definition of the shape of the data your application will store. Not every project needs this. A simple tool with one or two data types may not warrant it. But when it does appear, it is one of the most important sections in the plan. For the Reading List Manager, each book is stored as a simple object:

```
{
  "id": "OL12345W",
  "title": "The Name of the Wind",
  "author": "Patrick Rothfuss",
  "pages": 662,
  "status": "reading",
  "progress": 180,
  "notes": "Brilliant prose. Slow in places.",
  "dateAdded": "2026-02-15T10:30:00Z"
}
```

Defining this before implementation prevents the most common mid-build problem: discovering that your data structure cannot support a feature you thought was simple. The "last read" timestamp, for example, is trivial to add in the data model but requires rethinking every storage call if you try to retrofit it later.

Feature Requirements. The plan uses a MoSCoW structure (Must Have, Should Have, Could Have, Won't Have: a prioritisation framework borrowed from project management). For the Reading List Manager, explicitly ruling out user accounts, social features, and recommendations in the Won't Have list kept the MVP focused and gave the AI a clear boundary during the build.

Technical Approach. This section reflects the answers you gave during the Constraints pass of the ICE conversation. When the AI asked about platform, stack, and technical preferences, your answers determined the approach. For the Reading List Manager, the constraint was "plain HTML, CSS, and JavaScript", so the plan records that choice and its rationale: a static site with no build step, no framework, no added complexity. If you answered differently (a React app, a Python backend, a mobile-first PWA), that is what will appear here. The plan is not prescribing a technical approach; it is recording yours.

UI Wireframes. A specification for each screen and state that the AI can reference during implementation. For the Reading List Manager, this was produced as a separate HTML file alongside plan.md, capturing the tab structure, card layout, and button placement in a form that could be opened in a browser and reviewed before any application code was written. If something was wrong, the wireframe was the thing to fix. The planning section of this chapter covers how to produce it.

If you are building for someone else (a colleague, a client, a team), the HTML wireframe becomes a shared artefact. You can show them what the finished product will look like before any real code exists. That conversation will surface ideas, preferences, and concerns that would not have emerged until after the build. Fixing a wireframe takes minutes. Reworking a working application takes sessions. Ambiguity disappears: "build the book card" becomes unambiguous because both parties can see what "book card" means. It is already rendered.

Safety and Security Considerations. The plan records the outcome of a STRIDE analysis run before implementation. For the Reading List

Manager, three of the six STRIDE categories produced no realistic threat. The plan recorded that explicitly, so the build could focus effort where it actually mattered, as Table 7.3 shows.

Category	Applies	Notes
Spoofing	No	No identity model
Tampering	Yes	XSS via innerHTML, root cause of most threats
Repudiation	No	No transactions or consequences
Information Disclosure	Yes	XSS exfiltration, API leakage
Denial of Service	Marginal	localStorage quota edge case
Elevation of Privilege	No	No permission model

Table 7.3: STRIDE analysis for the Reading List Manager, reproduced from plan.md. Three categories are not applicable; two produce actionable requirements.

From that analysis, the plan extracted seven non-negotiable rules baked in from the start, not retrofitted after the build:

1. Never use `innerHTML` with user data; use `textContent` for all user-supplied content instead
2. Validate all URL fields on input, accepting only `http://` and `https://`
3. Wrap all localStorage writes in `try/catch` so a full store never fails silently
4. Require SRI hashes on any CDN dependency: no external script without integrity verification
5. Cover images use lazy fetch only, not an auto-query against Open Library on every add
6. Set a Content Security Policy via meta tag (default-src 'self')

7. Add clickjack protection with X-Frame-Options DENY

The implementation prompt referenced these rules directly. The AI did not have to be reminded of them mid-build because they were already in the plan it was reading from.

Open Questions and Decisions. Questions raised during planning that were not immediately resolved, with a record of how each was eventually answered. For the Reading List Manager, four questions remained open at the end of the planning session. The plan recorded them explicitly, and they were answered before the build prompt was written, shown in Table 7.4.

Question	Decision	Notes
Cover images	Manual URL paste	Auto-fetch rejected: leaks title and IP to Open Library on every add
Mark done behaviour	Brief undo window	Disappears after five seconds unless undone
Empty state	Just the add field	No instruction text, no chrome: clean
Hosting	Local file only	Open as file:// in browser, no server needed

Table 7.4: Open questions resolved before building. Each answer is recorded with its reasoning.

Recording the reasoning alongside the decision is as important as the decision itself. Six months later, when you return to the project and wonder why cover images use manual paste rather than auto-fetch, the answer is already there. You do not have to reconstruct it, or worse, inadvertently reverse a deliberate security decision.

7.4 Build and Launch

With a comprehensive plan document, implementation becomes a focused execution session. The conversation shifts from "what should we build?" to "build what the plan describes."

The Implementation Prompt

The implementation prompt for the Reading List Manager was a single instruction pointing at the plan:

- **Example prompt — implementation prompt:**

  > "Here is plan.md for a Reading List Manager. Build everything described in the Must Have section. Reference the wireframes for UI layout. Use vanilla HTML, CSS, and JavaScript as specified. Include the three demo books in the initial state."

For a project of this scope (one user, three files, no integrations), a plan document of a few hundred lines is sufficient for a single prompt to produce a working application. The AI has enough context to make consistent decisions throughout. The wireframes resolve every UI question. The data model prevents structural confusion. The Won't Have list prevents the AI from adding unrequested features. The prompt is this simple because the project is this simple. As projects grow in complexity, the handover from plan to build needs to grow with them: establishing documentation obligations, restating critical constraints, and creating checkpoints between phases. Chapter 8 covers what that looks like in practice.

What the Handover Looks Like

The AI's response to the kickoff prompt typically starts with a brief confirmation of what it has understood, followed by the code. Something like:

> "I'll build the Reading List Manager as specified. I'll create a single HTML file with embedded CSS and JavaScript, using the data model from the plan and implementing all Must Have features. Starting now..."

That confirmation is worth reading before the code arrives. If it states something you did not intend (a different architecture, or a feature you put in Won't Have), correct it now before the build begins. Once several hundred lines of code have been generated, changing course costs more than a single clarification before the first line.

The AI may also ask a small number of clarifying questions before starting, or flag an assumption that was not in the plan. Engage with these briefly and directly. They are usually signs that the plan has a gap the AI caught before it caused a problem. After that exchange, implementation flows without interruption. Questions belong before the first line of code, not scattered through it. If a question arises mid-implementation, ask the AI to pause, answer the question, then resume from where it stopped.

During the build, the AI may ask permission to create files, write to folders, or run commands. Read the request briefly. It should be consistent with what the plan describes. Then approve it. This is the practical meaning of what Andrej Karpathy said in Chapter 1: "I just accept the diffs." He was not describing carelessness. He was describing trust earned through planning. When the plan is thorough, the AI's requests during build are predictable extensions of decisions already made. You are not approving something unknown; you are confirming something you already agreed to.

What "Single Session" Means

"Build in a single session" does not mean a single prompt produces a flawless application. It means the implementation phase is compressed into a focused session where the primary activity is execution, not discovery. During implementation, you will still:

- Answer clarifying questions the AI raises
- Make micro-decisions about details the plan did not specify
- Test components as they are built
- Adjust when something does not feel right in practice

But you will not:

- Discover fundamental requirements you missed
- Debate architectural approaches mid-build
- Realise halfway through that the data structure is wrong
- Rebuild features because expectations were unclear

The planning investment front-loads the discovery. Implementation becomes translation: converting the plan into working code.

What Comes Out

For the Reading List Manager, the application that emerged from the plan was a single HTML file with CSS and JavaScript embedded within it: the simplest possible structure for a tool with no build step and no server. The search connects to Open Library (a free, public book database requiring no registration or API key), with a debounced input so searches do not fire on every keystroke. Books are stored in the browser's local storage, which persists between sessions without any server. This is the architecture that followed from the constraints given: pure HTML/CSS/JS, local file, no framework. Different constraints produce different results; a reader who specified a React app or separate files during the ICE pass will receive a different structure. The plan governs the output.

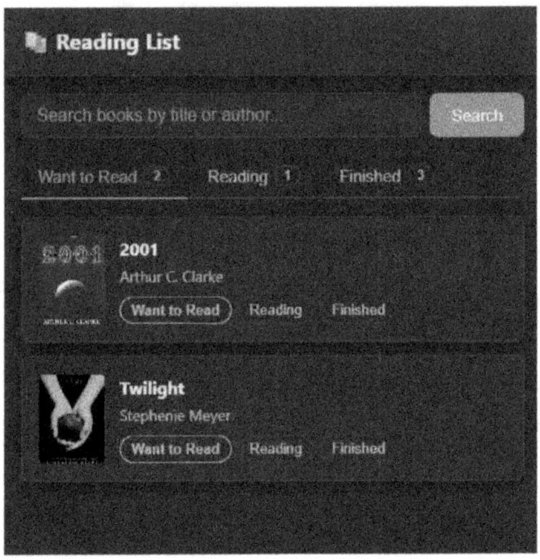

Figure 7.5: The completed Reading List Manager — built from a plan document in a single session.

All of that emerged from the plan document. None of it required mid-build debate. The implementation conversation was almost entirely execution.

7.5 Debug and Iterate

When the Reading List Manager loaded in the browser, the application appeared to work: the search found books, the cards displayed correctly, the layout held on mobile. This is exactly where the methodology does not allow complacency. Opening the developer console (press F12, then click the Console tab) is not optional: it is the first verification step, regardless of how well the application looks. One error was quietly waiting.

This is the normal experience. The application loads, it functions, and

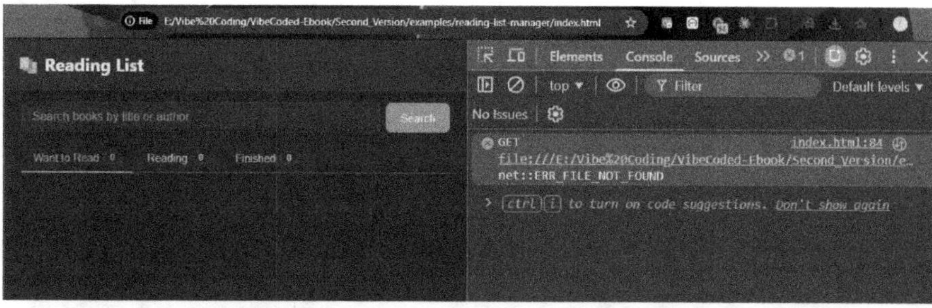

Figure 7.6: The browser console after the initial build. The application worked — but the console revealed an issue to address.

the console reveals errors the visible behaviour concealed. You do not need to understand what the errors mean. You need to show them to the AI. There are two ways to do this: select the error text and copy it directly from the console, or take a screenshot of the console and send the image. Either works. The AI will read both.

- **Example prompt — console error prompt:**

> "My application is running but the browser console is showing these errors. Can you explain what each one means and whether it needs fixing?"

The AI will tell you which errors matter and which do not. Some are genuine bugs in the code. Some are limitations of the local file environment that will resolve themselves when the application is deployed to a proper host. Some are noise from browser extensions that have nothing to do with your application. For the Reading List Manager, the AI identified one genuine bug to fix (a malformed API call to Open Library), one deployment concern to note for later (a security header that requires a web server), and one extension conflict to ignore. Once the AI has categorised the errors, fixing what needs fixing is simple:

- **Example prompt — console fix prompt:**

> "Please fix the errors that need fixing and document any that I should address after deployment."

That single prompt fixed everything that needed fixing. The key discipline is to check the console before considering the build complete: a clean-looking application with a console full of errors is not finished. Make it a habit: build, open in browser, press F12, check the console. If there are errors, copy them to the AI. If the console is clean, you are done.

Keeping the Plan in Sync

Iteration is also where the project enters change territory. Each fix (a header removed, an API call corrected, a fallback added) is a deviation from the original plan. If those changes are not recorded, the plan document drifts out of sync with the application. Future sessions start from a description of what you intended to build, not what you actually built. The AI loses context. Prompts become less precise. Results become less reliable.

The minimal discipline is to commit each change to version control with a meaningful message, so the history of what changed and why is recoverable. Chapter 9 covers documentation and the danger of drift in full: what happens when the plan and the application fall out of sync, and how to prevent it.

- **Example prompt — commit prompt:**

> "Commit these changes with a descriptive message explaining what was fixed and why."

If you have connected a GitHub repository, add "and push to GitHub" to the prompt so the remote copy stays in sync with your local changes.

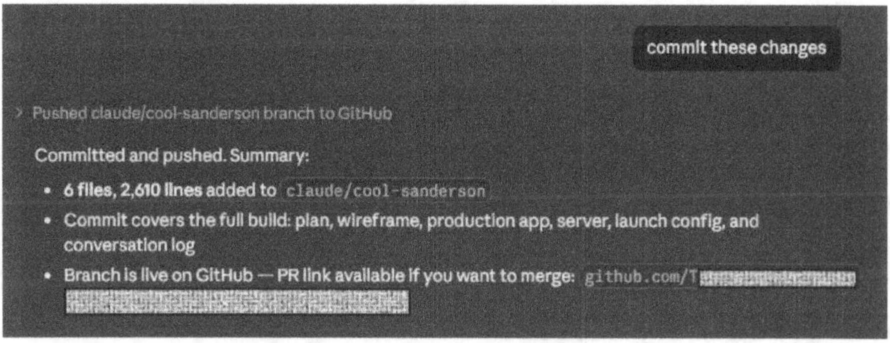

Figure 7.8: The commit following the Open Library API fix. The message records what changed and why – context that will matter in a future session.

When to Re-Plan

Sometimes iteration reveals that the plan was not just incomplete but fundamentally wrong: the approach itself needs to change, not just a detail within it. Signs that re-planning is needed rather than further iteration:

- A fix in one place consistently breaks something elsewhere, indicating the data model or architecture cannot support the feature
- The same problem keeps reappearing despite multiple attempts to resolve it
- What you have built and used reveals that the original intent was wrong: the application solves the stated problem but not the actual one

When this happens, return to planning mode. Update the plan document with what you have learned. Run ICE again on the revised requirements. Then implement the revised approach. This is not failure; it is the process working at a larger scale. The first plan was a hypothesis. Reality provided data. The revised plan incorporates that data, and the next build is faster because the discovery has already happened. In traditional development, a rebuild is expensive. In vibe-coding it is not: when AI can reconstruct a working application from a revised plan in a single session, starting fresh is often faster than trying to repair a fundamentally flawed build. If the fixes are becoming more complex than the original build, that is a signal worth heeding.

7.6 Security Review

Before considering the project complete, run a security review. This is not optional, even for a personal project. The habits you build now transfer to applications where the stakes are higher. Regardless of how the code was produced, the decision to deploy is yours, and with that decision comes responsibility for what happens next.

The Security Audit as a Deliverable

Most developers treat security as a checklist to tick before launch. Vibe-coders have a better option: ask your AI assistant to generate a security audit programme tailored to your specific application. Not a generic list of warnings, but a structured assessment that identifies your actual attack surface, prioritises findings by severity, and proposes mitigations proportionate to your project's risk profile.

The prompt follows the same pattern as everything else in this workflow:

- **Example prompt — security audit:**

> "Review this application for security vulnerabilities. Consider the OWASP Top 10 as a framework (a standard list of the most common web security risks). For each category, identify whether a realistic threat exists given this specific application's architecture and data. Prioritise findings as Critical, High, Medium, or Low. For each finding, describe the risk, the realistic impact, and a proportionate mitigation."

What comes back is not a generic security tutorial. It is a prioritised findings list specific to what you have built: the data that is stored, the external services called, the inputs that reach the screen. For a production application handling user accounts and payment data, this conversation can grow into a full testing programme with phases, automated test scripts, and a vulnerability reporting template. For a reading list manager, it surfaces the two or three things that actually matter.

For this project, the audit worked through each OWASP Top 10 category in turn. Six categories were not applicable at all: the Reading List Manager has no authentication, no server-side processing, no multi-user data flows. Four categories produced findings, shown in Table 7.5:

OWASP Category	Finding	Severity	Resolution
A02 Cryptographic Failures	localStorage is plaintext, visible in DevTools	Low	Accept risk: no sensitive data stored
A03 Injection (XSS)	User content inserted into DOM	Low	Already mitigated: plan's security rules required `textContent` throughout

OWASP Category	Finding	Severity	Resolution
A05 Security Misconfiguration	Inline script in HTML file	Medium	Move script to external `app.js`
A08 Software and Data Integrity	Cover image ID not validated before use	Low	Add validation before passing coverId to Open Library

Table 7.5: OWASP Top 10 audit findings for the Reading List Manager. Six categories were not applicable; four produced findings.

Two of the findings required no action at all. The XSS finding was already mitigated because the planning stage had required safe text handling before any code was written. The localStorage finding was accepted: a personal reading list stores nothing sensitive. That left two items to fix.

- **Example prompt — fixing audit findings:**

> "Please fix the two remaining findings: move the inline script to a separate app.js file, and add validation on the cover image ID before it is passed to Open Library."

If the findings use technical language you do not fully understand, you do not need to decode them first. Paste the audit output back to the AI and ask it to explain which findings need fixing and what to ask for. It will tell you exactly what to say. One prompt, both changes made, the application rebuilt and retested in the same session.

Regardless of what the audit finds, three XSS test inputs are worth running manually on any application that accepts user text. They take thirty seconds and confirm that user-entered content cannot execute as code in the browser:

1. In any text field: `<script>alert('XSS')</script>`
2. As a title or name: `<img src=x onerror=alert('XSS')>`
3. In any notes field: `<a href="javascript:alert('XSS')">click</a>`

If no alert box appears and the text displays literally on screen, the input handling is safe.

Risk Proportionality

Security effort should match the stakes, and the rule is simple: never deploy to production with unresolved Critical or High findings. For a personal project the consequences of getting this wrong fall only on you. For anything that touches other people's data (accounts, payments, personal information), it is non-negotiable. Traditional security frameworks assign remediation timescales measured in days or weeks because human developers must schedule, implement, test, and deploy fixes. With an AI assistant, a Critical finding can be resolved, tested, and committed in the same session. The severity categories still matter; the queuing logic does not.

Severity	Meaning and required response
Critical	System or data compromise likely: fix before launch
High	Significant vulnerability, exploitable: fix before launch
Medium	Moderate risk, requires specific conditions: fix or consciously accept
Low	Minor concern, limited realistic impact: document and monitor

Table 7.6: Security severity levels: what each rating means and the required response.

Documenting What You Find, and What You Accept

When you identify a vulnerability, write it down. You do not need to draft this yourself: the AI has just conducted the audit and has all the context it needs. Ask it to record the findings for you.

- **Example prompt — documenting security decisions:**

  > "Please update the Security Considerations section of plan.md with the audit findings. For each item, record the severity, the risk, the decision we made, and the reasoning. Include the findings we accepted as well as the ones we fixed."

When you consciously decide to accept a risk rather than fix it, record that too: not for compliance, but for future-you and for anyone who later works on or inherits the project. The right place to record this is the Security Considerations section of `plan.md`, the same document that captured your STRIDE analysis. If the project is significant enough to warrant a separate file, use `security.md` in the project root. Either way, the record travels with the project, not with your notes. A minimal record for each finding:

```
## Security Decisions

### [Finding name]
**Severity:** Low / Medium / High / Critical
**Risk:** What could go wrong, and under what conditions.
**Decision:** Fix / Accept / Defer
**Reasoning:** Why this decision is appropriate for this
project.
**Mitigation:** What reduces the risk even if not fully
resolved.
```

When someone later asks "did you consider this?" you have a written record of the decision and the reasoning behind it. That is professional risk management. The Reading List Manager has no user accounts, no passwords, and no personal data beyond what the user chooses to store in their own browser. The one Medium finding was fixed in a single prompt; the Low findings were accepted or quick-patched. Document what you accepted and why.

7.7 Scaling ICE Up: Reading List Manager vs LockedPillar

The four planning stages are not fixed in scope. They scale with the complexity and consequences of the project. The Reading List Manager is a low-stakes personal tool with no user accounts, no sensitive data, and no commercial dependencies. LockedPillar is a subscription SaaS platform serving paying customers. The same four stages apply to both.

What changes is the depth of each answer and the consequences of getting it wrong.

Table 7.4 shows how the same planning questions produced materially different outputs across these two projects. The LockedPillar answers are reconstructed from the retrospective in Chapter 10, not from a planning document that existed at the time. LockedPillar was built without a formal ICE session. The retrospective makes clear what a planning session would have surfaced. That is the point.

Planning Stage	Reading List Manager	LockedPillar
Stage 1: Initial ICE	Track books across reading states. No backend, static files, free hosting. No user accounts in MVP. Mobile-first layout.	Subscription web app for actors memorising performance scripts. Needs user accounts, authentication, payment processing, and licensing. Multi-device access. UK-based commercial deployment.
Stage 2: Deep ICE	User's emotional state: aspirational reader who feels guilty about the stack of unread books. Default view should reflect aspiration, not obligation. Tab order and default state determined here.	User's emotional state: under performance pressure, often time-critical before auditions. Speed and reliability are non-negotiable. Failure at the wrong moment is not a minor inconvenience. It is a professional problem.

Planning Stage	Reading List Manager	LockedPillar
Stage 3: Critical Persona	Sceptical user surfaced the design brief: "One thing, one job, no friction. Hear about a book, open app, type title, press enter, done. Under five seconds." Everything in the MVP either served that or was cut.	A hostile operations manager would have surfaced the 40% operator scope: licence management, subscription lifecycle tooling, category management. None of this appeared in the original plan. Every item was built reactively after its absence became a problem.
Stage 4: Pre-Mortem and STRIDE	Three of six STRIDE categories not applicable. XSS already mitigated by planning-stage requirement for safe text handling. localStorage accepted as low-risk for a personal tool.	STRIDE would have flagged credential management (Azure Key Vault: the right answer, but arrived at by iteration rather than design), payment webhook completeness (failed charges, cancellations, refunds, each a business decision not just a technical one), and session security for a paying-customer product. The payment event mapping lesson came from mid-build discovery, not pre-mortem analysis.

Table 7.4: The same four planning stages applied to two projects of different scale and consequence.

The comparison is not to suggest that LockedPillar failed. It did not. The platform worked, found paying customers, and the commercial infrastructure eventually caught up. The point is what "eventually" cost: reactive builds into an already-large codebase, mid-build course corrections, and three additional weeks of post-launch stabilisation that a planning session would likely have eliminated. The planning stages matter more for complex projects because the consequences of skipping them are higher.

7.8 Key Takeaways

- **Invert the ratio:** Spend more time planning than implementing. Comprehensive plans eliminate rework that costs more than the planning investment.
- **Recursive ICE:** First pass surfaces *what*; second pass surfaces *why*. The emotional state of the user at point of use shapes design decisions the surface requirements never reach.
- **Critical personas:** Ask the AI to review your plan as a sceptical user, a security auditor, or a hostile critic. This surfaces weaknesses that helpful AI would otherwise overlook.
- **The pre-mortem:** Before defining Expectations, ask "how could this fail?" Two passes (human-led happy path, then AI-challenged edge cases) surface the unknowns that specifications miss. STRIDE provides a structured taxonomy for security-relevant pre-mortems.
- **The plan document:** Wireframes, data models, feature lists, safety considerations: all captured before implementation begins. The plan is the specification.
- **Build and launch:** With a comprehensive plan, implementation is a single focused session. Discovery happened during planning; implementation is translation.
- **Iterate on reality:** No plan survives contact with users. Budget for iteration, but keep it surgical rather than architectural.

- **Security is not optional:** Ask your AI assistant to generate a prioritised security audit against your specific application. Resolve Critical and High findings before launch. With AI assistance, this is a single session, not a scheduled project. Document every risk you accept.

Notes

43 Shostack, A. (2014). *Threat Modeling: Designing for Security*. Wiley. ISBN: 978-1118809990. The standard reference for the STRIDE framework, originally developed at Microsoft by Loren Kohnfelder and Praerit Garg (1999).

CHAPTER 8

Building in Practice — What You Encounter When You Build

8.1 Introduction

Chapter 7 gave you the framework. This chapter gives you the experience. Every step of the sequence Chapter 7 described — explore, plan, set up, build, debug, sustain — looks different once you have done it against real constraints: a third-party service that ignores your code because the credential is wrong, a bug that has nothing to do with the code at all, a security audit that generates ninety pages of documentation you now have to work through. These are not refinements of the theory. They are the things the theory does not prepare you for, and they are what this chapter covers. The sequence in this chapter revisits Chapter 7's steps not to repeat them but to add what experience teaches about each one.

8.2 The Sequence in Practice

Chapter 7 introduced the sequence as a framework. What follows is the same sequence annotated with what practice actually reveals: the step most people skip, the discipline that only makes sense after something has gone wrong, and the places where the framework is right in principle but more complicated in execution. Each step creates the foundation the next depends on.

Step 0 — Explore the problem space. Use a chatbot loosely to decide whether you actually need to build anything. The answer might be a process change, not software.

Step 1 — Set up the project infrastructure. Create the project folder, initialise version control, and open a stub project memory file before the design conversation begins.

Step 2 — Run ICE and produce the plan. The planning conversation can span multiple sessions and produce multiple artefacts: a plan, wireframes, a data model, a security assessment. Commit each as it is produced.

Step 3 — Update the project memory file as the catalogue. The plan will outgrow the memory file. Turn it into the index (a governance file pointing to each planning artefact) so every new session starts with full context.

Step 4 — Hand off to build. Send the kickoff prompt. The build begins against a prepared, version-controlled foundation.

Step 5 — Debug and iterate. Some bugs are in the code; others are in the environment. Describing symptoms accurately is the core skill.

Step 6 — Sustain the project over time. Plans drift. plan.md and history.md, kept current, are what prevent it — Chapter 9 covers the full discipline.

Step 0 — Exploring: What Experience Teaches

The most expensive mistake in any project is building the wrong thing well. Step 0 exists to catch that before a line of code is written. For surfacing non-technological solutions, talking to people is often more useful than talking to an AI. Colleagues, future users, or a non-technical friend asked to describe the problem in their own words can surface things an AI will miss, because AI thinks technologically. It will tend towards technical answers and is poorly placed to suggest that the real solution is a culture change, a clearer policy, or doing nothing at all. A reporting tool that saves time on a process that should not exist is not a success. A dashboard that papers over a team communication problem will not fix it.

Where a chatbot is useful at this stage is as a stress-test: ask it to argue against building, to describe what failure looks like, or to list the non-software alternatives. Used critically, it can sharpen your thinking. Used uncritically, it will helpfully design you a system you did not need. Vibe-coding makes building fast, which makes skipping this question easier than ever. Step 0 is the deliberate pause that protects against that.

Step 1 — Setting Up: What Experience Teaches

The discipline of setting up version control and a project memory file before the first design conversation sounds procedural until you experience what happens without it. The ICE conversation itself can run to thousands of words across multiple sessions. Decisions get made, revised, and made again. Without version control, that entire record exists only in a conversation log that will eventually be compressed or lost. With it, every meaningful exchange is a commit: a recoverable, readable record of how the project's thinking evolved. The mechanics are simple. Create the project folder, open it in your AI coding tool, and ask it to initialise everything for you:

- **Example prompt:**

> "initialise this project folder for git and create a stub project memory file"

Chapter 6 covers the setup in detail if you prefer to understand what is happening under the hood.

The project memory file (CLAUDE.md in Claude Code, or a system prompt or custom instruction file in other tools) does not need to be elaborate at this stage. A few lines establishing the project name and one or two non-negotiable constraints is enough to govern the earliest conversations. It grows as planning produces decisions worth preserving. By the time the plan is complete, the memory file has been accumulating context throughout: it is not written after planning, it matures during it.

Step 2 — Planning: What Experience Teaches

Chapter 7 introduces the double ICE technique, critical persona reviews, the pre-mortem, and wireframing as planning tools. What experience adds is a sense of when they earn their time and what they reliably surface that the first pass always misses. It also teaches you to expect a multi-document outcome. A thorough planning conversation does not produce a single file. It produces a plan (plan.md or equivalent), wireframe files you can open in a browser, a data model, a security assessment, a list of open questions, and possibly more. Each is a separate artefact, committed to version control as it is produced. Taken together, they are the complete design record of the project. On any meaningful build, two passes through ICE is a minimum, not an aspiration. For simple tools, two is usually enough. For complex problems — those with significant unknowns, competing constraints, or user needs that are difficult to articulate — the questioning may need to go deeper, in the way that asking "why" repeatedly uncovers causes that the first answer concealed. Three to five passes are not unusual when the problem genuinely warrants it. The test is simple: if each pass is still surfacing decisions you would have got wrong, keep going.

The second ICE pass earns its time disproportionately, and experience reveals two distinct reasons, not one.

The first reason is what you expect: it surfaces things you missed. The second is less obvious and more important to a practitioner: it audits the plan itself for errors the AI introduced. A first-pass planning document reads well. It is coherent, detailed, and structured. What it may also contain is a recommended library that has been deprecated, an integration approach that does not work the way the AI described, or a performance claim with no basis. These do not stand out because they are written in exactly the same tone as everything accurate around them.

Running a second pass as a deliberate challenge, not "continue the plan" but "interrogate it", is the most reliable way to find these before they become build problems. Ask why a particular technology was chosen over its alternatives. Ask what would happen if a key assumption turned out to be wrong. Ask whether the recommended approach is current. The AI that confidently asserted something in the first pass will sometimes, under direct questioning, walk it back entirely. That moment is uncomfortable. It is also exactly what the second pass is for.

The second pass also surfaces what the first genuinely cannot: why the tool matters to the person using it. Their state of mind at the moment of use, the real job they are trying to accomplish beneath the stated requirement, and the ways the tool could make their situation worse rather than better. These insights do not emerge from requirements lists. They emerge from asking "what is the user actually feeling when they reach for this?" and sitting with the answer long enough for it to reshape design decisions. I have not run a second ICE pass that did not change something meaningful about the plan.

Adversarial reviews earn their time when they produce findings you do not want to hear. When a sceptical persona tells you a feature will become a chore or a data model will not survive real usage, the instinct to argue or quietly exclude the finding is the instinct to protect comfort at the cost of quality. Treat discomfort as a signal.

One practical hazard: the challenge technique can produce 15 questions at once, and 15 unanswered questions is paralysing. Ask your AI assistant to work through them one at a time. The questions are the same; the difference is that one at a time is a conversation and all at once is a wall.

Steps 3 & 4 — Catalogue and Handover: What Experience Teaches

Chapter 6 introduced the project memory file as a tool: a short instructions document the AI reads at the start of each session, so you are not re-explaining the project every time. What experience teaches is that the catalogue function of the memory file matters as much as the governance function — and it is the one most often skipped.

The governance structure that the memory file provides (maintain history.md, never deviate from plan.md without flagging, record verification evidence as you go) is largely the same across every project and quickly becomes habitual. What varies, and what the memory file must contain if it is to work, is a map of where everything lives. The AI begins every new session by reading the memory file. If that file tells it that the plan is in plan.md, the wireframe is in wireframe.html, the data model is in data-model.md, and the security assessment is in security-notes.md, it can navigate the full project context immediately. If the memory file contains only standing rules with no map of assets, the AI will begin each session partially blind: unaware of decisions and constraints that exist in files it has not been told to read.

The practical discipline is simple. Before the first build conversation opens, commit the plan and generate the memory file from it. The planning context is still live at that moment; that is precisely when to do it. Sessions end, context compresses, weeks pass. A prompt carries intent for one conversation; a well-constructed memory file carries it for every conversation that follows, whether it is the first build session or a return to the project six months later. Ask your AI assistant to generate it now. The result is a governance and navigation document drawn from your own ICE conversation — not something you draft from scratch, but something the AI produces from decisions already made.

Over time, the standing sections become largely reusable. Only the project-specific catalogue changes. Setup that initially took a full session eventually takes minutes.

Step 5 — Debugging: What Experience Teaches

The most disorienting debugging experiences are not the ones where the code is wrong. They are the ones where the code is right and something else is wrong. An ad-blocker silently blocking a file. A dashboard open in test mode while checking live results. Configuration pointing at the wrong server. In each case, the AI analyses the code exhaustively and finds nothing, because the problem is not in the code.

Debugging through AI works best when you give it both the error and the symptom. Copy the error text or screenshot it: the AI can read both, and the technical detail matters. Pair it with a plain description of what you are seeing. "The page loads but the data does not appear" gives the AI context that an error message alone does not. One tells it what went wrong technically; the other tells it what the experience of the failure actually is. Together they are more useful than either alone.

The deeper lesson is to direct how the AI thinks before it starts. Left to its own instincts, an AI will reach for the most obvious explanation and start fixing. That can cost time if the obvious explanation is wrong. Instead, ask it to stop and consider the full picture first:

- **Example — full-environment diagnosis prompt:**

  > "Before you suggest a fix, I want you to think broadly about what could be causing this. Consider the code, but also the environment, the browser, any external services, credentials, and configuration. List the possible causes in order of likelihood before we start changing anything."

That one instruction changes the conversation from reactive to analytical. The AI that was about to rewrite a function may instead identify that the problem is a misconfigured setting that has nothing to do with the code at all.

Step 6 — Sustaining: What Experience Teaches

The projects that remain useful over time are not the most technically sophisticated. They are the ones that stay comprehensible. A tool you cannot explain to your AI assistant in a fresh session is a tool you cannot extend. A project whose decisions exist only in your memory is a project that degrades every time you step away from it.

The habit that makes the difference is writing things down at the moment they happen, not afterwards. A history.md entry written at the end of a session takes a single prompt: ask the AI to summarise what changed and why, and it will. Written two weeks later, it is a reconstruction from memory that misses half the decisions and none of the reasoning. The same applies to verification: recording that something works at the moment you verify it takes seconds; reconstructing that evidence later is often impossible.

Vibe-coding's speed is also its main threat to longevity. You can generate fifty changes in an afternoon; without discipline, that afternoon produces a project that works today and is mysterious in a month. The sequence in this section is not overhead imposed on top of building. It is what building with AI actually looks like when it is done well.

8.3 Data Storage

Every tool that does anything meaningful must answer one question before it can do anything else: where does the data live? Data storage is how your application holds information that needs to survive after the user closes the tab or the application stops running: a list of tasks, a set of records, a history of calculations. Without a deliberate storage decision, that information simply disappears. The right choice depends on who will use the tool, how many of them, and what happens if the data is lost. This decision belongs in the Constraints phase of ICE before any code is written. Ask your AI assistant directly:

- **Example prompt:**

  > "Given these constraints, what data storage approach would you recommend, and why?"

The answer will typically surface options you had not considered, and reasons to start simpler than you were planning.

Local files are the simplest option. A JSON file (a lightweight, plain text format that AI handles fluently) is entirely adequate for personal tools used on one machine. No accounts, no infrastructure, no costs. The limitation is simple: the file lives on one machine and cannot be shared. Save it inside an OneDrive or Dropbox folder and you get cross-device sync for free.

Browser storage works for tools that run entirely in the browser with no server behind them. The data lives on the user's device, never leaves it, and costs nothing. The catch: clear the browser cache and it is gone. For browser-based tools, ask your AI assistant to add an export/import pair from the start: two buttons, no infrastructure, and the backup cycle is under your control.

Git as a data store is less obvious but genuinely useful. GitHub Gists (individual files hosted on GitHub) function as a lightweight remote store: synchronised, versioned, free, and accessible from any device. Think of it as local JSON with built-in sync, suitable for personal tools where each user's data can live in a private Gist.

Cloud databases become necessary when a tool needs to serve multiple users or grow beyond what a file can hold. A database organises data into structured tables, handles simultaneous users without corruption, and enforces access controls. Supabase is the platform I recommend for most vibe-coded projects: free for small projects, well-documented, and reliably understood by AI assistants. Be aware that the free tier pauses inactive projects after seven days. Azure SQL suits enterprise environments already running Microsoft infrastructure; AWS and Google Cloud offer equivalent services.

Option	Best For	Multi-user?	Cost	Complexity
Local JSON file	Personal tools, experiments	No	Free	Very low
Git / GitHub Gist	Personal tools, cross-device	No (limited)	Free	Low
Browser storage	Single-device browser tools	No	Free	Low
Supabase	Early-stage products, consumer apps	Yes	Free tier	Moderate
Azure SQL / AWS / GCP	Enterprise, existing cloud ecosystems	Yes	Paid	High

Table 8.1: Data Storage Options at a Glance

The principle that crosses all storage choices: start simple and add complexity only when the use case demands it. I started almost every project with local JSON files. When a tool graduated to multi-user, I migrated to Supabase. When enterprise requirements entered, Azure SQL. And regardless of the storage layer, treat modification and deletion with care. Reading data is low risk, but a wrong delete is irreversible. Before running any script that changes existing data, ask your AI assistant to explain exactly what each step does, and test against a copy before touching live data.

8.4 Third-Party Integrations

Payments, email delivery, mapping, document generation, translation, identity verification: all of these are available as third-party services that your tool can connect to rather than build from scratch. Traditional developers use them too. The difference is that connecting one has always required reading dense technical documentation, writing connection code, and understanding integration patterns that are rarely obvious. Most people without a development background would not attempt it. With AI, you describe what you need and it produces the connection code, explains the configuration, and walks you through the account setup. Capabilities that once required specialist knowledge to integrate are now accessible in an afternoon. Most vibe-coders underuse them simply because they do not realise how much is available.

For most major services, your AI assistant can generate architecturally correct connection code and walk through the configuration required. But knowing the structure of an integration and knowing whether it will work in your specific environment are different things. The limitation, consistently across all integrations, is that AI knows the structure but not the specifics of your account. It will generate code that looks complete and fail silently because a credential is missing, an environment setting is wrong, or the documentation it trained on has since changed. That gap between "the code is correct" and "the system works" is the central lesson of every integration experience.

Decide which third-party services your tool will use during the ICE conversation, not mid-build. Rather than trying to remember the right questions yourself, ask the AI to lead the conversation. A prompt like this hands the work to where it belongs:

- **Example — integration ICE prompt:**

> "I am planning to build [description]. What third-party services would you recommend, and what questions do you need to ask me before we design the integrations?"

The AI will take it from there, asking about credentials, failure handling, structural isolation, and free-tier options without the user needing to know those terms exist. A 22,000-line tool I built broke within weeks when a social platform changed its API, because the structural isolation question was never asked. One prompt at the planning stage would have prevented it.

Payments are where delegation matters most. Stripe handles the mechanics of accepting card payments: card data never touches your server, security compliance is Stripe's responsibility, and test mode lets you build without processing real transactions. The integration cost is trivial compared to the liability avoided. Be aware that subscription state management is more complex than it first appears: the lifecycle from trial to active to overdue to cancelled has edge cases that surface only when real customers start paying.

One term worth knowing before you get to a payments integration: a **webhook**. Most third-party services, Stripe included, need a way to tell your application when something happens on their end, a payment succeeds, a subscription renews, a card fails, without your application having to constantly ask. A webhook is how they do it: the service sends your application a message the moment the event occurs. Ask your AI assistant to set this up as part of the integration; Chapter 10 covers webhooks in the context of deploying and connecting a live application.

Email sent from a tool is not the same as email sent from your inbox. The code can be correct and emails still fail to arrive, landing in spam or being silently rejected. A dedicated email platform handles the authentication configuration that makes messages look legitimate to receiving servers. For transactional email (password resets, receipts, notifications), Resend is the platform I recommend: clean API, reliable deliverability, and well understood by most AI assistants. For marketing email, note that data protection law imposes legal obligations (consent records, unsubscribe mechanisms) that are Constraints, not technical choices. GDPR (the General Data Protection Regulation) governs UK and EU recipients; CAN-SPAM applies in the US; equivalent legislation exists in most major markets. These obligations apply regardless of where you are based if your users are in those jurisdictions. State them in ICE or they will not appear in the code.

The failure mode that Constraints alone cannot prevent is what I call the credentials trap. AI generates integration code that looks complete, runs without errors during testing, and then fails silently against the real service because the credentials it assumed were configured have not been. The code is not wrong. The environment is not ready. Test with real credentials in the real environment before assuming any integration works.

> ***What I Actually Did:*** *For every integration, I now test with real credentials in the correct environment before assuming the code works. The lesson cost me hours of debugging a Stripe integration that was working perfectly — in test mode, against a dashboard I was not looking at.*

Figure 8.1: The Wrong Dashboard — hours of debugging for a problem that had nothing to do with code.

8.5 Authentication and User Management

Authentication (usually shortened to "auth") is the system that answers the question: who is this person, and are they allowed to be here? Every tool that has more than one user, or that stores data belonging to specific individuals, needs an answer to that question. Without authentication, anyone who finds the link to your tool can access everything in it.

In practice, authentication covers several related problems. Identity verification: how does the tool confirm the person logging in is who they claim to be? Session management: once logged in, how does the tool remember that, so the user is not asked to prove their identity on every click? Access control: once inside, which parts of the tool can this person see and use? Password security: if the tool stores passwords, how are they stored so that a data breach does not expose them? Account recovery:

what happens when a user forgets their password or loses access to their device?

Each of those is a system with its own failure modes and security implications. For most vibe-coders, the instinct is to ask AI to build a login page, and AI will oblige, producing something that looks entirely convincing. The problem is that a login system that looks correct and a login system that is secure are not the same thing. The gaps between them are precisely where attackers look first. This is not a reason to avoid building tools that require users to log in; it is a reason to understand the decision you are making before you make it, and to use the ICE conversation to surface that decision explicitly.

Authentication is where the principle of delegation applies most forcefully. Specialist auth providers (services whose entire purpose is solving the identity problem securely) have dedicated security teams, compliance certifications, penetration testing programmes, and incident response capabilities. Your vibe-coded implementation has you. That asymmetry should inform every decision you make about user login systems.

The market offers several strong options, each with generous free tiers that make the cost argument irrelevant for most projects.

Provider	Strength	Free Tier	Best For
Clerk	Developer experience	10,000 monthly users	Modern apps, quick setup
Auth0	Enterprise features	7,000 monthly users	Complex requirements
Supabase Auth	Integrated with database	Unlimited	Already using Supabase
Firebase Auth	Google ecosystem	Unlimited	Mobile apps
Nex-tAuth.js	Self-hosted flexibility	N/A (self-hosted)	Next.js projects

Table 8.2: Authentication Provider Comparison (correct at time of writing; verify current pricing and free tier limits before selecting a provider)

Each of these providers handles the components that matter most: storing passwords securely, managing sessions, allowing users to log in via an existing Google or GitHub account rather than creating a new password, two-factor verification, and account recovery. Each of those is a system with edge cases and failure modes that take months to implement correctly. Using a provider is achievable in an afternoon.

Two-factor authentication (2FA — the extra verification step where a user confirms their identity via a code sent to their phone or generated by an app like Google Authenticator) illustrates the build-versus-buy decision most clearly. With a provider, you turn it on. It works. Building it yourself means asking AI to implement half a dozen interlocking components, each with its own security requirements, several of which are genuinely high-risk if implemented incorrectly. AI will produce code for all of them. The question is whether a flaw in any one of those components will be visible to you before someone exploits it. For most vibe-coders, the answer is no. Use a provider, turn on the option, and move on.

For minimum viable products, magic links offer security without complexity. No passwords to store or hash. No 2FA needed because email is the second factor. AI implements these well, and users are familiar with the pattern. A prompt as simple as the following produces a working implementation:

- **Example prompt:**

  > "Add magic link authentication: user enters email, system sends login link valid for 15 minutes, clicking link creates session"

> ***What I Actually Did:*** *For every project that needed user accounts, I used a provider. The ICE Constraint I state in every such conversation is simple: "Use an established authentication provider — do not build login systems from scratch." That single Constraint removes an entire category of security risk from the project before a line of code is written.*

The principle is to match authentication complexity to actual risk. A reading list app does not need the same auth as a tool handling medical records or financial data. Most providers are free for small projects, and at the scale where they start charging (typically seven to ten thousand active users per month) you have a real business and can afford the modest subscription cost. That is cheap insurance compared to the cost of a security breach, the reputational damage that follows, and the legal exposure that GDPR creates when personal data is involved.

8.6 Taming the Black Box: Harnesses

One of the most common anxieties in vibe-coding is deceptively simple: how do you know the code your AI assistant wrote actually works? You did not write it line by line. You may not fully understand every part of it. And yet you are about to rely on it.

The answer is not to become a traditional developer and audit every line. The answer is a harness.

A harness is a small piece of code you build around AI-generated code to test, control, or run it safely before trusting it with real work. It is the scaffolding that lets you verify behaviour without needing to fully understand the implementation inside. In traditional software engineering, harnesses have existed for decades as testing infrastructure. In vibe-coding, they take on a broader and more immediate role: they are how you maintain oversight of code you did not write.

There are four practical types. A test harness feeds known inputs to an AI-generated function and checks that the outputs match what you defined as correct. An execution harness runs AI-generated code inside a controlled environment with timeouts, restricted access, and captured output, containing any damage if the code misbehaves. A prompt harness wraps an API call with retry logic, output parsing, and safe defaults, making an inherently unpredictable response reliable enough to use in subsequent steps. An evaluation harness runs multiple AI-generated candidate solutions against the same test suite and selects the winner objectively, so you never need to read competing implementations in detail.

The division of labour is consistent across all four types: your AI assistant writes the thing inside the harness; you write the harness itself. In practice, your AI assistant can write the harness too, provided you ask with sufficient structure. Which is where ICE earns its place.

A weak harness prompt – "write a test harness for this function" – produces a harness that confirms the function works when everything goes right. It tests the happy path, invents plausible-looking mock data, and passes confidently. It will not tell you anything useful about how the function behaves when input is malformed, boundaries are breached, or something unexpected arrives.

An ICE-structured prompt changes this substantially. Intent tells your AI assistant what confidence you are trying to achieve, not just what to produce. Constraints are where most of the harness-specific thinking lives: which test cases to use, what failure behaviour looks like, what scope is permitted, and critically, which adversarial inputs to include, such as malformed data, boundary values, and empty fields. Your AI assistant will not add these unprompted. Expectations define the output format precisely enough to be useful: a standalone script, clear PASS/FAIL output per case, a non-zero exit code on failure so it can sit inside an automated pipeline.

> ***What I Actually Did:*** *For all projects I now create, on any function that handles external data or user input, I ask my AI assistant to write a test harness before the function touches anything real. The constraint I include in that prompt is: "Include adversarial inputs – malformed data, boundary values, empty fields. The harness should fail loudly when something goes wrong." A harness that passes on perfect data only is not a harness. It is a false sense of security.*

The harness prompt is one of the cleaner demonstrations of why ICE works. The difference between a vague prompt and a structured one is not philosophical: it is immediately visible in whether the harness you receive would actually catch a problem, or merely reassure you that everything is fine.

8.7 Debugging Beyond Code

The website stopped loading correctly. Claude analysed everything it could see: the code, the structure, the logic. Hours of investigation, every diagnosis pointing to problems that did not exist. The actual problem was an ad-blocker. A browser extension installed on the user's computer was silently blocking part of the page because its name contained the word "analytics." The code was perfect. The environment around it was the problem. And Claude, which can only see the code itself, spent hours looking in the only place it knew to look.

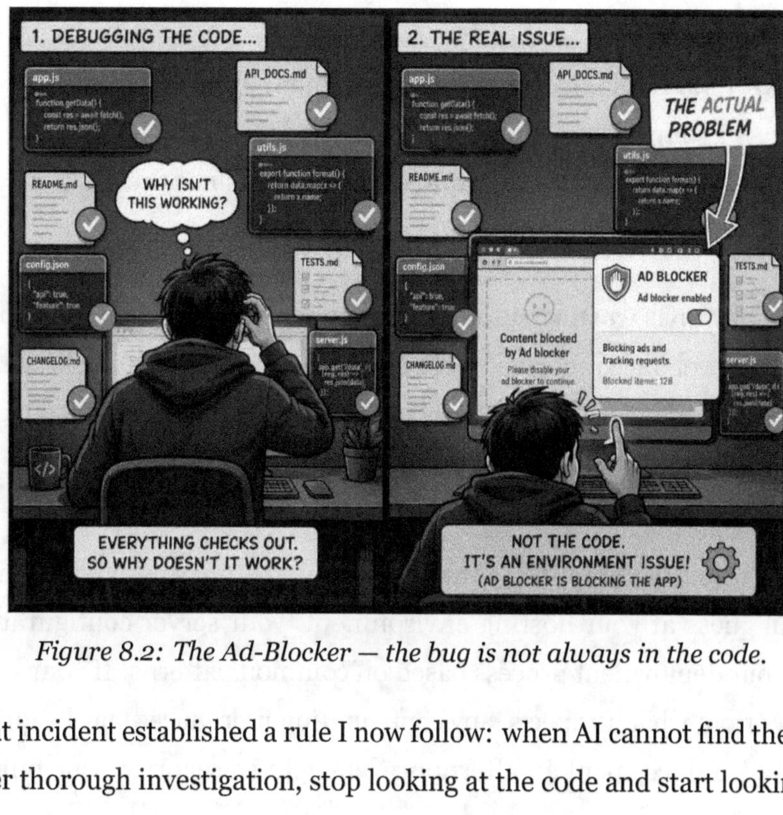

Figure 8.2: The Ad-Blocker — the bug is not always in the code.

That incident established a rule I now follow: when AI cannot find the bug after thorough investigation, stop looking at the code and start looking at everything around it. The most common culprits are things AI cannot see:

- **Browser extensions:** ad-blockers, privacy tools, and security plug-ins can silently interfere with how a website loads or behaves. They are invisible to AI and easy to forget are running.
- **The gap between testing and live:** an app that works perfectly on your own computer may behave differently once it is published online. The two environments are rarely identical, and the differences are often the source of the problem.
- **Outdated copies:** browsers and hosting services keep temporary copies of web pages to load them faster. If you fix a problem and it seems to persist, you may be looking at an old copy, not the current one.
- **External service changes:** if a payment processor, email service, or API your app depends on has changed its behaviour, updated its rules, or experienced an outage, your code is not the problem and changing your code will not fix it.

A similar trap is trusting automated testing tools uncritically. A security scanning tool once reported a problem I had already fixed weeks earlier. The fix was in place. The tool was out of date. Automated tools, like AI, can be wrong, and they can report stale results confidently. Verify the finding exists before spending time fixing it.

AI also makes assumptions about your setup that may not match reality. It will guess at your hosting environment, your server configuration, and your deployment process based on common patterns. If your setup differs from what it expects, any configuration it produces may be quietly ignored. I once spent an afternoon debugging a security issue only to discover that the configuration file Claude had helpfully created was written for a different hosting platform entirely. The file existed, looked correct, and did nothing.

> ***What I Actually Did:*** *After the ad-blocker incident, I started every debugging session by asking "Is this a code problem?" before letting Claude analyse anything. Half the time, the answer was no. That single question has saved more hours than any debugging technique.*

When AI is stuck and the code looks right, run through these questions before going further. Is this definitely a code problem, or could it be something in the environment (an extension, a cached copy, an external service)? Does the problem happen both on your own computer and when published online, or only one of them? Have you recently changed anything outside the codebase (a hosting setting, a service subscription, an account password)? Is AI looking at the current version of your files, or could it be working from something outdated?

8.8 Security at Scale

Chapter 7 walked through a security audit on the Reading List Manager: a handful of OWASP findings, two things to fix, two things to accept. That is what security looks like on a small, low-stakes project. LockedPillar was different. When I asked my AI assistant to produce a security testing package for a commercial application handling subscription payments, the scale of the output was unlike anything I had encountered in the Reading List Manager.

Enterprise-grade security documentation, generated in hours rather than the weeks a consultant would require. But generating documentation and executing it are different activities. A 66-page testing schedule means nothing if it sits unread. The human must still run the tests, interpret the results, and make decisions about what to fix and what to accept.

Document	Scale	Purpose
Executive Summary	13 pages	Leadership/business overview
Full Testing Schedule	66 pages	Phase-by-phase methodology
Quick Start Guide	14 pages	Immediate actions, Day 1 tasks
Python Test Suite	576 lines	Automated security testing

Table 8.3: Security Testing Package Generated by AI

Before launching LockedPillar, I ran the testing package as part of the pre-launch review. The findings divided neatly into three categories: issues requiring immediate attention before any user saw the application, issues needing to be addressed before launch, and controls that were already in place from the initial build. Running the tests told me which was which, and gave me a defensible record that the review had happened.

The critical items got fixed before launch. The high-priority items got fixed before launch. But the scanning report also flagged issues where the effort of fixing would have been disproportionate to the risk. Two of the findings related to browser security policy rules that, if resolved, would have required significant refactoring of the entire codebase. For an application that stores no sensitive user data, where Stripe handles all payment information, and where the attack value is minimal, these were high-effort changes for low-return improvements.

Figure 8.3: The Security Stack — generating the documentation is not the same as running the tests.

This is where risk management as a discipline, not just a concept, matters. I documented the decision formally: given that no sensitive information is present and overall risk is very low, these failings are high effort for low return. That documentation protects against future questions. It is not an excuse for laziness; it is evidence of deliberate risk-based decision-making. The format for recording that decision is the same one Chapter 7 introduced: severity, risk, decision, reasoning.

Issue	Effort	Risk	Decision
Remove browser policy restriction (inline scripts)	High	Low	**Accept**
Remove browser policy restriction (dynamic evaluation)	Medium	Low	**Accept**
Add cross-origin access headers	Low	Low	**Optional**

Table 8.4: Risk Acceptance Decisions for LockedPillar

The cost spectrum for security testing reinforces why risk-based thinking matters. In-house testing using free tools costs £0 in fees but requires time and judgement. External penetration testing from a professional firm varies significantly by scope, accreditation, and market. As a rough UK guide in early 2026, scoped web application tests from CREST-accredited firms typically run into the tens of thousands of pounds. A hybrid approach, where you do the initial work and bring in professionals for targeted review, sits at a fraction of that cost. For a solo practitioner building a low-risk application, the in-house approach with AI assistance is rational. For anything handling personal data, financial information, or operating in a regulated industry, professional review is not optional.

> ***What I Actually Did:*** *I fixed the critical and high-priority vulnerabilities, accepted the medium-risk items with documented rationale, and spent the security budget on the areas with highest return. Total professional cost: £0 for security testing (in-house with AI), £480 for legal advice on copyright. The security documentation became part of the project's verification evidence — the record that confirms it does what it was supposed to do.*

Security is contextual. A line-learning application is not a banking application. The framework is in Chapter 7. The lesson here is about scale: when a project grows beyond a personal tool, the same structured approach produces a proportionately larger body of work, and the discipline of executing rather than just generating it is what separates a defensible security position from a false sense of security.

8.9 Workflow Patterns That Compound

The clearest discovery across three years of practice is that small workflow investments compound. Lean memory files, version control discipline, knowing when to intervene: none of these is dramatic on its own. Together, they change the daily experience of vibe-coding from reactive to systematic.

When a friction point in your workflow appears once, note it. When it appears a second time, note it again. When it appears a third time, fix it: adjust the project memory file to prevent the problem, or encode the solution as a reusable skill. The threshold of three prevents over-engineering while ensuring genuine patterns get addressed. Chapter 9 covers the full range of tools available for encoding these patterns.

Version control discipline matters more than it does in traditional development, precisely because iteration is so fast. Commit before testing to preserve AI's first interpretation. Branch before risky changes. Write commit messages that explain why, not what. When you can generate fifty commits in an afternoon, the commit history becomes your only record of how the project evolved. Make it readable.

> ***What I Actually Did:*** *I keep a running list of workflow friction points. When the same friction appears three times, I build a skill or*

adjust the project memory file to eliminate it.

The refactoring trap deserves a specific warning. AI sometimes wants to rewrite everything when a surgical fix would suffice. The signs are recognisable: "Let me restructure this for better maintainability." Changes spanning files unrelated to the bug. New abstractions appearing mid-fix. When you see these patterns, intervene. "Just fix the specific issue without refactoring surrounding code." Left unchecked, a simple bug fix becomes a rewrite that introduces new bugs while solving the original one.

8.10 Deployment Lessons

Deployment options (static hosting, serverless functions, containers, mobile wrapping, and self-hosting) each suit different types of project. What follows are the practitioner lessons that no deployment guide covers: the things that went wrong despite the code being correct.

Offline apps can hide your updates. A Progressive Web App (PWA), a website that can be installed on a phone or desktop and used without an internet connection, works by saving a copy of the app on the user's device. The problem is that the same mechanism that makes it work offline can also make your updates invisible: users may continue running a saved copy for days without receiving changes you have already deployed. The first time a user reported a bug I had already fixed, I spent an hour re-investigating before realising they were running last week's version. Build a strategy for forcing devices to fetch the latest copy into your deployment from the start, not after users complain.

Packaging tools add complexity that must earn its keep. Docker is a tool that bundles your application and everything it needs to run into a self-contained package, so that it behaves identically whether running on your laptop, a colleague's machine, or a remote server. It solves a real problem ("it works on my machine but not in production") but introduces a new category of problems in return. AI can set Docker up competently, but the issues that arise from it require understanding that goes beyond what AI can easily diagnose. Use it when you genuinely need consistent behaviour across multiple environments. Do not use it because it feels like the professional choice. Simple web projects rarely benefit.

On-demand code has a wake-up delay. Serverless functions are small pieces of code that run in the cloud only when called, rather than running continuously on a dedicated server. The hosting provider starts them on demand and shuts them down when idle, which keeps costs low. For container-based serverless platforms (AWS Lambda, Google Cloud Functions), the catch is that a function which has been idle for a while takes several seconds to start up the first time it is called. This delay does not appear when testing on your own machine, where the code is always ready. Edge-native platforms like Cloudflare Workers use a different architecture and do not exhibit this delay. If you are on a container-based platform, this catches most vibe-coders eventually: the feature works perfectly in development, then feels sluggish in production for the first user of the day. Test in a live environment before assuming the experience matches what you saw locally.

The app store tax is real. Converting a web app into a mobile app for distribution through an app store is achievable with AI. The submission process is not. Apple Developer account carries an annual fee; Google Play charges a one-time registration fee. Both stores have review processes where rejection is common for first submissions. Every update requires a new submission. Unless your users specifically need device APIs or an app store presence, stay web-only.

> ***What I Actually Did:*** *During the LockedPillar build, I asked my AI assistant to map out the likely deployment path: what hosting would serve the early version, what its limits were, and what the upgrade route looked like. That conversation surfaced the PWA requirement early enough to influence the architecture. LockedPillar launched on static hosting with a managed database as a deliberate decision rather than a default. For all projects I now create, mapping the deployment path is part of the planning conversation, not something I return to after the build is under way.*

Self-hosting requires sysadmin skills you may not have. AI can help configure a VPS (Virtual Private Server, your own rented server in a data centre), but debugging production issues at 3am requires understanding that goes beyond what AI can scaffold. Start with managed platforms. Graduate to self-hosting when you hit their limits, not before.

8.11 Key Takeaways

- **Planning compounds:** Front-loading discovery displaces rework. When planning reveals a problem, the cost of changing course is a conversation; when implementation reveals it, the cost is rebuilding. Set up version control and the project memory file before the first design conversation. Commit the ICE plan before building begins.
- **Data storage:** Start with the simplest option that meets your needs. AI builds quickly; verify infrastructure assumptions before going live.
- **Third-party APIs:** AI knows the structure but not your credentials, current versions, or rate limits. Build assuming external services will change.
- **Authentication demands delegation:** Auth providers have secu-

rity teams; you do not. Use an established auth service for any app with user accounts.

- **Harnesses verify what you cannot audit:** A harness is a small piece of code that tests AI-generated code against known inputs before it touches real work. Structured with ICE, it catches failures the happy path never will.
- **Debug beyond code:** When AI cannot find the bug, check the environment: browser extensions, cached copies, external service changes. Tools can be wrong.
- **Security is contextual:** Apply controls proportionate to risk. Document decisions. Delegate what you can. Know when professional review is essential.
- **Workflows compound:** Small investments in memory file discipline, version control habits, and knowing when to intervene multiply over time.
- **Deployment rewards simplicity:** Start with the simplest hosting that works. Each upgrade should be driven by an actual limitation, not an anticipated one.

CHAPTER 9

Documentation and Advanced Tools

9.1 Introduction

Building a project that works is one achievement. Building a practice that sustains over months and years is another. Chapter 8 covered what you encounter while constructing a real project. This chapter covers what determines whether that project, and the ones that follow, remain coherent, maintainable, and improvable over time.

Two forces shape long-term practice. The first is documentation drift: the inevitable tendency for what was planned and what was built to diverge, silently, until the gap is too wide to bridge without archaeology. The second is capability compounding: the tools and habits that, once established, make every subsequent project faster, more reliable, and less effortful than the one before. This chapter addresses both: first the discipline that keeps projects coherent, then the advanced capabilities that make the work itself faster and more powerful.

9.2 Documentation Drift

Three weeks after finishing a file management utility, I asked Claude to review the plan to confirm a feature was included. Claude read the original `plan.md` and told me "recommendations only" was the specification. The implemented application had full deletion capability. I had built a feature that contradicted my own specification, and neither I nor Claude had noticed until I went looking.

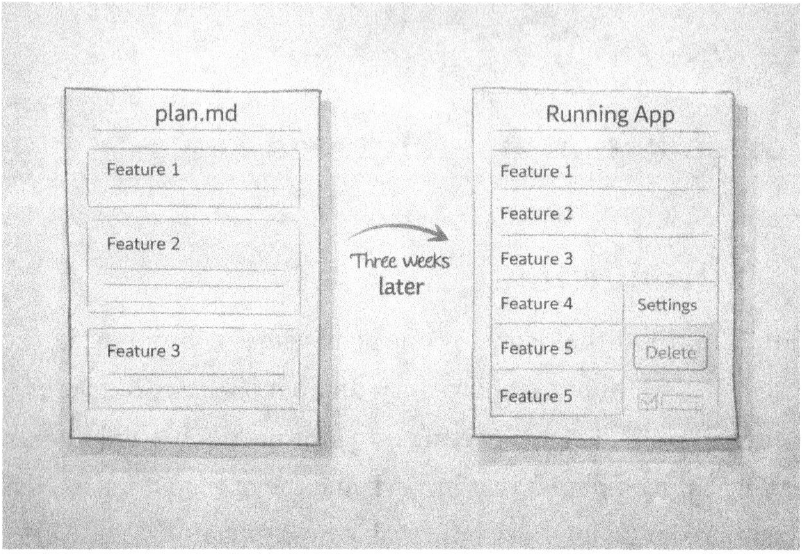

Figure 9.1: Documentation Drift — the plan and the reality diverge without anyone noticing.

This is documentation drift, and it is the inevitable consequence of vibe-coding's speed. You generate ideas faster than documentation can keep up. A static plan becomes stale almost immediately. Maintaining perfect documentation slows momentum. But without documentation, you lose track of what the project is supposed to do versus what it actually does. Every vibe-coder faces this tension.

Chapter 8 introduced the practical countermeasures: CLAUDE.md as persistent project memory, history.md as the development journal, and the phase pause that keeps both current. This section explains why those countermeasures matter — what documentation drift actually is, how it happens, and what it costs when left to accumulate.

The drift happened naturally. The original specification called for the application to identify files that could be deleted, but for the user to act manually. Safety through inaction. During development, Claude suggested a "Test Removal" feature: rename files to make them inaccessible, let the user verify nothing breaks, then permanently delete. This was genuinely better than the original approach. I implemented it. What I did not do was update the plan.

The underlying problem is that Claude Code maintains its own working plan in a `.claude/plans/` folder during complex work. This plan evolves with implementation. Your `plan.md` may not. Neither document is wrong; they serve different purposes. But assuming they say the same thing causes confusion. When you ask Claude to "check the plan," you need to clarify which plan you mean.

Approach	Benefit	Cost
Update plan.md constantly	Always accurate	Slows momentum, feels bureaucratic
Never update plan.md	Fast iteration	Drift becomes invisible
Ignore documentation entirely	Maximum speed	No record of decisions

Table 9.1: The Documentation Tension

None of these extremes works. The solution I settled on is two documents with distinct purposes.

plan.md is the authoritative specification: what the project is supposed to do. You update it only when you consciously decide to change scope. When implementation diverges from the original spec, add a "Current Scope" section at the top rather than rewriting the original. The original sections become historical reference, showing where the project started and why certain decisions were made. The delta between the two tells you how far you have drifted.

history.md is the development journal: what actually happened during development. You update it after each significant session or feature. It is chronological, conversational, and captures decisions, pivots, features added or removed, and most importantly why. An entry might look like this:

```
## Session 5: Test Removal Feature

SCOPE CHANGE: Added deletion capability (not in original spec)

Implemented "Test Removal" feature:
- In-situ rename approach (.backup suffix)
- Manifest-first safety for crash recovery
- Instant undo capability

Rationale: Original "recommendations only" approach created
friction.
Test Removal provides safety through reversibility rather than
inaction.
```

The workflow is simple. Before starting work, check `plan.md` for scope. When ideas emerge during development, note them in history.md with a "PROPOSED:" prefix. When scope actually changes, update `plan.md`'s Current Scope section first, then implement. After each session, write a brief history.md entry summarising what was done.

This works because each document answers a different question. `plan.md` answers "What does this app do?" which is useful for onboarding, reviews, and returning after a break. `history.md` answers "How did we get here?" which is useful for understanding decisions, debugging regressions, and writing case studies. Together, they give you just enough documentation to catch drift without the overhead of maintaining perfection.

Here is a practical trick that reduces the friction further: use AI to write the documentation. At the end of a session, ask your AI assistant to summarise what was built or update the plan. Your AI assistant has full context of the conversation and can produce a first draft in seconds. This removes the most common excuse for skipping documentation, which is that it takes too long.

- **Example prompt — updating history.md:**

> "Summarise what we built today for history.md."

- **Example prompt — updating plan.md:**

> "Update the Current Scope section of plan.md to reflect what we just implemented."

But apply the same trust calibration to AI-generated documentation that you apply to AI-generated code. Your AI assistant will sometimes describe what it intended to build rather than what was actually built. It may omit a feature that was discussed but not implemented, or include one that was planned but deferred. It may describe the architecture as cleaner than it actually is. Review the AI's draft against what you actually see in the project. Internal documentation that misrepresents reality is worse than no documentation at all, because it gives you false confidence when you return to the project months later.

The ICE Pack

The two-document approach solves the drift problem. But there is a broader question: when a project is finished, what should you have to show for it? Not as decoration or compliance theatre, but as evidence that the work was done deliberately.

The answer is three things, which together I call the **ICE Pack**:

1. **plan.md**, the specification written before the work. Intent, Constraints, Expectations. What you set out to build, why, and what "done" looks like. This is the *before* artefact.
2. **The delivered product**, the working application, document, analysis, or tool. This is the *during* artefact. It exists because you built it.
3. **Verification evidence**. This is the *after* artefact, and the one most easily skipped.

Verification evidence answers the question: how do you know it works, and how do you know it works the way you intended? Not "I ran it and it seemed fine." Something deliberate. Something you could show someone else. For LockedPillar, verification evidence included the security testing package described in the Security section of Chapter 8 (executive summary, full testing schedule, and the Python test suite), the risk acceptance decisions documented there, the history.md entries recording what was built in each session, and screenshots confirming that the Expectations defined in the original ICE conversation were met. Together they form a coherent record: here is what I set out to build, here is what I built, and here is my evidence that the two correspond.

Verification evidence does not need to be elaborate. For a small internal tool, a history.md entry that works through the original Expectations one by one is sufficient. For a public-facing application handling real users, it should include security review findings, tested edge cases, and documented risk decisions. For anything in a regulated domain, professional review belongs here. The principle is proportionality: the verification evidence should be commensurate with the stakes. What matters is that it exists — that you asked "does this do what I said it would do?" and recorded the answer. If you have been following the workflow from Chapter 7, you already produce all three artefacts as natural byproducts. The ICE Pack simply names what you are already doing.

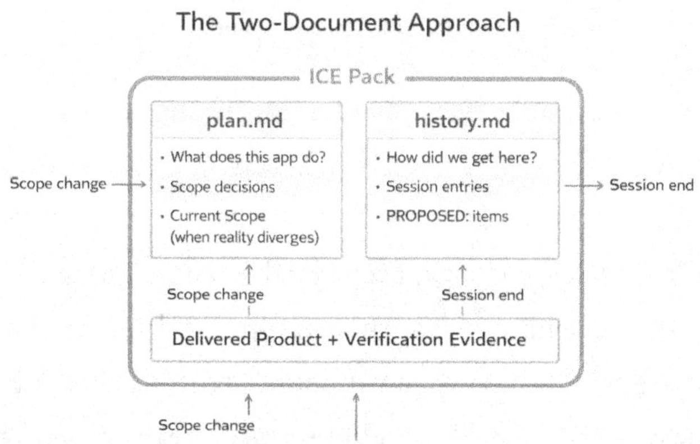

Figure 9.2: The Two-Document Approach — plan.md answers "What does this app do?" and history.md answers "How did we get here?" Together they form the foundation of the ICE Pack.

Situation	What the ICE Pack provides
Returning to a project after months	plan.md tells you what it was supposed to do. history.md tells you what actually happened. You can resume without archaeology.
Handing a project to someone else	The specification, product, and verification evidence give them everything they need to understand, maintain, or extend the work.
Defending a decision	"Why did you build it this way?" has an answer: the plan.md documents the reasoning. The security review documents accepted risks.

Situation	What the ICE Pack provides
Building a portfolio	Ten projects with ICE Packs demonstrate systematic practice. Ten projects without them demonstrate ten experiments.

Table 9.2: When the ICE Pack Matters

This connects to a broader risk. Chapter 3 introduced cognitive debt: the gap between what the code does and what the practitioner understands. The ICE Pack is cognitive debt insurance. If your plan.md describes the architecture, your history.md captures the decisions, and your verification evidence confirms what works, then the mental model is not locked inside your head or lost in expired conversations. It is documented. Any competent person, or AI, picking up the project can reconstruct the reasoning. The residual risk is narrower than the critics suggest: it reduces to whether you actually maintained the documentation, which circles back to the discipline of this section. Cognitive debt is real. It is not inevitable. But it is only prevented by the practices you sustain, not the ones you intend.

> ***What I Actually Did:*** *After the drift incident described above, I adopted the two-document approach for every non-trivial project. At the end of each session, I ask Claude to draft the history.md entry. It takes thirty seconds to review and adjust. The documentation that seemed like overhead became the cheapest insurance I carry.*
>
> *But having the habit is not the same as keeping it. Session after session, I found myself finishing the work and moving straight on to the next thing. The build was done, the result was in front of me, and updating the journal felt like an afterthought to a task I had*

already mentally closed. For me, that moment was saving the work to a repository, the technical equivalent of pressing send. But the feeling is the same whatever form it takes: the work is done, the moment of completion has passed, and anything that comes after feels unnecessary.

The fix was not to write the rule down more firmly. What worked was building the journal check into that closing routine itself, so it happened automatically before I could move on. Once the check was part of the routine rather than something I had to remember separately, I stopped skipping it. That distinction between a rule you rely on remembering and one embedded in what you already do matters more than it sounds. We return to it when we look at skills.

9.3 Advanced Capabilities — Tools That Compound

If you are not actively building projects yourself, this section is optional. The capabilities below are for practitioners who have working projects and want to extend them. If you are directing a team rather than building personally, or if you are still getting started, the documentation discipline in the first half of this chapter is what matters most right now. Return here when your practice is established.

The first half of this chapter was about keeping projects coherent: catching drift before it becomes archaeology, building documentation habits that sustain rather than slow. That discipline is the foundation. This second half is about what you build on top of it.

The vibe-coder who has the documentation habits in place does not experience AI as a conversation partner they occasionally consult. They experience it as a development environment actively working with them across multiple surfaces simultaneously, with accumulated institutional knowledge and a toolkit refined over months of practice. The four capabilities below are what create that shift: not steps to follow in sequence, but tools to adopt one at a time, each compounding the last. Not all will be relevant right now. Treat this section as an inventory of what is possible, and return to it as your practice matures.

MCP: Giving Your AI Assistant Access to Your World

Every integration you have built so far required code as the bridge: your application called an external service, and AI helped you write that code. MCP (Model Context Protocol) removes the code entirely. Claude connects directly to the service and acts on it autonomously during your conversation.

A concrete example: without MCP, asking Claude to fix a bug in your GitHub repository means describing the code, copying relevant files into the conversation, receiving the fix, and manually applying it. With the GitHub MCP server configured, you say: "The function in src/customers.js that calculates overdue accounts is returning wrong results when the account has no orders. Fix it and commit." Claude reads the file directly from your repository, identifies the problem, writes the fix, and commits it. No copy-pasting, no intermediary code, no context lost in translation. The same session can span multiple services simultaneously: Claude can read your codebase via GitHub, check your error logs via Sentry, update a task in Notion, and post a summary to Slack. All from a single conversation.

In this chapter, MCP is a tool for the vibe-coder during development: configuring servers so your own AI assistant can reach GitHub, Sentry, Notion, and similar services while you build. That is not MCP's only role – the same protocol can also connect an AI feature inside your deployed application to live external services at runtime, which Chapter 10 touches on. Here, though, think of it alongside git and CLAUDE.md as part of the development environment you configure before serious work begins. Setup in Claude Code is a single command per service. The protocol is free and open-source, introduced by Anthropic in November 2024; by late 2025 thousands of servers had been published covering GitHub, Notion, Slack, Stripe, Figma, databases, and the local filesystem.[40][41]

One caveat warrants more than a brief mention. Community-built servers vary in quality, and the most serious risk is prompt injection: a server that fetches web pages, reads email, or processes untrusted documents could deliver instructions that cause Claude to act against your intent: reading files it should not, making commits you did not authorise, or sending data to external destinations. This is an active area of exploit research for AI agent systems, not a theoretical edge case. Review carefully what each MCP server can access, and never grant filesystem or git write permissions to a server that also reads external content. Treat installing an MCP server with at least the same caution as installing any third-party software.

Skills and Slash Commands: Encoding Your Best Thinking

You have already encountered the patterns that skills encode. In Chapter 5, the discovery conversation (asking your AI assistant to surface requirements before writing a single line of code) was presented as a technique. In Chapter 7, the adversarial persona and pre-mortem prompts were presented as planning steps. Both are genuinely useful. But each time you use them, you write the prompt again from scratch, or hunt back through notes to find the version that worked.

A skill removes that friction. It is a defined prompt template stored as a file, invoked with a short command rather than rewritten each time. The discovery conversation becomes `/q`. The adversarial review becomes

`/challenge`. The verification pass becomes `/verify`. Claude Code calls these skills; other AI tools have equivalent concepts under different names. The label varies; the principle is the same.

The value compounds quietly. Every time you find yourself writing the same kind of prompt ("review this for a non-technical reader", "run an adversarial review", "generate a commit message", "check this against the plan") you are doing cognitive work that could be done once and reused indefinitely. A skill encodes that work permanently.

This book was written with skills. The adversarial editor skill runs five hostile perspectives across any chapter on demand. The flesh-out skill transforms a skeleton outline into publication-ready prose. The commit skill creates structured git commits. The reference audit skill checks every citation. None of these prompts are written fresh each time: they are invoked with a slash command and applied to whatever is in the current context.

AI can help you write skills. Describe the task you want to encode and your AI assistant will produce a skill definition you can store and use immediately.

- **Example prompt — creating a skill:**

  > "I want a skill that reviews any section of writing for jargon that a non-technical reader would not understand, then suggests plain-English replacements."

The barrier to creating skills is lower than most vibe-coders assume. Whenever you write a prompt that produces a genuinely useful result, ask yourself whether you will want this again. If yes, ask your AI assistant to turn it into a reusable skill. After a few months of practice, the skills you have accumulated represent a personalised toolkit that reflects your specific working style and the projects you build.

The most useful skills are not always shortcuts for things you already do well. Sometimes they are guardrails for things you reliably forget. If there is a step you know matters but keep skipping, the answer is probably not more willpower. Build the check into a skill that runs at the moment you are most tempted to move on, and the problem tends to solve itself.

Agents: Working in Parallel

An agent is a separate AI process you dispatch to work on a task independently, with its own context window, that reports back when it finishes rather than occupying your main conversation while it works. Claude Code calls this capability agents (dispatched with the Task tool, or its equivalent in the interface you use); other AI tools have similar concepts under different names. The label varies, the principle does not: a human developer working alone is fundamentally serial, one train of thought at a time, while a vibe-coder working with agents can be genuinely parallel, with several independent lines of work proceeding at once.

Agents add the most value on tasks that are clearly scoped and genuinely independent of your main conversation. While your primary conversation builds a feature, a second agent can review the security implications of a design decision, or research the documentation for an integration you will need next. The same pattern extends to auditing existing material rather than building something new: this book's own editing process used three agents dispatched simultaneously against every chapter of the manuscript, each checking a different thing (word-frequency patterns, internal cross-references, terminology consistency) and returning an independent report. What makes a task suitable is independence: it does not need your live context, and it does not need an answer before you can keep working on something else. “Figure out why the authentication is broken” is a poor fit for a project the agent has no context of; “audit this codebase for hardcoded secrets and report file and line references” is.

Figure 9.2: Serial vs Parallel — the single conversation is the bottleneck, not the thinking.

The words in your prompt do not launch an agent by themselves; the tool has to actually dispatch one. Ask for it explicitly:

- **Example prompt — dispatching an agent:**

> “Dispatch an agent to read the authentication flow in src/auth/, compare it against the session-handling requirements in plan.md, and report back any place where the implementation diverges from the spec, with file and line references. Run this in the background while I continue here.”

Once several agents are running, the result you actually want is not four separate reports but one synthesised answer. Give each agent a distinct, non-overlapping scope so their findings do not duplicate each other, then review what comes back with the same scrutiny you would apply to any

AI output before combining it yourself, or asking your main conversation to combine it for you, into a single result. The orchestration is your job: agents divide the work; they do not decide how the pieces fit together.

Model Selection: Matching Capability to Task

Not every conversation requires the most capable model available, and the most capable model is not always the best choice even when it is available. Different models have different strengths, speeds, and costs, and treating every task as identical is a common source of both unnecessary expense and unnecessary waiting.

As a general principle: use the most capable model for tasks where quality of reasoning matters most: complex planning conversations, architectural decisions, adversarial reviews, anything where a subtle error has significant consequences. Use faster, lighter models for routine tasks where speed matters more than depth: generating boilerplate code, summarising documentation, writing commit messages, formatting output.

The ICE planning conversation that shapes the entire build warrants the best reasoning available. The commit message for a minor style fix does not. Developing the instinct for which category a task falls into both improves the quality of important work and reduces the cost and latency of routine work.

The AI landscape is also evolving quickly. Model capabilities that represent the frontier today will be routine within a year. The habit to develop is not memorising which model to use for which task, but regularly revisiting your assumptions about what the available models can do, because the answer changes faster than most practitioners realise.

Building the Practice

None of this happens overnight. The right approach is to add one capability at a time, let it become habitual, and only then add the next. A practice built gradually holds up better than one adopted all at once and partially understood. Start with skills: they have the lowest barrier and the most immediate return. Add MCP when you find yourself repeatedly moving information manually between services and your conversation. Explore agents when you notice yourself waiting for sequential tasks that could run in parallel. Revisit model selection once the others are habitual and you start noticing where speed or cost is the constraint.

> ***What I Actually Did:*** *The skills in this book's development — adversarial editor, flesh-out, reference audit, commit — were not built all at once. Each one was created at the moment it was first needed, usually after writing the same prompt manually two or three times and recognising the pattern. That is the right moment to encode a skill: when repetition has confirmed the prompt works and the need is real.*

9.4 Key Takeaways

- **Documentation drifts without discipline:** Plans become stale faster than you expect. Maintain two documents: `plan.md` for authoritative scope (updated only on conscious scope decisions), and `history.md` for what actually happened. The goal is not perfect documentation; it is visible drift.
- **Use AI to write the documentation:** At the end of each session, ask your AI assistant to draft the history.md entry. It takes seconds to review and costs nothing extra. The most common excuse for skipping documentation is that it takes too long.

- **The ICE Pack:** Specification (plan.md), product (the delivered artefact), and verification evidence. Three things that emerge naturally from good practice. Apply when stakes justify it; skip for throwaway work.
- **MCP extends Claude's reach:** Rather than writing integration code, configure MCP servers to give Claude direct access to GitHub, Notion, Slack, and other services. A single conversation can orchestrate across multiple tools simultaneously.
- **Skills encode your best thinking:** Every prompt you write more than twice should become a skill. Skills accumulate into a personalised toolkit that reflects your working style and the projects you build.
- **Agents remove the serialisation constraint:** An agent is a separate AI process that works independently and reports back. Dispatch one explicitly for clearly scoped, independent work; review what comes back with the same scrutiny as any other AI-generated result; combine the results yourself. Waiting for AI is optional.
- **Match model to task:** Use the most capable model for reasoning-heavy work. Use faster, lighter models for routine tasks. The instinct to develop is not which model to use today, but to revisit your assumptions regularly as capabilities evolve.
- **Build capabilities one at a time:** Skills first (lowest barrier, immediate return), then MCP when manual information-moving becomes friction, then agents when you notice yourself waiting for sequential tasks. A practice built gradually holds up better than one adopted all at once.

Notes

40 Anthropic (2024). "Introducing the Model Context Protocol." *Anthropic News*, November 25, 2024. `anthropic.com/news/model-context-protocol`

41 Piñeyro, L. (2025). "A Year of MCP: From Internal Experiment to Industry Standard." *Pento*, December 23, 2025. `pento.ai/blog/a-year-of-mcp-2025-review`

Part Three: The Practitioner

CHAPTER 10

From Code to Product

10.1 Introduction

Most vibe-coding guides end when the code works. This chapter begins there. The risks of vibe-coding do not end at launch – they change character. During building, the risks are technical: wrong architecture, missing constraints, unverified output. After launch, the risks are operational: dependency on infrastructure you do not fully understand, obligations to users you did not fully anticipate, and the slow drift of a live system away from the state in which you built it.

This chapter is about the transition from builder to operator, and the risks that come with it. Some of those risks are commercial – payments, licensing, user acquisition. Others apply equally to anyone who has built something that people depend on, whether that is a paying customer base or a team inside an organisation. Where the commercial specifics arrive, read them as examples of a broader principle: every decision made after launch carries an obligation, and obligations that were not planned for become the surprises that cost most.

The good news is that your AI assistant can handle almost all of the technical execution. Your job is to know the right questions to ask and the mistakes worth avoiding. That is what this chapter covers.

10.2 The Platform Spectrum

When I began vibe-coding in 2023, the market was simpler, and the complexity you had to absorb was higher. You generated code with an AI assistant, then figured out deployment entirely yourself: hosting, databases, authentication, deployment pipelines. That friction was real, and it filtered out many people before they got to a working product. The reason this book teaches pure vibe-coding (code you own, deploy, and control) is that working through infrastructure at least once builds the understanding you need to make every subsequent choice intelligently. That includes the choice of whether to do it again.

By early 2026, the landscape had fragmented into three distinct categories. A note before we proceed: this market moves fast. Platforms are acquired, pricing changes, and new entrants appear. The specific products and prices mentioned here are accurate as of January 2026 and are offered as illustration, not recommendation. The categories and trade-offs they represent are durable; the names are not.

Approach	Examples	You Own	You Manage
Pure vibe-coding	Cursor, Windsurf, Claude Code	Full source code	Everything (hosting, database, deployment)
Platform vibe-coding	Lovable, Bolt.new, Replit	Code (exportable)	Very little (platform handles infrastructure)
Managed platforms	Base44, Coderick AI	Limited/no export	Nothing (fully managed)

Table 10.1: The vibe-coding spectrum — from full ownership to fully managed.

Pure Tools, Builders, and Managed Platforms

At one end sit pure vibe-coding tools: AI-native development environments that help you write code but provide no infrastructure. You own everything; you manage everything. This is the approach this book teaches. It suits you if you want full ownership and are building something that may need to grow or change in ways you cannot yet anticipate.

In the middle sit full-stack app builders like Lovable, Bolt.new, and Replit, which combine AI code generation with hosting, database, and deployment. Describe your application; they generate the code and run the infrastructure. The backend complexity largely disappears. Code export is available on most paid plans, so you are not permanently locked in. These platforms suit builders who want to move fast and accept some platform dependency in exchange.

At the far end sit managed no-code platforms, which handle everything but offer limited or no code export. Base44 (reportedly acquired by Wix for $80M in June 2025)[42] and similar tools suit projects that are internal or experimental. They are the right choice for a specific kind of project; they are the wrong choice if you think you might want to sell, scale, or modify the application in ways the platform does not support.

The Trade-Off That Matters

The meaningful distinction between these categories is not speed or price: it is what happens when the platform's constraints become your constraints. A project that starts on Lovable can export its code when it outgrows the platform's limits. That export is work, but it is possible. A project built on a managed platform without export cannot migrate its code directly, though the application can be rebuilt in a proper coding environment, using the working product as a live specification. The decision you make at the start determines the decisions you can make later.

This book teaches pure vibe-coding not because managed platforms are inferior, but because understanding infrastructure at least once makes you a better decision-maker regardless of which platform you eventually choose. The interloquial skills (articulating intent, ICE analysis, critical persona review) transfer across every platform. A comprehensive plan works identically whether you implement with Cursor or Lovable. If you choose a platform approach, you can move directly to the sections on costs and payments, which apply regardless of how your code is hosted.

10.3 Where Your Code Lives

If you have chosen pure vibe-coding, your code needs somewhere to live. The right choice depends on what you have built. Start with the simplest option that works. Many vibe-coders over-engineer deployment because more complex approaches feel professional. In most cases, they are not needed. If you followed the ICE process, your hosting approach will already be named in your plan. When the time comes, ask your AI assistant:

- **Example prompt:**

> "I've built a browser-based application with no server or database. What's the simplest way to deploy it so users can access it at a custom domain?"

Your AI assistant will recommend the appropriate service and walk you through the steps. You do not need to memorise the options; you need to describe what you have built and let it guide you.

As your applications grow, you will encounter terms worth understanding briefly. **Static hosting** serves applications that run entirely in the browser with no server processing: the simplest and cheapest option, often free. **Serverless functions** let you add small pieces of backend logic without managing a server yourself, useful when you need one or two specific capabilities. **Managed application hosting** suits applications with more complex backend requirements. Each step up adds capability and cost. Your AI assistant will tell you which applies to your project when you describe what it does.

Most vibe-coded applications live in the browser and stay there. For the minority that need to go further (a mobile app users can install, a desktop application with offline access), your AI assistant can handle the technical path once your plan specifies the requirement. Be clear-eyed about the overhead: publishing to the Apple App Store, for instance, involves a £79-per-year developer account, a complex review process, and first-submission rejection is common. Unless an app store presence is a genuine requirement rather than an aspiration, staying web-based is almost always the simpler and faster choice.

10.4 Connecting Your Application

A deployed application is just a starting point. Most real applications need to connect to external services (payment processors, databases, email providers), respond to events, automate tasks on a schedule, and give you the tools to manage what you have built. This section introduces the key patterns. Your ICE session will have identified which of these your application needs; your plan will already name them as specific build tasks. None of this needs to be figured out on the fly.

Keep Your Secrets Safe

Every external service your application connects to will give you a secret key: a private password that authorises your application to use that service. This is where many beginners make an expensive mistake: those keys end up written directly into the code, committed to a code repository, and exposed to anyone who can read it. The consequences range from unexpected bills to serious security incidents. The fix is simple and your AI assistant will implement it: secret keys belong in a separate configuration file that never gets shared, not in the code itself. Name this as a task in your plan the moment you identify any external service dependency. When you build it, ask:

- **Example prompt:**

> "Set up secure configuration for this application so that my API keys and database credentials are stored separately from the code and won't be accidentally shared."

Events, Schedules, and Automation

Two patterns appear in almost every commercially active application. The first is **webhooks**: a way for external services to notify your application when something happens. When a payment succeeds, Stripe sends your application a message so it can update the user's account immediately, without the user having to wait. When you ask your AI assistant to integrate a payment processor, webhook handling should be part of that build task, not an afterthought. The second is **scheduled tasks**: your application acting automatically at a set time regardless of external events. Nightly database cleanup. A weekly digest email. A daily report. These make a tool feel genuinely useful over time. Both patterns belong in your plan named alongside the features they support:

- **Example prompt:**

> "Add a scheduled task that runs every night at midnight and removes records older than 90 days. Also add a webhook endpoint that listens for payment confirmation events from Stripe and updates the user's subscription status."

AI Inside Your Application

Everything so far has used AI as your development tool. A separate and powerful pattern exists: AI as a feature *inside* the application you are building, working on behalf of your users. A document summarisation tool, a question-answering interface over your own data, an automatic classification engine: in each case, your application sends a user's request to an AI provider and returns the result. A more advanced version of the same pattern connects that in-product AI to live external services at runtime (an MCP server, introduced in Chapter 9, that lets it look up a customer's order or act on a connected system on the user's behalf) rather than just processing text it was handed. The mechanics are simple, but three things belong in your plan before you build any of this.

Cost scales with usage, so a feature that costs pennies at a hundred users needs to be modelled at ten thousand before you commit to it. AI responses take time, so your interface needs a visible loading state from day one.

Most importantly, when your application sends user data to an external AI service, that data leaves your infrastructure entirely. What happens to it is governed by the AI provider's terms of service and legal jurisdiction, not yours. Sending a user's confidential documents to an external AI for summarisation may breach your confidentiality obligations, even if the provider never misuses the data. If those users are in the UK or EU, GDPR applies. The obligation follows your users, not your location. A tool summarising public news articles sits in a very different risk category from one processing client contracts or personal records. Chapter 3 covers this risk in full. Read it before you build any feature that sends user-provided content to an external AI service.

AI Pipelines: Serious Efficiency at Low Cost

One of the most powerful and most overlooked applications of AI in a vibe-coded product is using it to automate your own operational work, not just your users' experience. Any process you currently do manually and repeatedly is a candidate: categorising incoming data, transforming content from one format to another, generating reports, extracting structured information from unstructured text. What takes a person hours can often be reduced to seconds. The economics are striking: a batch operation that might cost a freelancer £500 can cost pennies in AI API fees.

LockedPillar is a concrete example. The product is a memorisation tool for speeches and scripts. Every piece of content needed to be transformed into a precise internal format before users could practise with it: speakers identified, lines annotated, text broken into learning segments. Doing that manually for each script was not viable at scale. An AI pipeline did it automatically: four stages, each validating its output before passing to the next, requiring no manual intervention. The pipeline was operator-only, so end users never triggered an AI call, which kept costs predictable and data protection clean. The principle transfers to any domain. Ask your AI assistant:

- **Example prompt:**

  > "I have a repetitive data preparation task that currently takes me [X hours]. Here is what the input looks like and what the output needs to be. Design an AI pipeline to automate this."

The efficiency gains from this pattern are often larger than anything else in this chapter.

You Are Building Two Applications

There is a distinction that product specifications almost never make but that every commercial application requires: you are building two applications, not one. The first is the product your users see. The second is the back-end interface that lets you operate, administer, and monitor it.

When a user contacts support to say their account is not working, you need a screen to look it up. When a payment fails, you need tooling to suspend and reactivate that account. When you want to understand how people are using your product, you need a dashboard.

I discovered this the hard way, which is exactly the failure mode a thorough ICE session prevents. When I analysed LockedPillar's backend, roughly forty per cent of it was administrative infrastructure that users never see. I call this the **40% observation**: in a complex commercial application, plan for roughly forty per cent of your backend scope to exist for you as operator, not for your users. Your ratio will vary, but the principle holds. Include the operator interface as a first-class deliverable in your plan from the start.

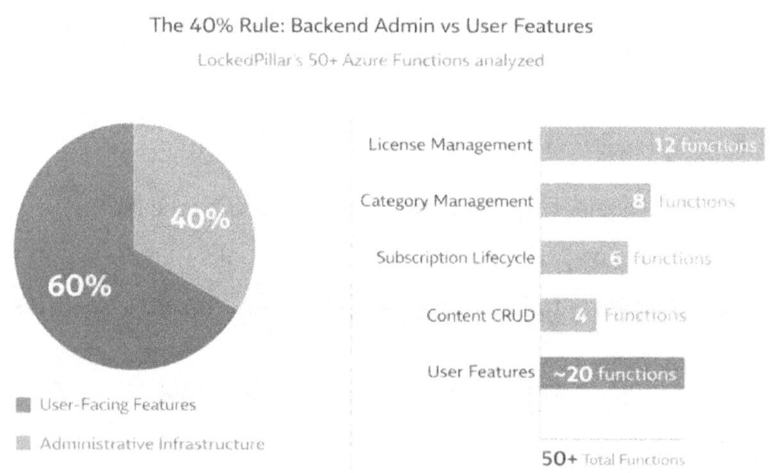

Figure 10.1: The 40% Rule in practice — roughly 40% of LockedPillar's backend existed solely for the operator. Plan for this from the start.

Ask your AI assistant during planning:

- **Example prompt:**

> "For each user-facing feature in this plan, what administrative tools will I need to manage it? What do I need to be able to look up, modify, suspend, or monitor?"

If you are directing a team rather than building solo, this prompt also tells you what to brief them on: the administrative surface area is scope that needs to be assigned, estimated, and delivered alongside the user-facing work.

10.5 Costs and the Limits of Free

Free tiers are generous, but they are not unconditional, and the condition is rarely spelled out where you would notice it before it bites. Some limits show up as a bill: bandwidth overage charges, a usage quota that is generous until you are close to it. Others show up as an outage: a service that simply stops working once you cross a line nobody told you about. Both are the same underlying problem wearing a different costume. Most vibe-coders discover these limits by hitting them rather than by planning around them.

The failure mode vibe-coders hit most often is not a bill at all. It is the database pause. Your application works during development. You launch, users sign up, then you take a week's holiday. When you return, the database has paused: some free tiers suspend the database after a period of inactivity, and users have been seeing errors for days. Nothing was overspent. Nothing was billed. The service simply stopped, because "free" came with a condition that was never in your plan. The fix is simple, an AI assistant can write a keep-alive check as part of your launch tasks, but the damage to user trust from days of silent errors is done regardless.

Cost modelling belongs in your ICE session for exactly this reason: your choice of services has both financial and reliability implications that should inform whether you choose them in the first place, not surprise you after you have. During planning, share your intended services with your AI assistant and ask it to model your exposure at different usage levels, and to name the free-tier conditions (inactivity suspensions, bandwidth caps, quota cliffs) that could stop the service working even when nothing is being overspent. This takes five minutes and can prevent both a billing surprise and an outage, months later:

- **Example prompt:**

  > "Given these services and this expected usage, what are the cost triggers I should watch for, and what are my options when I hit them? Also tell me about any free-tier conditions, like inactivity suspensions or hard caps, that could stop the service working even if I am not being charged more."

For a typical application with modest traffic, the database is the main cost at low traffic; most other components stay on free tiers. If your application uses AI on behalf of users, those costs sit outside your hosting bill and scale faster than anything else. One user asking a hundred questions a month could cost £1 to £5 in AI fees alone. Platform approaches like Lovable or Bolt.new are more predictable but less flexible.

Figure 10.2: The Holiday Test — the system that runs itself until it doesn't.

10.6 Payments and Licensing

Taking money from users sounds like the goal. It is, but it is not the problem. The problem is everything that surrounds the transaction: the invoice the user needs for their accounts department, the refund they are entitled to under consumer law, the credit you owe when they cancel mid-cycle, the account you must suspend when a payment fails. These are ICE-stage decisions, not implementation details to figure out later. The processor choice, the pricing model, the refund policy, and the tax approach should all be settled in planning. I built LockedPillar before I understood any of this. The payment processor worked on day one. The surrounding infrastructure took months to get right.

The Tax Decision Comes First

Before you choose a payment processor, decide what kind of relationship you want with tax. Standard payment processors like Stripe move money to your account and leave tax entirely to you: calculating the correct VAT or sales tax for each customer's country, filing returns, remitting to the relevant authority. For a UK-only application with modest sales, this is manageable. For anything sold internationally, it grows into a significant compliance burden.

Merchant of Record services (Paddle and LemonSqueezy are the most widely used) sit between you and the customer legally. They handle tax, issue invoices, and process refunds. You receive net revenue after their fee (around 5%, versus roughly 1.5% for standard processors). For a solo vibe-coder selling to multiple countries, that higher fee often buys the removal of an entire compliance layer. Choose the category before you choose the product.

Pricing Model and Payment Events

How you charge affects how you build. One-time purchase is simple but requires continuous new sales. Subscription generates recurring income but requires ongoing value delivery. For most vibe-coded applications, start with the simplest model that fits. The transaction itself is five seconds of a customer's relationship with you. Everything surrounding it (refunds, failed payments, cancellations, account suspension) is everything else, and each of these flows must be planned before a single line of payment code is written. Use this prompt during your ICE session:

- **Example prompt:**

> "I'm building a subscription application. Walk me through every payment event I need to handle: successful charge, failed charge, cancellation, refund, and plan upgrade. For each, tell me what my application should do and what the user should see."

Your AI assistant will produce a comprehensive map. The business decisions (refund window, suspension timing) are yours. The implementation is a conversation.

Licensing Your Software

A software licence tells users what they are allowed to do with your product. Without one, the legal position is ambiguous. Two licences cover most vibe-coders: the **MIT Licence**, which lets users do almost anything with the code and is appropriate for tools you want to distribute freely, and the **proprietary licence**, which is the default for paid software and reserves all rights to you. Both can be generated by your AI assistant. The licence must travel with the product: in the footer of your web application, on the sign-up screen, or embedded in the files of a downloadable tool.

A licence is not the same as a privacy policy or terms of service, though the three often appear together. A privacy policy covers how you handle personal data, required by law in most jurisdictions. Terms of service covers the broader relationship with users. All three are necessary for a commercial product and all three can be drafted with AI assistance. Ask:

- **Example prompt:**

  > "Draft a privacy policy, terms of service, and proprietary licence for a subscription web application that processes user data in the UK."

> ***What I Actually Did:*** *For a vibe-coded Excel tool I distribute freely, I used the MIT Licence, generated by AI and embedded in the source code as commented lines at the top of the file. For LockedPillar, a commercial web application, I used a proprietary terms of use, linked in the footer and presented at checkout with an explicit acknowledgement checkbox. Same principle, applied differently depending on what the product is and who it is for: the licence travels with the product.*

10.7 What LockedPillar Actually Cost

The rest of this chapter describes how to approach platform decisions, costs, payments, and commercial infrastructure. LockedPillar is the project that made those lessons necessary. This section is the retrospective that the preceding chapters never quite assembled: what was decided, what it cost, and what I would do differently.

The platform choice was made without deliberate analysis. I was building with VS Code and Claude from the start because it was what I knew. The hosting stack (Azure Functions for the backend, Azure SQL for the database, Azure Key Vault for secrets management, Azure CDN for delivery) was assembled incrementally as each need arose, not planned as a coherent system in advance. There was no moment of choosing this stack against alternatives. There was a series of moments of choosing the next thing that seemed to fit. The result worked, but the coherence was retrospective, not designed.

What I would do differently: define the deployment architecture in the ICE session before the build begins. One conversation: "given this application's requirements, what is the simplest stack that can grow to ten thousand users without a full rewrite?" would have produced a better answer than the one I arrived at through iteration. The stack would probably have been the same. The important difference is that the choice would have been examined rather than accumulated.

The documented costs were: £613 in AI API fees over the eleven weeks of development; £480 for a legal consultation on copyright. The legal cost was the one I had not anticipated and had no framework for anticipating. The question was not whether LockedPillar itself infringed copyright – a tool that helps users memorise scripts is not inherently infringing, in the same way that a word processor does not infringe copyright simply because a user could type out a copied book. The question was whether the application, by enabling users to work with performance scripts, could be used as a vehicle for infringement by those users, and what obligations that created for me as the developer. The consultation resolved the question: the liability follows the user's act, not the tool's capability. But the consultation was necessary, and I had not budgeted for it.

Stripe and its webhook system were easy to integrate. What required genuine thought was not the technical implementation but the range of payment events that a real commercial product has to handle: failed charges, cancellations, refunds, account suspension on non-payment, and plan changes. Each of those is a business decision as much as a technical one. The advice earlier in this chapter (asking the AI to walk through every payment event before a line of code is written) came directly from the experience of realising mid-build that I had not thought through what should happen when a customer's card declines. The integration itself was not the problem. The problem was not having mapped the full event space before starting it.

The 40% observation was not a design principle when I built LockedPillar. It was a post-build measurement: I counted the Azure Functions when the build was complete and discovered that 22 of approximately 50 were administrative infrastructure that users never touched. Licence management, category management, subscription lifecycle tooling: none of it was in the original plan because I had not thought to ask for it. Every single one of those functions was built reactively, after the absence of the tool became a problem. Planning for the operator interface from the start would not have reduced the scope. It would have reduced the cost: each reactive addition required understanding a codebase that was already large and had accumulated context I had to reconstruct rather than remember.

The sequence of decisions, and their consequences, is easier to see in summary than in the narrative above. The table below reconstructs the build timeline from the git commit history. It is not a complete record, but it shows the pattern: the reactive builds cluster in the middle and late stages, precisely where a planning session would have put them at the beginning.

Week — Decision	What Went Wrong	What I Would Do Differently
Wk 1 — Chose VS Code and Claude as the build environment: the tools I already knew.	Nothing went wrong here. Familiarity was the right criterion.	No change.

Week — Decision	What Went Wrong	What I Would Do Differently
Wk 2–3 — Assembled Azure stack incrementally: Functions, SQL, Key Vault, CDN. Each added as the need arose.	No coherent architecture decision was ever made. The stack was accumulated, not designed.	One ICE conversation asking "simplest stack that scales to 10,000 users without a full rewrite" before touching a deployment tool.
Wk 4–5 — Built user-facing features: script display, highlight tracking, progress state.	The operator-facing functions were not in scope. The absence was not noticed.	Apply the 40% rule from day one: for every user function, ask what the operator equivalent is and plan it alongside.
Wk 6 — Integrated Stripe for payments.	The payment event space was not mapped before integration. Failed charges, cancellations, refunds, and plan changes were discovered mid-build, each requiring a business decision under time pressure.	Ask the AI to enumerate every payment event before writing a line of payment code. This is now in Chapter 10 as standard practice.

Week — Decision	What Went Wrong	What I Would Do Differently
Wk 7–8 — Built administrative infrastructure reactively: licence management, category management, subscription lifecycle.	Twenty-two of approximately fifty Azure Functions were operator-facing, none of them planned. Each was built into a codebase that was already large, requiring context reconstruction rather than fresh development.	Plan the operator surface in week one alongside the user surface. The scope does not shrink; the cost does.
Wk 9 — Legal consultation on copyright position.	Had no framework for anticipating this cost or timing it correctly. The question (whether enabling users to work with performance scripts created developer liability for user infringement) was not on the pre-mortem.	Add a legal review milestone to the plan before build begins for any product that touches third-party content.
Wk 10–11 — Final build, launch preparation, deployment.	Post-launch stabilisation took three additional weeks as gaps in the operator tooling and payment handling became visible under real usage.	With the planning discipline described in this book, the stabilisation period would have been shorter. The gaps were foreseeable.

Table 10.3: LockedPillar build timeline, reconstructed from git history. Reactive builds cluster in weeks 6 to 9, the period where planning would have had the most impact.

The professional development comparison is instructive. A traditional development engagement for a subscription SaaS platform with authentication, payment processing, and administrative infrastructure would typically require 1 to 2 developers over 3 to 6 months, at UK market rates. The equivalent cost would be in the range of £80,000 to £150,000. The direct documented costs of LockedPillar were £613 in AI API fees and £480 for legal consultation: just over £1,000 in out-of-pocket expenditure. The gap between those figures is why the capability matters. Even accounting for the eleven weeks of the author's time, the cost differential is substantial and the capability delivered is comparable.

The plain summary: LockedPillar worked. It generated its first paying customer. The documentation, the payment infrastructure, the legal position, and the operational tooling all caught up eventually. But "catching up eventually" is expensive in time, disruptive to users in the early weeks, and entirely avoidable with the planning discipline this book describes. The version of LockedPillar that would have been built with an ICE session, a formal plan, and the commercial architecture questions asked in advance would have taken the same eleven weeks to build and perhaps three fewer weeks to stabilise after launch. Three weeks of a working commercial product is not nothing.

10.8 Key Takeaways

- **The platform choice determines future choices:** Pure tools give you full ownership. Full-stack builders trade some control for speed. Managed platforms trade most control for simplicity. The meaningful question is not which is best, but which you will regret when the platform's constraints become your constraints.
- **Secrets never go in code:** API keys and credentials belong in a separate configuration file, never in your code repository. Your AI assistant will set this up. Make it a named task in your plan from the first external service dependency.
- **Plan for events and automation:** Webhooks (notifications from external services) and scheduled tasks (automation on a timer) cover most production needs. Both belong in your plan before you build, not after you launch.
- **Free tiers have specific traps:** Databases can pause after inactivity. Bandwidth limits trigger overage charges. Model your cost exposure during planning and ask your AI assistant to identify the triggers before you commit to a stack.
- **You are building two applications:** The user-facing product and the operator's interface are both required. In a complex commercial application, roughly 40% of backend scope exists for the operator. Plan for it from the start.
- **The tax decision comes before the processor decision:** Standard payment processors are cheaper but leave tax compliance to you. Merchant of Record services cost more per transaction but handle tax entirely. Choose the category before you choose the product.
- **The planning transfers:** ICE analysis, a comprehensive plan, and

critical persona review apply to any platform. The skill is the planning; the platform is just where the output lives.

Notes

[42] Wix / GlobeNewswire (2025). "Wix Further Expands into Vibe Coding with Acquisition of Base44." *GlobeNewswire*, June 18, 2025. globenewswire.com/news-release/2025/06/18/3101508/0/en/Wix-Further-Expands-into-Vibe-Coding-with-Acquisition-of-Base44-a-Hyper-Growth-Startup-that-Simplifies-Web-and-App-Creation-with-AI.html

CHAPTER 11

Running What You Built

11.1 Introduction

Getting your application live is the beginning of a different kind of risk. The risks of building (wrong specification, unverified output, architectural drift) are largely within your control. The risks of running something that real people depend on are not. Users arrive with expectations you did not fully anticipate. Systems that worked reliably in development develop failure modes in production. The world changes around your application whether or not you are paying attention.

The risk that most vibe-coders underestimate is the gap between what they built and what they are now responsible for. A working prototype carries no ongoing obligation. A tool that users depend on, whether those users are paying customers or colleagues inside your organisation, carries obligations around reliability, responsiveness, data stewardship, and maintenance that do not appear in any tutorial. This chapter is about those obligations: what they are, how to manage them, and where vibe-coding reaches the limits of what one person can sustain.

The commercial specifics in this chapter (user acquisition, payments, licensing) are examples of a broader principle that applies to every post-launch context. If you built for your organisation rather than a market, the mechanism differs but the risk does not: something people depend on can break, drift, or become your permanent responsibility by default.

The question in both cases is the same: did you build with the awareness that you would have to run it?

None of this is covered in typical building tutorials, because tutorials end at launch. The vibe-coder who builds sustainable products is distinguished from the one who builds impressive prototypes that quietly stop working eighteen months later by one thing: they took operations seriously. The practitioner who survives this stage is the one who faces its obligations squarely rather than deferring them.

11.2 Operations as a Vibe-Coding Problem

The moment you launch, a different kind of work begins: the work of being found, being chosen, and keeping the people who chose you. Most builders treat this as a separate discipline: marketing over here, support over there, maintenance somewhere else entirely. It is just more problems. And you already know how to solve problems: clarify your intent, name your constraints, define what good looks like, and build the thing that does the work.

That is the insight this section is built around. The operational tasks that follow a launch (reaching users, handling their questions, keeping the software running) are tedious when you do them manually and entirely tractable when you treat them as vibe-coding projects in their own right. The same interloquial skills that produced your application can produce the tools that run it.

Getting Users

A working application with no users is an unread book. Getting users is the gap between "it's live" and "people are using it", and it is a gap that does not close by itself. The judgement about who your user is and why they should care is yours to make — no AI assistant can substitute for having spoken to the people you are trying to reach before you launch. But the execution of reaching them is exactly the kind of repetitive, well-defined work that vibe-coding handles well.

An onboarding email sequence is a good first example. Every new user deserves a welcome message, a prompt to complete their setup, and a follow-up if they go quiet. Done manually, this is unsustainable at any real volume. Done through a vibe-coded tool, it runs without you. But before writing a single prompt, run an ICE session. Your intent, constraints, and expectations need to be clear in your own mind before you ask your AI assistant to build anything. What does success look like at each stage of onboarding? What email provider are you using? What user actions trigger each message? What tone matches your product? The ICE conversation surfaces those answers. Once it has, the build prompt takes care of itself.

The same logic applies to content marketing. If writing and publishing to reach your audience is part of your strategy, the mechanical parts of that process — drafting, formatting, scheduling — can be partially automated. An ICE session that defines your audience, your message, and your publishing cadence produces a brief your AI assistant can execute against repeatedly. What it cannot replace is the underlying judgement: who specifically is this for, and what problem does it solve for them that they would pay to have solved? That question requires your own thinking, ideally informed by direct conversations with potential users. The automation serves the strategy. It does not substitute for having one.

The Support Burden

The moment you have users, you have support obligations, and not in a vague, theoretical sense. Someone will email you on a Saturday morning to say the thing they paid for is broken, and they will expect a reply. This is the cost most vibe-coders underestimate, partly because it is invisible during development and partly because no amount of planning makes it feel real until the first message arrives.

Users are creative in ways you are not. During development, you test the paths you designed. Your users find every other path — the browser you did not test, the data format you did not expect, the feature combination you never considered. Each of these is a valid use of your application. Each of them may produce a failure you have never seen. Before launch, ask your AI assistant to stress-test what you have built from the perspective of a confused first-time user:

- **Example prompt:**

> "What questions would a user have that the interface does not currently answer? What actions could they take that would produce a confusing or broken state?"

The list that comes back will identify gaps in your interface, your error messages, and your empty states. Fixing them before launch means fewer emails after it. It also means your AI assistant has reviewed the application through an adversarial lens that your own familiarity with it prevents you from applying.

When something does break in production, your first move is the same one that built the feature: paste the error into your conversation, describe what the user reported, and ask your AI assistant to diagnose the most likely causes. This works, but only if you can reproduce the problem. Structured error logging makes reproduction possible; without it, you are diagnosing blind, relying on users to describe what they saw before they closed the tab. Build this before you launch:

- **Example prompt:**

> "Add structured error logging to this application so that when something fails in production, the error message, the user's action, and the relevant state are all captured and visible in my hosting dashboard."

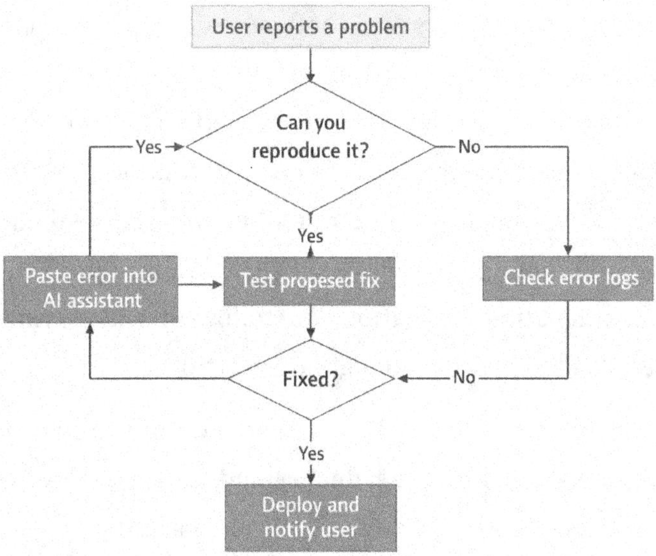

Figure 11.1: The Support Diagnosis Loop — a repeatable workflow for diagnosing and resolving production issues using your AI assistant.

The deeper opportunity is to reduce the support load before it arrives. A significant proportion of support emails are questions that a well-placed in-application answer would have prevented. A support triage tool — an intake form that categorises the user's question, checks it against your FAQ, and sends an automated response for known issues before a human ever sees it — is the kind of thing that transforms support from a morning-consuming interruption into a manageable hour per week. It is also its own vibe-coding project, with its own ICE session. If you are building your main application, support tooling belongs as a named workstream in that plan. If the application already exists, treat the triage tool as a separate project: define the intent, name the constraints (what FAQ do you have, what email provider, what logging do you need), and specify what good looks like before you start building.

When to Charge

Free software attracts users. Paid software attracts customers. A user of free software accepts, consciously or not, that the software is provided on a best-effort basis. A customer paid money, and that creates an expectation of reliability, responsiveness, and ongoing support that no terms and conditions fully extinguish. I discovered this with LockedPillar: the same slow first load that a free user would shrug off became a support issue requiring explanation, mitigation, and follow-up with paying customers. The code was identical. The obligation was not.

The practical rule is simple: if you cannot commit to supporting something, keep it free. Before you launch a paid product, ask yourself plainly whether you have the time and the systems to respond to support within a working day, fix bugs within a reasonable window, and keep the service running with acceptable uptime. Transparency about your constraints is not a weakness. A product page that states clearly this is built and maintained by one person, with support by email within five working days, sets an expectation that many users will accept at a lower price. Setting the expectation correctly at the start prevents the complaint later.

Maintenance Realities

Software does not stay working by itself. The underlying cause is always the same: the world changed and your application did not. Table 11.1 summarises the four categories of change and what to do about each.

Figure 11.2: The Saturday Morning Email — every solo vibe-coder's rite of passage.

None of them require deep technical knowledge to manage — they require attention and a regular habit of asking your AI assistant to check.

Risk	What Changes	Mitigation
Dependencies	Library versions drift; some break silently	Ask your AI assistant to audit dependencies before reopening any project you haven't touched in months
APIs	Third-party endpoints, pricing, and rate limits change without warning	Subscribe to the status pages of every service you integrate

Risk	What Changes	Mitigation
Security	Vulnerabilities emerge in frameworks you rely on	Run periodic security audits; verify fixes address the root cause, not just the alert
Platforms	Free tiers, hosting providers, and database behaviour evolve	Set a quarterly calendar reminder to review your infrastructure costs and configuration

Table 11.1: The Four Maintenance Risks

A project that took forty hours to build might need four to eight hours per year just to keep working. That is the cost of running something people depend on — and for the vibe-coder, it is mostly a series of short, well-defined conversations rather than deep technical work.

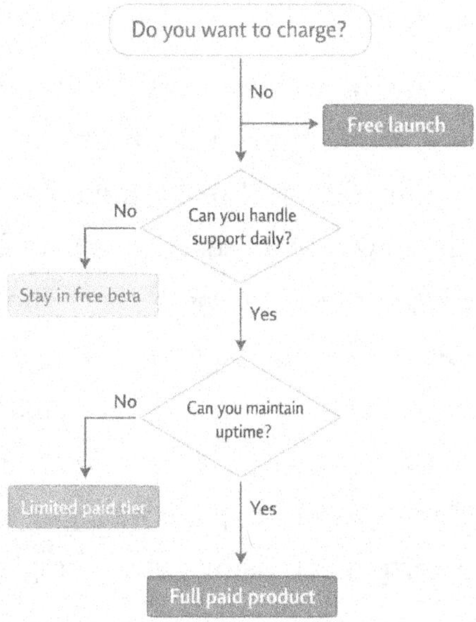

Figure 11.3: The Free-vs-Paid Decision — work through this before you set a price.

11.3 Running What You Built Inside an Organisation

Not every vibe-coder is building a product for a market. Many of the most useful applications of vibe-coding happen inside organisations: a process automation tool built by an Operations Manager, a reporting dashboard built by a Finance Analyst, a data pipeline built by someone who saw a problem and solved it. These tools work. People use them. And then their creator discovers something that no tutorial prepared them for: they have become the permanent custodian of something they built in a weekend.

The post-creation risks here are distinct from the commercial ones covered in the previous section. Internally-built tools have colleagues who depend on them, and dependency without a commercial structure creates obligations that are often invisible until they become problems.

The single point of failure. If you built it, you are the only person who can fix it when it breaks. If you change roles, take annual leave, or leave the organisation, the tool breaks and nobody else knows why. This is the most common way that useful internal tools die: not because they stopped working, but because the person who understood them stopped being available. The mitigation is documentation written for someone who has never seen the project: not a technical specification, but a plain-language account of what the tool does, why it was built, and what to do when the most likely things go wrong. Your AI assistant can produce this from your project history with a single prompt. Write it before you are asked.

Scope creep through success. A tool that works attracts requests. Colleagues notice what it does and ask whether it could also do something adjacent. Each individual request is reasonable. Cumulatively, they transform a focused tool into something sprawling that nobody fully understands, including its creator. The mitigation is a clear written definition of what the tool is and is not. When the next request arrives, evaluate it against the written scope rather than the path of least resistance in a corridor conversation.

Data governance. Internal tools built quickly often handle data that has governance implications the builder did not consider at the time. Does the tool store personal data about colleagues? Does it access systems that have access controls for a reason? Does it connect to data sources that have classification requirements? These are not technical questions. They have organisational answers: your information security team, your data protection officer, or whoever owns the relevant policy. The conversation to have is not "I built a thing, is this okay?" It is "I am planning to build a thing that will access X and store Y. What do I need to know?" That conversation happens before the build, not after the tool has been running for six months.

Handoff. At some point, you will not want to be the custodian of this tool. You may want to hand it to IT to maintain properly, to a successor, or simply to be done with it. The ease of that handoff is determined almost entirely by the documentation you maintained while building and running it. A tool with a clear project plan, a decisions log explaining why significant choices were made, and a plain-language operating guide can be transferred in an afternoon. A tool with none of these requires weeks of archaeology and may simply be rebuilt from scratch, discarding everything you built.

The interloquial skills developed throughout this book apply directly to each of these. Articulating intent precisely is how you write a scope document that holds under pressure. Surfacing constraints is how you identify the data governance questions before they become problems. Defining expectations is how you write handoff documentation that transfers knowledge rather than just describing the interface. The sustained AI collaboration that built the tool can sustain its documentation, its evolution, and its eventual handoff.

The simplest version of good practice here is a single conversation before you share any internally-built tool with colleagues: ask your AI assistant to help you identify the three most likely failure modes, the one governance question you should check before deployment, and what a new user would need to know to use it without your involvement. That conversation costs twenty minutes and can save months of disruption later.

11.4 When Vibe-Coding Is Not Enough

This book makes a strong case for what vibe-coding enables. It would be incomplete without an equally clear-eyed account of where it reaches its limits. Those limits are real, and the vibe-coder who does not recognise them is exposed. Knowing where to stop is part of the skill.

Technical Boundaries

Your AI assistant is very good at implementing known patterns against a clear specification. It has absorbed an enormous quantity of code and documentation, and it can reproduce working implementations of almost anything that has been done before. What it cannot do is optimise what it does not understand, or innovate at the level of computer science research. These are descriptions. Understanding them tells you where human expertise remains essential.

Performance-critical systems are the clearest example. Your AI assistant can produce code that sorts a list, processes an image, or handles user requests. That code will usually be correct. It will often not be fast. The difference between code that works and code that works at scale — handling enormous volumes reliably in real time — requires engineering expertise that goes beyond what sustained dialogue can deliver. Whether the code runs within your system's performance constraints is a question that requires a human specialist, not an AI assistant.

Genuinely novel problems present a similar constraint. Your AI assistant excels at implementing solutions that already exist and are well-documented. If your application requires something that has not been done before — a new approach to a data problem, a mathematical method that does not yet exist, a security protocol specific to your domain — the AI can help you explore the problem space, but it cannot invent the solution. That work requires a specialist. The AI is a collaborator for building and for learning; it is not a substitute for someone who has spent years solving problems in your specific field.

Large and complex systems are often cited as a hard ceiling for vibe-coding, but that framing mistakes the problem. Complexity does not defeat the approach; undisciplined documentation does. The vibe-coder's answer to complexity is to externalise it. A well-maintained project plan that captures the architecture, a decisions log that records why choices were made, and structured documentation for each component mean that your AI assistant can engage with any part of the system in context, because the context is written down rather than assumed. The failure mode in large systems is the vibe-coder stopping maintenance of the documentation that makes coherent collaboration possible. At sufficient scale, that discipline requires as much effort as the coding itself.

Professional Review Requirements

There is a second category of limitation that is not about technical capability but about accountability. Some domains carry regulatory frameworks or professional standards that exist because mistakes in them harm people. In these domains, the question is whether that code can be deployed without independent professional review. The answer, in these domains, is always no.

Healthcare applications that provide medical advice, manage patient data, or interface with clinical systems are subject to regulation in every major jurisdiction. In the UK, the MHRA (Medicines and Healthcare products Regulatory Agency) regulates software as a medical device. In the US, the FDA (Food and Drug Administration) applies similar frameworks. These frameworks are the accumulated consequence of things that went wrong when software in clinical settings was not properly reviewed. Vibe-

Figure 11.4: Where Vibe-Coding Reaches Its Limits — know which zone your project is in before you build.

coding can speed up the development of a healthcare prototype. The prototype cannot be deployed without clinical and regulatory review, regardless of how it was built.

Financial applications that handle investments, provide regulated advice, or process certain payment types operate within frameworks (the FCA, or Financial Conduct Authority, in the UK; the SEC, or Securities and Exchange Commission, in the US) that impose obligations around code quality, auditability, and change management. Your AI assistant can build a functioning integration with a payment processor. Whether that integration meets the standards required for a regulated financial product is a question for a qualified reviewer, not an AI assistant.

Safety-critical systems such as automotive software, aviation systems, medical devices, and industrial control carry standards (ISO 26262, DO-178C, IEC 62304) that mandate specific development and verification processes. These standards exist because software failures in these contexts can kill people. The standard does not distinguish between code written by a human engineer and code generated by an AI. It requires that the code be verified to the standard. Vibe-coding cannot substitute for that verification.

Figure 11.5: Knowing when to call a professional — preferably before the professional calls on you.

The vibe-coder's enthusiasm for what their AI assistant can produce is legitimate. The risk is that enthusiasm causes a misjudgement about which category a project falls into. If you are building an internal tool for your own team, the accountability question is different from building patient-facing software for a hospital. The self-assessment that matters here (*is this a domain where professional review is required?*) is not a question the AI can answer for you.

The Handoff Point

There is a third situation that is neither a technical limitation nor a regulatory requirement but a practical judgement: the project has grown beyond the point where solo vibe-coding is the right vehicle for it. It means the concept was worth building, users found it worth paying for, and the application has reached a scale or complexity where the appropriate next step is to bring in professional engineering resource.

The vibe-coded prototype, at this point, has done exactly what it was supposed to do. It validated the concept, defined the requirements through iteration, and created a working reference implementation that communicates intent to a development team more clearly than any document could. A team that inherits a working prototype and a clear brief is in a far better position than one handed a specification and a budget. This applies equally if you are not building a public product: a working prototype presented to an IT team, a development agency, or a budget committee makes the case for investment more powerfully than any slide deck. The vibe-coder who arrives at that conversation with something that already works is in a categorically stronger position than the one who arrives with a plan.

The handoff does not mean the vibe-coder becomes passive. Your AI assistant remains useful throughout the professional development process. You can use it to review technical documentation, to understand architectural decisions being made about your product, to evaluate proposals, and to communicate more precisely with the development team about what you need. The skills you have developed (asking precise questions, understanding systems well enough to evaluate them critically, iterating on a specification through dialogue) are as useful in a client relationship with a development agency as they are in front of a code editor.

Vibe-coding expands what non-engineers can build, but it does not eliminate the need for engineering expertise in domains where that expertise matters. The appropriate response to recognising a boundary is the same pragmatic judgement that drives every other decision in this chapter: using the right tool for the job, including the tool of knowing when to bring in someone who has capabilities you do not.

11.5 The Operator's Mindset

There is a shift that happens when you move from building to running. During development, you are a creator: adding, iterating, expanding. Once you have users, a second identity emerges alongside the creator: the operator. The operator's job is to keep the thing working, to respond when it does not, to manage the relationship with users, and to make the unglamorous decisions that determine whether the product survives.

The skills of this book (articulating intent precisely, thinking through constraints before they become problems, defining expectations clearly) are skills of the creator. They are also, with only a small shift of perspective, skills of the operator. The discipline that produces a well-specified project plan before development begins is the same discipline that produces a structured approach to support, a quarterly infrastructure review, a documented policy on refunds. The practitioner who applies ICE to code specification can apply the same rigour to operational decisions. It is the same underlying habit: thinking before doing, externalising what matters, naming constraints plainly rather than glossing over them.

If you are directing a team that builds with AI rather than building yourself, the same questions apply — and they are yours to own. Who is responsible for keeping the application running? Who handles support escalations when something breaks? Who monitors costs as usage grows? Who decides when a dependency needs updating? The operator's mindset applies to anyone accountable for something that runs.

The vibe-coder's particular advantage in this transition is that the AI relationship does not stop at launch. Your AI assistant can help you draft support responses, analyse patterns in user feedback, review your dependency audit, model the cost implications of a pricing change, and review a proposed architecture change for a second version. The sustained collaborative relationship that built the product can sustain the product. The context you have accumulated — the project plan, the decisions log, the documentation — is the operating manual.

The best preparation for running something is building it with the awareness that you will have to run it. The operator's needs (the reporting dashboard, the audit trail, the cost model, the support policy) are requirements, present from the start, as legitimate as any feature the user will ever see. The final chapter returns to the practitioner and to practice; but the lesson of this chapter is worth carrying forward.

Figure 11.6: The Creator–Operator Identity Shift — the same person, the same skills, a different screen.

11.6 Ending

The previous sections cover what it takes to keep an application running. This one covers what it takes to stop. Endings are part of the lifecycle of every product, including small ones built by a single person in their spare time. Most of the books written about software products are about growth, acquisition, and scale. This chapter would be incomplete if it only described those trajectories, because most products do not end that way. Most end quietly: a user base that did not grow, a market that moved on, or simply a builder whose circumstances changed. None of those outcomes make the work a failure. They make it finished.

Recognising When It Is Over

The sunk-cost trap is the most common reason people run products they should have closed. Sunk costs are resources already spent that cannot be recovered, and the trap is allowing them to influence forward-looking decisions. The time and money spent building an application are sunk costs. They are real, and letting them go is genuinely difficult, but they are not a reason to continue operating something. The only question that matters is forward-looking: does continued operation, at its current cost in time and money, still produce enough value to justify it?

The signs that an application has reached its natural end are usually visible before they feel conclusive. User numbers have plateaued or declined despite reasonable effort. The maintenance burden has grown to the point where it competes with paid work or personal time in a way that no longer feels sustainable. A well-resourced competitor has entered the space and solved the problem more completely than you can. The original purpose has been achieved and the tool is no longer needed. Or simply: you have moved on, and the application has not moved with you.

Any one of these can be sufficient. None of them requires an apology. Judging what a product is still worth calls on exactly the same skill as judging what a project needs to do before you build it.

Closing is also not the only option. Before winding something down, it is worth asking whether someone else would benefit more from running it than from closing it.

Winding Down

If the decision is to close, the sequence matters as much as the decision itself. The way you close leaves a lasting impression on everyone who used what you built.

Users first. Paying users have the clearest claim on your attention. Notify them early (thirty days is a minimum for anything embedded in someone's workflow), explain the closure clearly, and refund any unused subscription time without requiring them to ask for it. Free users deserve notice too. The appropriate lead time depends on how central your tool has become to what they do. A tool people use daily warrants more warning than one they visit occasionally. The communication itself should be direct and human: what is closing, when, what happens to their data, and where they might go instead if an alternative exists. Your AI assistant can help you draft this notice; the draft should go through your own review, because the right tone is something only you can judge.

Data obligations. What happens to user data on closure is not optional. GDPR (the General Data Protection Regulation, which governs how personal data must be handled throughout the European Union and, post-Brexit, under equivalent UK legislation) requires that users are informed how their data will be handled when you stop operating. The practical minimum: export user data to them where possible, commit to a specific deletion date, delete the data on that date, and document that you did so. Your AI assistant can help you generate a data-deletion checklist and draft user-facing language that covers the key requirements. As with anything touching legal obligations, review what it produces carefully and, where your data situation is complex, take qualified advice.

Third-party services. The decommission sequence has a specific order that is easy to get wrong, and the cost of getting it wrong is usually a surprise invoice months later from a service you thought you had already closed. Prepare a checklist before you begin: every paid service your application depends on, with its renewal date and what needs to happen to it. Work through it in order rather than from memory. Your AI assistant can help you generate this list from your project documentation, provided that documentation exists and has been kept current.

Communication tone. A well-handled closure protects the relationship with users who might follow you into the next thing you build. Users who receive clear, direct communication about a closure are far more likely to trust you again than those who received silence until the service stopped working. Closing with care is a practical consideration.

Selling or Transferring

Not every application ends at closure. Some are worth more to someone else than the cost of continuing to run them, and a sale or transfer is the better outcome for both builder and users.

What you are actually selling. A vibe-coded application is a bundle of assets: the codebase, the domain, any brand recognition, the active user base (with appropriate data-transfer agreements in place, as GDPR imposes obligations on transfers of personal data as well as closures), and the documented system. That last element is often underestimated. A well-maintained project plan, a clear decisions log, and structured documentation mean that a buyer can orient themselves quickly and take over with confidence. An undocumented codebase, even a working one, is significantly harder to value and to transfer. The documentation discipline this book argues for throughout is, in a sale context, an argument with a direct financial return.

Realistic expectations for small tools. Micro-acquisitions (the sale of small, independently operated software tools) are a genuine market, particularly for tools with consistent monthly recurring revenue (MRR). This is the income that renews each month from subscribers, and it is the metric most commonly used to value small tools, with buyers typically paying a multiple of it. The market for these transactions is real but variable. Expectations should be modest: a small tool with stable revenue is worth something, but the figure depends on the niche, the growth trajectory, the quality of the documentation, and how much operational involvement the buyer will inherit. Listing platforms for small software acquisitions exist and are findable with a search; approaching potential buyers directly (individuals in the same niche, or adjacent businesses) is often just as effective. Before listing anything, state plainly what the application actually generates and what a buyer would actually need to do to run it.

The handover itself. A sale does not end at the point of payment. Transferring ownership — the codebase, the domain, the connected services, access to everything the new owner needs to run it — takes time, and so does the period during which you are available to answer questions they will inevitably have. The quality of this transition is what distinguishes a sale that leaves both parties satisfied from one that generates resentment. Your AI assistant can help you prepare a handover pack: a technical overview, a list of all external services with their configuration and renewal dates, a known-issues log, and any operational decisions that exist only in your memory. Writing that last category down is usually illuminating. It also reveals how much undocumented knowledge has accumulated that a buyer would otherwise only discover by running into problems.

Open-sourcing as an exit. Where commercial sale is not realistic (because the revenue is too small, the niche too narrow, or the tool too specialised to attract an acquirer) open-sourcing is a legitimate and sometimes genuinely useful exit. The code continues to serve users through community maintenance, without ongoing obligation on the original builder. The practical steps: choose a licence that reflects your intentions, write a clear README with setup and deployment instructions, and mark the repository as archived if active development has ceased. An archived open-source repository is a handover to a different kind of ownership, and for tools that solve a real but narrow problem, it can extend the useful life of the work long beyond what solo maintenance would have sustained.

The ending of an application, handled well, is the final expression of the operator's mindset. It requires the same qualities as the best moments of building: clarity about what the situation actually is, plain speaking about what you are and are not able to commit to, and care for the people who depended on what you made. The work does not have to be permanent to have been worth doing.

11.7 Postscript: What Happened to LockedPillar

LockedPillar was cancelled. The code worked. The application handled user accounts, subscriptions, and the AI pipeline that processed scripts for practice. The problem was the market.

The original route-to-market strategy was to approach Masonic organisations. The reasoning seemed sound at the time: members regularly deliver formal speeches and ritual texts from memory, the need for a memorisation tool was genuine, and the organisations have the infrastructure to communicate with their membership at scale. What I had not adequately considered was the nature of those organisations. The texts Masons commit to memory are not casual: they are confidential, bound by obligations of discretion that preclude recording them in any external system. A tool that required users to upload their scripts to a cloud application was structurally incompatible with the obligations those users had already made. The market existed. It simply could not use the product as built.

The second limitation was the content creation problem. LockedPillar required users to create or upload their own scripts before they could practise. For actors with a text in hand, this was manageable. For the general user who wanted to improve their public speaking without a specific script, it created a barrier that most did not cross. The tool solved the practice problem well. It did not solve the content problem at all, and without content, practice cannot begin.

The third failure was structural. A memorisation tool for performance texts sits directly within the interest of publishers who hold the rights to scripts, speeches, and performance material. Licensing that content — creating a library users could practise from without having to source material themselves — would have transformed the product's usability. Every publisher approached declined. The reasoning, where they gave any, was consistent: a tool that reduces the need to buy a physical text undermines the sales model the rights exist to protect. The product's value proposition to users was precisely its threat to the publisher's business model. That is a structural problem, not a negotiating one.

LockedPillar could be viewed as an expensive failure. Against the cost of a professional development team to build the same product, it was cheap: £613 in AI API fees, £480 in legal consultation, eleven weeks of evenings and weekends. Against the value of what it taught — about vibe-coding as a methodology, about commercial architecture, about the gap between a working product and a viable business — it was a cheap training course in both software development and business. This book is the most durable output of those eleven weeks, and that was not the plan.

11.8 Key Takeaways

- **Marketing is the second project:** Building something is necessary but not sufficient. Reaching your intended users takes time and sometimes money in quantities comparable to the original build. Budget for it before you launch, not after you wonder why nobody came.
- **Support is the hidden cost:** Users find failure modes you never anticipated. Add error logging before launch, not after. A good FAQ and clear error messages prevent more support emails than any amount of post-launch firefighting.
- **Maintenance never ends:** Dependencies update, APIs change, platforms evolve. A forty-hour project typically needs four to eight hours per year just to keep working. Build that expectation in from the start.
- **Charging creates obligations:** A paying customer expects reliability and responsiveness that a free user does not. Know your support capacity before you go paid, not after the complaints arrive.
- **Transparency is not weakness:** Explicitly limited support (one person, five-day response, no guaranteed uptime) is a fair offer that

many users will accept at a fair price. Set expectations before they become complaints.

- **Internal tools carry the same obligations as commercial ones:** If colleagues depend on something you built, you are its custodian. Document it for someone who has never seen it, check the data governance questions before sharing it, and treat handoff as part of the build.
- **Some projects exceed vibe-coding:** Performance-critical, safety-critical, and regulated applications require professional review regardless of how they were built.
- **The handoff is a success outcome:** A working prototype that a professional team can take further is a better starting point than a specification document. You defined the what; they deliver the how-at-scale.
- **The operator's mindset is the creator's mindset applied differently:** ICE analysis, precise specification, plain constraint-surfacing: the same habits that build good software also run it well.
- **Endings are part of the lifecycle:** Most tools have a natural lifespan. Closing or selling an application is a completion. The forward-looking question is whether continued operation is still worth the cost, not how much was invested in building it.
- **Wind down with the same care you launched:** Paying users deserve a refund and early notice; free users deserve clear communication. GDPR obligations survive the closure decision. A decommission checklist prevents orphaned costs.
- **Documentation is what you are selling:** A well-maintained project plan and decisions log are the most transferable assets in any transfer or acquisition. Undocumented code is significantly harder to

value, harder to transfer, and harder to sell. The same documentation discipline that enables complex vibe-coding makes any system manageable — and any exit cleaner.

CHAPTER 12

Building Your Practice

12.1 Developing Interloquial Skill

Interloquial communication, like any form of communication, improves with deliberate practice. You would not expect to become a skilled negotiator, presenter, or writer without sustained effort over time, and interloquial skill is no different. The good news: every project you build is practice. The better news: unlike learning to code, where years of study precede useful output, interloquial practice produces useful results from the start. This chapter provides a framework for intentional improvement: how to structure your practice, recognise your growth, and continue developing long after you finish this book.

But improvement requires more than repetition. Typing thousands of prompts does not automatically make you better, any more than sending thousands of emails makes you a better writer. What separates practice from mere repetition is reflection: noticing what works, understanding why, and deliberately applying those insights to the next interaction. Chapter 2 introduced the Interloquial Maturity Curve — six levels from unstructured to fluent — as a map for understanding where you are. This chapter is about how to move through it.

Deliberate Practice

Knowing the levels is useful. Moving through them requires deliberate effort. Here are four practices that speed progression:

- **Review your failures.** When an AI interaction produces poor results, resist the temptation to simply re-prompt. Instead, ask: what was wrong with my specification? Was the intent unclear? Did I omit a constraint the AI needed? Were my expectations vague enough that the AI chose a reasonable interpretation that happened to be wrong? This five-second reflection teaches more than fifty re-prompts.
- **Compare your specifications.** After a successful project, compare your initial ICE specification with what was actually built. Where did the plan change? Were those changes improvements (the AI or the process surfaced better approaches) or drift (requirements were underspecified)? The pattern of divergence reveals your specification weaknesses.
- **Vary your domains.** If you only build one type of project, your interloquial skill becomes narrow. Build a tool, then write a document, then generate a data analysis. The underlying skill (articulating intent, surfacing constraints, defining expectations) transfers across domains. Each new domain exposes assumptions you did not know you were making.
- **Teach someone else.** Nothing reveals gaps in your understanding like explaining your process to another person. When a colleague asks "How did you get the AI to do that?" and you cannot articulate the answer beyond "I just asked it," you have identified a skill that is intuitive but not yet conscious. Making it conscious is how you move from L3 to L4.

12.2 Healthy Boundaries

Chapter 3 explored the psychological risks of intensive AI collaboration: idea monomania, parasocial attachment, automation complacency, the bleed of interloquial habits into interpersonal communication. This section is about managing them in daily practice.

The first boundary is temporal. Set limits on session length. Not because there is a magic number of hours beyond which harm begins, but because extended sessions erode the critical distance you need to evaluate AI output. After four hours of collaborative building, the AI feels like a partner. Its suggestions feel right because you have been agreeing with each other all afternoon. That feeling is not evidence of quality; it is evidence of entrainment. Take breaks. Work on something unrelated. Return with fresh eyes. The bugs you catch after a break are the ones you would have accepted during the session.

The second boundary is emotional. When you find yourself defending the AI's output to a human critic ("No, it's right, the AI said so") you have crossed a line. The AI's output is a draft, not an authority. If a colleague questions something, engage with their concern rather than citing the AI as a source. The moment you treat AI output as settled rather than provisional, you have stopped exercising the judgement that makes vibe-coding work.

The third boundary is identity. You built the tool. You specified the intent. You defined the constraints. You verified the output. The AI generated code, but you engineered the outcome. This distinction matters in both directions. Do not diminish your contribution by saying "the AI did it." And do not inflate your contribution by claiming expertise you do not possess. If someone asks "Can you maintain this codebase?" the accurate answer may be: "I can collaborate with AI to maintain it, but I cannot

Figure 12.1: The AI Said So — when AI output becomes authority rather than draft.

read the code line by line." That honesty is a strength, not a weakness. It sets accurate expectations.

The fourth boundary is social. If your primary intellectual relationship is with an AI, something has gone wrong. AI collaboration is powerful precisely because it augments human capability, but it does not replace human connection. Discuss your projects with colleagues, friends, or online communities of practice. Seek feedback from humans who will disagree with you in ways an AI will not. The AI is agreeable by design. Humans are not. You need both.

These boundaries are the conditions that make sustained practice possible. The practitioners who burn out or produce poor work are almost always the ones who treated vibe-coding as a marathon with no rest stops. The ones who sustain high-quality output over years are the ones who build recovery into their rhythm.

Protecting Your Professional Capacity

Chapter 3 introduced cognitive erosion as a risk distinct from cognitive debt: not the incomplete understanding of a specific project, but the gradual degradation of your underlying professional capabilities through sustained AI reliance. This section examines the evidence base and the practical strategies for protecting against it.

The mechanism is well described. Cornelia Walther formalises it as *agency decay*: a process operating like muscle atrophy, progressing through four stages: experimentation, integration, reliance, and finally addiction, a state of chosen blindness. What makes the progression dangerous is that it operates outside the performer's awareness. You do not notice your critical judgement weakening; you notice only that the AI keeps being right. The neuroscience is consistent with this model: neural networks that are not regularly activated weaken through synaptic pruning. The capacities most affected are precisely those most essential when automation fails: meta-cognition, novel problem-solving, independent judgement. AI can simultaneously create the illusion of enhanced agency while actually diminishing it. A professional using AI to synthesise complex information may feel more capable than ever while the hard-won pattern recognition built through years of independent work quietly contracts.[44]

The research evidence is early-stage but directionally consistent. A 2024 peer-reviewed study by Macnamara and colleagues identified two distinct threats: *skill decay* in experts, who lose existing capabilities through AI-assisted disuse (the aviation evidence is instructive: pilots relying heavily on autopilot retained procedural skills but showed significant decline in situation awareness and emergency handling); and *skill development hindrance* in learners, who may never build independent capability at all because AI handles the effortful processing through which skill develops.[45] More recent work corroborates the direction: a 2025

MIT preprint found lower independent performance after repeated AI-assisted writing sessions; a 2026 evidence synthesis calls for operational definitions and multi-site studies before mechanisms are scientifically settled. The defensible position is this: repeated cognitive offloading reduces active engagement with demanding tasks and produces measurable performance differences when assistance is removed. That is the claim the evidence actually supports. Whether it constitutes lasting damage is not yet established.

The practical implication follows directly. There are three illusions that make the risk hard to see from the inside: an illusion of explanatory depth, believing you could explain the reasoning behind an AI recommendation when you could not; an illusion of exploratory breadth, believing you have considered the full option space when you have only seen what the AI surfaced; and an illusion of objectivity, failing to account for the biases embedded in the model's training and its developers' choices. Each illusion makes you less likely to seek independent verification and less likely to challenge recommendations that should be challenged. This is the mechanism by which cognitive erosion becomes professionally consequential: not through dramatic failure, but through the gradual narrowing of what you think to question.

The stakes are not merely personal. Individual cognitive erosion aggregates. The professionals who will need to evaluate AI-driven decisions in 2032 — to challenge an algorithmic recommendation, to identify when a model's output does not fit the context, to hold a board accountable for automated decisions they cannot explain — are being shaped right now by whether they are actively thinking or passively offloading. When AI systems encounter novel situations outside their training parameters, employees find themselves ill-equipped to respond. If those employees have experienced agency decay, they may lack the critical judgment to intervene at all.[44] Cognitive erosion is not a personal hygiene issue. It is a professional liability issue. At scale, it is an organisational resilience issue.

Walther's prescription is "cognitive fitness regimens": deliberate practices designed to maintain human agency. In practical terms: never arrive at a dialogue empty-handed. Bring a problem you have worked, a position you have formed, a question you have genuinely tried to answer. Specify intent before asking for execution. Verify outcomes against your own judgement, not just against the AI's internal consistency. Schedule regular "manual mode" sessions where you work through problems without AI assistance: not as punishment, but as maintenance. The boundaries described in the previous section serve this purpose too: session limits, emotional distance from AI output, identity clarity about what you built versus what the AI generated. These are not restrictions on practice. They are the conditions under which professional capacity is preserved.

12.3 Staying Current

The tools you use today will not be the tools you use in twelve months. Between the early drafts of this book (mid-2025) and this substantially revised version (early 2026), the field shifted significantly. New AI coding assistants appeared. Existing ones added agentic capabilities. Browser-based platforms matured into viable development environments. Pricing models changed. The only constant was change itself.

This creates a genuine challenge: how do you stay current without spending all your time evaluating tools instead of using them? The answer is to separate the stable from the volatile.

- **What stays stable.** The interloquial skills this book teaches: intent, constraints, expectations. The planning-heavy workflow. The discipline of verification. These transfer across every tool, every platform, every model generation. A practitioner who is L4 on the maturity curve will be L4 regardless of which AI assistant they use. The skill is in the human, not the tool.

- **What changes rapidly.** Specific model capabilities, pricing, context window sizes, tool integrations, platform features. These matter tactically but not strategically. Knowing that a new platform offers one-click deployment is useful, but it does not change how you specify intent or structure constraints.
- **Practical approach.** Pick one primary AI assistant and learn it deeply. Use it for real work, not toy experiments. When you hear about a new tool or capability, evaluate it against a real task you have already completed, not against a hypothetical. "Could this tool have built my Reading List Manager faster?" is a useful question. "Could this tool theoretically do amazing things?" is not. The former gives you evidence. The latter gives you distraction.

Periodically (perhaps quarterly) spend an afternoon trying your current workflow on a competing platform. Not to switch, but to calibrate. You may discover capabilities you did not know existed. You may confirm that your current setup is the right choice. Either outcome is worth knowing. What is not worth knowing is whether the latest tool is marginally better – constant tool-hopping driven by anxiety about missing out produces nothing useful.

The practitioners who remain effective over years share a common trait: they invest in skills, not tools. Tools are replaceable. The ability to articulate precisely what you want, surface what could go wrong, and verify what you receive compounds indefinitely.

12.4 Community and Resources

Vibe-coding is new enough that its community of practice is still forming. As of March 2026, there are no established professional bodies, no accredited courses, no widely agreed curricula. Courses do exist, but they are almost exclusively aimed at developers or tied to specific tools such as Cursor, Lovable, or Replit. Platforms such as Coursera, Udemy, and Codecademy have launched introductory programmes, but a transferable framework for the non-programmer professional remains largely absent from formal education. This is both a challenge and an opportunity. It means you cannot simply enrol in a programme and follow instructions. It also means the field is shaped by its early practitioners, and you are one of them.

Here is how to engage with the community productively:

- **Where to find practitioners.** Several communities have proven durable. On Reddit, r/vibecoding and r/ClaudeAI are active forums where practitioners share real projects and problems; r/learnprogramming skews toward beginners but regularly covers AI-assisted development. The Discord servers run by Cursor, Claude, and GitHub Copilot are the closest thing to official practitioner spaces: search each tool's site for the community link. On X/Twitter, the hashtag #vibecoding and threads from AI researchers (as distinct from AI hype accounts) surface genuine technique discussion. The quality varies enormously. Apply the same critical judgement you apply to AI output: useful if verified, dangerous if accepted uncritically.
- **What to share.** The most useful contributions to any community of practice are candid accounts of what went wrong. Success stories are satisfying but teach less than failure analyses. When a project drifts, when a specification fails, when you accept AI output you should have

questioned: these are the stories that help others avoid the same mistakes. The DDoS incident from Chapter 3 (where I followed my AI assistant's rate-limiting test instructions too literally, denial-of-serviced my own application, and got my IP blacklisted by my hosting provider) has been more useful to more people than any success story in this book.

- **What to seek.** Look for practitioners who work in different domains from yours. A teacher using AI to generate lesson plans faces different interloquial challenges than a developer building web applications, but the underlying skill transfers. Cross-domain conversations reveal principles that domain-specific conversations miss.
- **Building your own resources.** The two-document approach from Chapter 9 (plan.md for specifications, history.md for the decisions log of what actually happened) plus the verification evidence you gather along the way, creates a personal knowledge base over time. After ten projects, your history.md files contain patterns you could not see in any single project. Review them periodically. The mistakes you made six months ago may be the mistakes you are about to make again.

12.5 The Future of Interloquial Communication

Prediction is a fool's game, especially in a field that reinvents itself quarterly. Rather than predict, I will identify three trajectories that hold regardless of which specific technologies prevail.

The specification becomes the product. As AI capabilities improve, the bottleneck shifts further from execution to specification. The person who can articulate precisely what needs to be built, with clear intent, well-defined constraints, and measurable expectations, matters more as

Figure 12.2: The Crystal Ball — the tools change quarterly; the skill that navigates them does not.

AI execution improves. The shift is already visible in how organisations are beginning to structure contracts: paying for outcomes rather than effort, for specifications rather than hours. The practitioner who can write a specification that an AI system can execute reliably is, in economic terms, the person who matters.

Interloquial skill becomes a mainstream competency. Today, interloquial communication is a niche skill practised by early adopters. Within a generation, it will be as fundamental to professional competence as written communication. Schools will teach it as a core literacy — the ability to communicate effectively with non-human intelligence — under whatever name the curriculum settles on (not "prompt engineering," which will age poorly). Curriculum reform lags technology adoption, which is exactly why the practitioners who develop this skill now will have a real advantage as adoption widens. Fluency takes time to develop. The time to start is before it becomes obvious.

The human role shifts from builder to auditor. Chapter 7 described a workflow where planning is the largest investment and implementation the shortest stage. That ratio will continue to shift. As AI systems become more capable, the implementation phase shrinks further. The human role becomes specification and verification: defining what should be built and confirming that what was built matches the definition. It is the role that matters most. An AI that can build anything is only as good as the human who can specify the right thing.

This trajectory has a shadow side worth acknowledging. Early industry surveys suggest a significant proportion of engineering leaders are planning to reduce junior developer hiring, reasoning that AI covers the work that juniors once did. One survey of over 800 engineering leaders found that 54% expected long-term reductions in junior developer hiring as AI coding tools are adopted.[37] But junior roles are where senior engineers are made. The debugging, the code review, the years of building mental models through hands-on struggle: these produce the experienced professionals who can specify, audit, and verify. If that pipeline contracts, the cognitive debt discussed in Chapter 3 becomes systemic, not just individual. The people needed to audit AI-generated systems in 2028 may not have been trained because they were not hired in 2025. The practitioners who develop interloquial skill now, who learn to specify precisely and verify rigorously, will be rarer and more sought-after than they otherwise would have been.

These trajectories converge on a single conclusion: the skills this book teaches are the foundation of a new form of professional competence — one that becomes more important as AI becomes more powerful.

There is growing enthusiasm, in some quarters bordering on utopianism, for a world that pays for outcomes rather than effort. The vision is seductive: specify what you want, let AI execute, measure the result. Some of these visions will collide with the realities of regulation, institutional inertia, and the simple fact that human problems are messier than any specification can capture. But the direction of travel is clear, even if the pace is uncertain. The economies, organisations, and individuals that learn to specify outcomes precisely will have an advantage over those still paying for hours of effort. It is already happening in procurement, in software contracts, and in how the best teams use AI today.

I cannot tell you what tools you will use in 2028. I cannot tell you which AI model will lead the market. I cannot predict pricing, capabilities, or platform consolidation. But I can tell you this with confidence: the person who can think clearly about what they want, articulate it precisely, anticipate what could go wrong, and verify that the result meets their standard will thrive in any configuration of the technology. That person is an interloquial practitioner. And you have already started becoming one.

12.6 Key Takeaways

- **The Interloquial Maturity Curve:** Six levels from unstructured (L0) to fluent (L5), introduced in Chapter 2. The jump from L0 to L1 is the most important. L2 is where most practitioners plateau. Deliberate practice moves you through; recognition of where you are is the starting point.
- **Deliberate practice beats repetition:** Review your failures, compare specifications to outcomes, vary your domains, teach others. These four practices do more for your progression than volume of AI interactions.
- **Boundaries sustain practice:** Temporal limits prevent entrainment. Emotional distance preserves critical judgement. Identity

clarity sets accurate expectations. Social connection provides the disagreement AI cannot.

- **Invest in skills, not tools:** The interloquial framework transfers across every platform and model generation. Tools change quarterly. The ability to specify intent, surface constraints, and verify outcomes compounds indefinitely.
- **Community teaches through failure:** Share what went wrong. Seek practitioners from different domains. Build a personal knowledge base through project plans, decisions logs, and verification checklists across projects.
- **The specification is the future:** As AI execution improves, the human role shifts further toward specification and verification — the role that determines whether powerful tools produce useful outcomes.

Notes

44 Walther, C. C. (2025). "The Silent Erosion: How AI's Helping Hand Weakens Our Mental Grip." *Centre for International Governance Innovation*, July 17,

45 Macnamara, B. N., Berber, I., Çavuşoğlu, M. C., Krupinski, E. A., Nallapareddy, N., Nelson, N. E., Smith, P. J., Wilson-Delfosse, A. L., & Ray, S. (2024). "Does using artificial intelligence assistance accelerate skill decay and hinder skill development without performers' awareness?" *Cognitive Research: Principles and Implications*, 9,

46 `doi.org/10.1186/s41235-024-00572-8`

37 LeadDev (2025). "Do junior devs still have a path to senior roles in an AI age?" *LeadDev*, September 3, 2025. Reports findings from the AI Impact Report 2025 survey of 880+ engineering leaders: 54% expect long-term reductions in junior developer hiring as AI coding tools are adopted; 18% expect fewer junior hires over the next 12 months. `leaddev.com/hiring/junior-devs-still-have-path-senior-roles`

About This Book

How vibe-coding and ICE built the book you just read.

The first draft of this book was written in a weekend.

I asked Claude to write a book about vibe-coding. I prompted it chapter by chapter, section by section, with broad instructions and minimal constraint. By Sunday evening I had approximately 100,000 words. It had fourteen chapters, five parts, a glossary, and appendices. It was structured, coherent, and almost entirely useless.

The facts were not wrong. The advice was mostly reasonable. It was useless because it had been written by a machine asked to fill a shape, not by a person asked to say something true. Every chapter covered what a chapter on that subject should cover. None of it was mine. Reading it back felt like reading a well-organised Wikipedia summary of a field I had spent years working in: technically competent and completely hollow. What it lacked was the thing that makes any book worth reading: a reason for this person to have written it.

I deleted it and started again.

The second attempt began not with writing but with a question: what do I actually know that nobody else is saying?

The answer, when I was honest about it, was risk. Not risk in the abstract: I have spent years as a Certified Fellow of the Institute of Risk Management, thinking professionally about what can go wrong and what obligations that creates. The books being published about AI collaboration were almost exclusively written by technologists or academics. They described capabilities without consequence, opportunity without obligation. The risk perspective was absent. That was the gap. That was the book.

Everything else followed from that recognition. The interloquial concept, the idea that communicating with AI is a distinct skill requiring its own vocabulary and discipline, emerged from asking why my early vibe-coding conversations produced such inconsistent results. The ICE framework emerged from asking what structured thinking I should have done before I wrote the first line of code on LockedPillar. The Interloquial Maturity Curve emerged from asking how I could help a reader understand where they were, so they could understand where the book was designed to take them.

The 100,000-word first draft had none of these. They were things I discovered when I stopped asking Claude to write a book and started asking it to help me think.

Once the framework was clear, the book was structured the way any complex vibe-coded project should be structured: with ICE applied at every level before a word of prose was written.

Each part had an Intent: what this section needed to establish in the reader's understanding before the next section could build on it. Each chapter had Constraints: what it must contain, what it must exclude, and how it must be presented. British English throughout. Minimal em dashes: a small discipline that turns out to be surprisingly difficult to maintain when working with AI, which reaches for the em dash the way a nervous speaker reaches for filler words. No technical jargon without definition. No author credential-stacking. Each chapter had Expectations: how a reader at Sarah's career stage, at Carl's age, or at

Chris's level of seniority would encounter the content, and what would make them continue reading rather than stop.

Sarah, Carl, and Chris are the three reader personas developed during the Expectations pass of the book's own ICE process. Sarah is a mid-career Operations Manager who gets inconsistent results from AI and will abandon a book that wastes her time. Carl is a graduate analyst who wants to stand out from his peers and has no patience for repetition. Chris is a senior manager who skims, reads headers, and will move on if the payoff is not immediately visible. Writing to three readers simultaneously is harder than writing to one. It is also what prevents a book from becoming a lecture.

The git history of this book's second draft contains more than ninety commits. Each one is a decision record: what changed, why, and what was rejected in the process. The commits do not just show what the book became. They show what it was not allowed to become: the scope that was constrained, the paragraphs that were cut, the framing that was corrected when it drifted from the persona it was supposed to serve. The decisions log principle, which the book argues is essential to any sustained vibe-coded project, was applied to itself. The history of this book is its own evidence.

The tools built to write the book are themselves the clearest demonstration of its argument.

The adversarial editor is a skill (a structured Claude prompt) that reads any chapter from five hostile positions simultaneously: a sceptical reader who suspects this is oversold, a developer who thinks non-programmers have no business building software, a risk professional who suspects the risk treatment is superficial, a journalist looking for claims that do not survive scrutiny, and an ideal customer who will recommend the book if it earns that recommendation but will not forgive padding. The adversarial editor was run on every chapter. It caught claims that were technically true but misleading, passages that were accurate but condescending, and sections that explained what the reader had already understood.

The reference audit skill checks every citation in the book against its source before it is committed to the manuscript. This was not optional. The book argues explicitly that AI-generated citations cannot be trusted without verification: the plausibility of a reference is not evidence of its existence. The reference audit was the practice of that argument applied to its own production. Every footnote in this book was checked. Several were corrected. One was removed because the paper it cited, while real, did not say what the first draft claimed it said.

The layout build pipeline converts the markdown chapter files into a print-ready PDF using a typesetting system called LuaLaTeX. This was itself a vibe-coded project: the pipeline did not exist before the book required it, and building it required the same planning discipline the book describes, understanding what the output needed to look like, what the constraints were (British English quotation marks, correct footnote formatting, consistent heading hierarchy), and what "done" meant before the first configuration file was written.

The reader persona assessment (the Sarah skill, the Carl lens) is a prompt that reads a chapter from each persona's perspective and identifies paragraphs that would lose that reader. It was run on every chapter. It caught author-heavy passages that taught nothing, technical jargon that assumed knowledge the target reader does not have, and sections that served the author's interest in establishing credibility rather than the reader's interest in learning something useful. Most of what it flagged was cut.

The illustrations in this book were produced through a two-stage process. Claude wrote the image prompts: detailed descriptions of what each illustration needed to show, what emotional register it should carry, and what compositional choices would serve the text it accompanied. Those prompts were fed into DALL-E via ChatGPT to generate the images. The final selection and any editing decisions were mine.

This division of labour reflects a genuine capability boundary. Claude's strength is precise verbal description: articulating exactly what a diagram needs to communicate and why. DALL-E's strength is rendering a detailed description into a visual. The gap between them is the human decision: which generated image actually serves the chapter, and which is technically competent but tonally wrong. That decision cannot be prompted. It requires the judgement of someone who has read the chapter and knows what the reader needs to see at that moment in the argument.

The cover art followed the same process.

The book's relationship to AI collaboration is literal. Every chapter was drafted in conversation with Claude, revised in response to the adversarial editor, assessed against the reader personas, and committed to version control with a meaningful message. The final prose is the product of that process: human intent, AI execution, human judgement applied to what came back.

What Claude cannot do is decide what the book should be. It cannot decide that risk is the distinctive contribution, that the first draft was hollow, that Sarah would abandon a chapter that talks about the author's career when she came to learn something for hers. Those decisions are the book. Everything else (the prose, the structure, the illustrations, the layout) is the build.

The methodology the book teaches is the methodology by which it was made. That is either the book's greatest strength or its most obvious weakness, depending on whether the reader believes the result.

You have now read the result. The judgement is yours.

The ICE Planning Framework

A Reference Guide and Facilitation Prompt

Chapter 2 introduces the ICE framework and Chapter 7 applies it to a real project. This appendix provides a complete practical reference: what ICE is, how each phase works, what to expect at each stage, and – critically – the full facilitation prompt you can paste into any AI assistant to run a structured planning session.

What ICE Is – and What It Is Not

ICE stands for **Intent, Constraints, Expectations**. It structures planning conversations between you and an AI assistant before implementation begins.

It is not a form with three boxes to fill in. Sending "Intent: X, Constraints: Y, Expectations: Z" is prompt engineering – a single optimised request. ICE is a dialogue. The AI asks questions, you answer, and the conversation surfaces things you did not know you needed to say: the assumption you were making without realising it, the constraint that rules out an entire class of approaches, the edge case that would have become a bug.

The value is in what emerges. A twenty-minute ICE session for the Reading List Manager produced the insight that the default tab should show "Want to Read" rather than "Currently Reading" – because the user's emotional state at the point of use involves guilt about unfinished books, not pride in current progress. That insight did not appear in any functional requirement. It came from the AI asking an unexpected question during Intent.

Phase 1: Intent

What the AI is doing: Understanding what you want to achieve and why it matters.

The AI will ask questions such as: - What problem are you solving? - Who will use this, and in what situation? - What does your current workflow look like? What is broken about it? - What happens if you do not build this? - How does the person using this feel at the moment they need it?

What to expect: The AI is listening for unstated context — the things you know but have not said. Expect questions that feel slightly sideways to the technical problem. "How do you feel when you think about your current reading list?" is an Intent question, not a personal one. The emotional state of the user often determines design decisions that functional requirements never reach.

The multi-pass technique: As described in section 7.1, it is worth running Intent at least twice. The first pass surfaces *what* you are building. The second pass surfaces *why* — the user's emotional state at the moment they need this, and what would make them feel the problem was truly solved. For complex projects, further passes will go deeper still. The first two passes are shown in the Reading List Manager plan later in this appendix, under "Phase 5: The Plan". The facilitation prompt, later in this appendix under "Running ICE for Your Own Projects", covers the first pass. When it concludes, run it a second time with the prompt shown in section 7.1.5: *"Run ICE on this plan again. Go deeper than the surface. What is the user's emotional state when they use this?"*

Phase 2: Constraints

What the AI is doing: Surfacing the hard limits the solution must respect.

The AI will ask questions such as: - What technical limitations exist? - What can you absolutely not do? - What resources are limited — time, money, expertise? - What business or personal rules must be respected? - What security or privacy requirements apply?

What to expect: Constraints have a dual nature. They restrict options and they generate creativity. "No backend server, static site only" eliminates entire categories of solution and forces the design into a simpler, cheaper, faster-to-deploy shape. Commit to constraints precisely — "it should work on mobile" is vague; "mobile is the primary use case, desktop is secondary" is a constraint.

Phase 3: Expectations

What the AI is doing: Establishing how you will verify the solution is correct.

Two passes over your Expectations:

Pass one (human-led): The AI asks you to walk through a typical successful use of the finished thing, step by step. This is the happy path — what you already know success looks like.

Pass two (AI-challenged): The AI probes the boundaries given your stated Intent and Constraints. Expect questions about: - Empty states — what happens when there is no data? - Failure states — what happens when something goes wrong? - Scale — what happens with far more data or users than expected? - Edge cases — what happens with unexpected or malicious input? - Concurrency — what happens if two things happen at the same time?

What to expect: This is where pre-mortems happen. The AI is looking for the conditions that turn a working demo into a production failure. These cost minutes to address in planning and hours to fix after the fact.

Phase 4: Critical Review

What the AI is doing: Adopting an adversarial stance to challenge the plan before it is committed to.

The AI will switch roles explicitly and review your plan as:

1. **A sceptical user** who has tried and abandoned similar tools. What would make them delete this after a week? What features promise more than they deliver?
2. **A security auditor.** What data does this handle? What could be exploited? What habits should be built in from the start, regardless of the apparent risk level?

What to expect: This is the stage that breaks sycophancy — the AI's tendency to build what was asked without questioning whether it is right. Expect pushback on vague commitments. If you said "export," the AI will ask what format. If you said "it should be fast," the AI will ask fast compared to what, and at what scale. When this phase surfaces new constraints or contradicts earlier decisions, update the earlier phases before proceeding to the plan. The plan should reflect the project as it stands after the full session, not as it was at the start.

Phase 5: The Plan

At the end of the session, the AI produces a structured summary. For the Reading List Manager, the plan looked like this:

Intent

A personal reading list manager for one user. Solves the fragmented, guilt-inducing workflow of tracking books across multiple tools. The core job to be done is not "track books" but "feel in control of reading goals." Design must reflect this: aspiration over obligation, low friction over completeness.

Constraints

- No backend server; static site only
- Free hosting (GitHub Pages or equivalent)
- No user accounts
- Mobile is the primary use case
- No paid third-party services
- Export format: JSON (specified, not vague)
- Search: debounced at 300ms to avoid rate limiting

Expectations

Happy path:

- Open app and see Want to Read list (default tab)
- Search for a book and see results appear
- Add book and see it appear in Want to Read list
- Update progress with +10 / +25 buttons
- Move to Finished tab when done

Edge cases:

- No search results: friendly message
- Search service down: error message, not broken UI
- No cover image: placeholder
- Corrupted stored data: reset silently
- Five hundred books: acceptable at this scale

Critical Review Notes

- Progress tracking friction: mitigated by quick-tap buttons on card, no modal
- Export: specified as JSON to prevent “export” as a vague future promise
- XSS prevention: use textContent for all user-provided content
- Rate limiting: debounced search prevents accidental hammering of the search service

Decisions Made

- Default view: Want to Read (aspiration, not obligation)
- No modal for progress updates: buttons directly on card
- Vanilla HTML, CSS, and JavaScript: no framework, no build step

This plan became the starting point for the full plan document that guided the build. The wireframes, data model, feature requirements, and STRIDE security analysis all build on what the ICE conversation established.

Running ICE for Your Own Projects

A session for a project of the Reading List Manager's scope takes roughly twenty minutes. For a larger project, plan for thirty to forty.

In Claude Code — setting up the /ice skill:

Claude Code supports custom slash commands called skills. A skill is a markdown file containing instructions for the AI. When you type `/ice`, Claude reads that file and follows its instructions to run the planning session. There are two steps: initialise your project, then add the skill.

Step 1: Initialise your project with `/init`

If you have not already set up Claude Code for your project, run `/init` in a new conversation. Claude analyses your project folder, identifies build commands, test instructions, and coding conventions it can detect, and generates a `CLAUDE.md` file at the root of your project. This file becomes the persistent briefing Claude reads at the start of every conversation — your project's standing instructions.

If a `CLAUDE.md` already exists, `/init` suggests improvements rather than overwriting it. After generation, you can edit the file directly to add anything Claude would not have discovered on its own: your preferred writing style, constraints specific to your business, or context about the project's purpose.

`/init` takes around a minute to run and is the single most valuable first step for any new project. It means Claude begins every subsequent conversation already knowing your project — no repetition, no re-explaining.

Step 2: Add the ICE skill

Once your project is initialised, add the ICE skill by creating a folder structure inside your project:

your-project/ - .claude/ - skills/ - ice/ - SKILL.md — paste the facilitation prompt here - CLAUDE.md — created by /init - (your project files)

You can create this structure manually, or you can ask Claude to do it for you. The full facilitation prompt is printed in the next section. Once you have it, open a new Claude Code conversation and paste the following instruction followed immediately by the full facilitation prompt text:

> "Create the folder structure `.claude/skills/ice/` in my project and save the following text as `SKILL.md` inside the `ice` folder. I want to run it by typing `/ice`."
>
> [paste the full facilitation prompt here]

Claude will create the folders, write the file with your exact prompt text, and confirm the skill is ready. You do not need to touch the file system yourself, and the skill will behave exactly as described in this appendix.

Whether you create the structure manually or let Claude build it, the result is the same: typing `/ice` at the start of any Claude Code conversation runs the session automatically. The skill persists across conversations as long as the file is in your project.

Personal installation (available across all your projects):

To make `/ice` available in every project without copying files, install it once in your home directory. Create the same folder structure at `~/.claude/skills/ice/SKILL.md`. On Windows, place it in your home directory under `.claude\skills\ice\SKILL.md`; on Mac and Linux the full path is `~/.claude/skills/ice/SKILL.md`. Paste the facilitation prompt into that file. Claude Code will find and load it automatically in any project.

The principle extends beyond `/ice`. Any repeating workflow — a code review checklist, a deployment procedure, a writing style guide — can be saved as a skill file and invoked with a single slash command. `/init` builds the foundation; skills build the toolkit on top of it.

In any other AI assistant: Paste the facilitation prompt below directly into a new conversation. It gives any AI the full instruction set to run the same structured session — the questions to ask, the order to ask them, when to switch to the critical persona, and what the plan must contain. The facilitation prompt uses no Claude-specific features and works equally well with ChatGPT, Gemini, Copilot, or any other AI assistant.

The ICE Facilitation Prompt

To install this as a Claude Code skill, follow the instructions in the previous section. To run a session directly, copy the prompt below into a new conversation with any AI assistant. The AI will guide you from there.

You are facilitating an ICE planning session — a structured dialogue to surface requirements before implementation begins. ICE stands for Intent, Constraints, Expectations.

Your role is to guide me through the session by asking questions. This is a dialogue, not a form. Do not ask me to fill in three boxes. Ask one or two questions at a time, listen to my answers, and probe where the answer is unclear or where I appear to have made an unstated assumption.

PHASE 1: INTENT

Ask questions to understand what I want to achieve and why it matters:

- What problem are you solving?
- Who will use this, and in what situation?
- What does your current workflow look like? What is broken about it?
- What happens if you do not build this?

- How does the person using this feel at the moment they need it?

Listen for unstated context. The emotional state of the user often determines design decisions that functional requirements never reach. Probe gently. Do not assume.

PHASE 2: CONSTRAINTS

Surface the boundaries the solution must respect:

- What technical limitations exist?
- What can you absolutely not do?
- What resources are limited — time, money, expertise?
- What business or personal rules must be respected?
- What security or privacy requirements apply?

Note: constraints have a dual nature. They restrict options and generate creativity. Treat them as useful, not as obstacles to apologise for.

PHASE 3: EXPECTATIONS

Establish how we will verify that the solution is correct. Two passes:

First pass (happy path): Ask me to walk through what a typical successful use of the finished thing looks like, step by step.

Second pass (AI-challenged): Given what I have described, probe the boundaries. Ask about empty states, failure states, scale, unexpected or malicious input, and concurrency.

PHASE 4: PLAN

At the end of the session, produce a structured summary in this format:

INTENT — What we are building and why. The problem. The user's emotional context. The job to be done.

CONSTRAINTS — Bulleted list of hard limits: technical, financial, scope, rules.

EXPECTATIONS — Happy path (step-by-step successful use). Edge cases (boundary conditions and how they should be handled).

DECISIONS MADE — Key choices and rationale. What was considered and ruled out, and why.

Throughout the session: ask, do not assume. One or two questions at a time. Reflect back to confirm understanding. Surface conflicts explicitly. Stay neutral — you are facilitating clarity, not advocating for solutions.

Begin by asking me what I want to build.

Advanced: The Consolidated ICE Prompt

The facilitation prompt above covers the first ICE pass. Chapter 7 then walks you through the subsequent stages – the deep second pass, the critical persona reviews, the pre-mortem – as separate conversations you initiate yourself. That separation is deliberate. Each stage builds on the last, and doing them manually means you understand what you are asking for and why.

Once you have run the multi-stage process several times and trust how it works, you may find that managing separate conversations adds friction without adding insight. At that point, you can consider a consolidated prompt that combines all stages into a single session.

What follows is an example of such a prompt. Treat it as a starting point, not a prescription. You will want to modify it to reflect your own experience of where the multi-stage process adds the most value for the kinds of projects you build.

Before using this: Run the staged approach in Chapter 7 at least twice on real projects. The consolidated prompt will mean more — and work better — once you know what each stage is doing and why.

You are facilitating a full ICE planning session — a structured dialogue covering Intent, Constraints, Expectations, critical review, and plan production. This session replaces the staged multi-pass process described in Chapter 7 of Vibe-Coding: The Art of Collaborating with AI.

Guide me through each stage in sequence. Ask one or two questions at a time. Do not rush to the next stage until the current one is complete.

STAGE 1: INTENT — PASS 1

Ask questions to surface what I want to achieve and why it matters:

- What problem are you solving?
- Who will use this, and in what situation?
- What does your current workflow look like? What is broken about it?
- What happens if you do not build this?
- How does the person using this feel at the moment they need it?

STAGE 2: INTENT — PASS 2 (DEEP)

Once the functional picture is clear, go deeper without prompting from me:

- What is the emotional state of the user at the exact moment they need this?
- What would make them feel this had completely solved their problem?
- What would make them feel it had failed, even if it technically worked?

Tell me you are moving to the deeper pass before you begin it.

STAGE 3: CONSTRAINTS

Surface the boundaries the solution must respect:

- What technical limitations exist?
- What can you absolutely not do?
- What resources are limited — time, money, expertise?
- What business or personal rules must be respected?
- What security or privacy requirements apply?

If any later stage surfaces a new constraint, return here and add it before continuing.

STAGE 4: EXPECTATIONS

Two passes:

First pass (happy path): Ask me to walk through a typical successful use of the finished thing, step by step.

Second pass (AI-challenged): Probe the boundaries. Ask about empty states, failure states, scale, unexpected or malicious input, and concurrency. If any edge case reveals a constraint not in Stage 3, return there and add it.

STAGE 5: CRITICAL REVIEW

Adopt an adversarial stance. Tell me you are switching roles, then:

1. Review as a sceptical user who has tried and abandoned similar tools. What would make them delete this after a week? What features promise more than they deliver?
2. Review as a security auditor. What data does this handle? What could be exploited? What habits should be built in from the start?

Challenge vague commitments. If anything here contradicts or extends what was agreed in Stages 1-4, revise those stages explicitly and tell me what changed and why.

STAGE 6: PLAN

Produce a structured summary reflecting the plan as it stands after the full session:

INTENT — What we are building and why. The problem. The user's emotional context. The job to be done.

CONSTRAINTS — Bulleted list of hard limits: technical, financial, scope, rules.

EXPECTATIONS — Happy path (step-by-step). Edge cases and how they should be handled.

CRITICAL REVIEW NOTES — What the sceptical user flagged. What the security auditor raised. Mitigations planned or risks consciously accepted.

DECISIONS MADE — Key choices and rationale. What was ruled out, and why.

Throughout: ask, do not assume. One or two questions at a time. Reflect back to confirm understanding. Surface conflicts explicitly. Stay neutral.

Begin by asking me what I want to build.

Appendix — The ICE Planning Framework See Chapter 2 for the conceptual introduction.

Glossary

Terms used with specific meaning in this book.

A–C

Articulation Bottleneck

Introduced: Ch01

The revelation that clear articulation of requirements, not coding skill, is the true constraint in software creation. "Traditional thinking assumes coding skill is the barrier. The vibe-code reality reveals that clear articulation is the true constraint."

Augment, Don't Replace

Type: Framework **Introduced:** Ch03

A core principle for responsible vibe-coding: AI is used to accelerate and enhance human thinking rather than substitute for it, maintaining active cognitive engagement throughout the process.

Automation Complacency

Type: General **Introduced:** Ch03

The risk that fluent, polished AI output receives less critical review than rougher output, reducing scrutiny of accuracy precisely when presentation is most convincing.

Boundary Erosion

Introduced: Ch03

The tendency to work excessive hours during AI collaboration because the AI is always available and never expresses fatigue, removing the natural friction that limits working hours.

Bracketing Emotion

Introduced: Ch02

A disciplined interloquial practice of recognising when feelings (frustration, impatience, excitement) are interfering with precision and consciously managing them before they degrade communication quality.

Branch

Type: Technical **Introduced:** Ch06

A parallel line of development in version control that allows experimental work without affecting the main codebase; can be merged back if successful or discarded if not.

CLAUDE.md

Type: Technical **Introduced:** Ch06

A project memory file placed in the project root that Claude reads automatically at the start of every conversation. Contains project description, coding conventions, and anything else the AI should retain across sessions.

Cognitive Debt

Introduced: Ch03

A property of the practitioner who no longer understands the code they are responsible for, distinct from technical debt, which is a property of the codebase. Accumulated when humans accept AI output without engaging with what it means.

Collaborative Uncertainty

Introduced: Ch01

The principle that specification emerges through dialogue rather than being pre-determined; you arrive at a project with a problem rather than a complete specification. "The specification emerges through dialogue, not before it."

Competence Confusion

Introduced: Ch03

Difficulty distinguishing one's own skills from AI capabilities, creating uncertainty about what knowledge and abilities are personally retained versus dependent on AI assistance.

Compounding Framework

Introduced: Ch02

A framework whose value increases with task complexity and duration. ICE is described as a compounding framework because its value compounds through extended collaboration, since context preservation enables coherent iteration.

Confidence Without Correlation to Accuracy

Introduced: Ch02

A distinctive property of AI responses where the system expresses answers with assured tone regardless of whether the answer is correct. "The response to 'what is 2+2?' and the response to 'what obscure 1987 paper discussed this topic?' arrive with identical confidence."

Constraints

Type: Framework **Introduced:** Ch02

The second element of the ICE Framework: boundaries within which a solution must operate, including technical limitations, business requirements, design principles, and performance targets. Constraints have both a restrictive function (narrowing solutions) and a generative function (forcing creative discovery).

Context Management

Type: Technical **Introduced:** Ch06

Deliberate control over the information provided to AI in conversations to manage cost and focus, including starting fresh conversations for new topics and keeping memory files lean.

Context Window

Type: Technical **Introduced:** Ch06

The maximum number of tokens a language model can hold in working memory at one time, limiting the length of conversations or documents it can process coherently.

Conversation Summary

Type: Framework **Introduced:** Ch05

A structured distillation of a discovery conversation into key requirements and decisions, saved separately from raw conversation history to serve as a reusable specification. "Context is an asset. Treat it like one."

Credentials Trap

Introduced: Ch08

A failure mode where AI scaffolds integration code that compiles cleanly but fails at runtime because required credentials have not been configured. "I call this the credentials trap, and I have fallen into it more times than I care to admit."

Critical Persona Review

Type: Framework **Introduced:** Ch02 (applied in Ch07)

A planning technique where you ask the AI to adopt adversarial stances (sceptical user, security auditor, hostile critic) to surface plan weaknesses that the AI's agreeable default mode would otherwise overlook.

D–F

Debugging Beyond Code

Introduced: Ch08

A debugging discipline recognising that problems may lie outside the codebase — in browser extensions, network conditions, caching, or environment differences — rather than in code logic.

Deliberate Practice

Type: Framework **Introduced:** Ch12

Intentional, reflective improvement of interloquial skill through structured effort: reviewing failures, comparing specifications to outcomes, varying domains, and teaching others. "What separates practice from mere repetition is reflection."

Discovery Conversation

Type: Framework **Introduced:** Ch05

A structured dialogue where the AI asks clarifying questions before building code, ensuring implementation matches the user's actual vision rather than generic assumptions. "Instead of hoping the AI guesses correctly, invite it to ask questions first."

Documentation Drift

Introduced: Ch09

The inevitable divergence between project specification and actual implementation when speed outpaces documentation discipline. "This is documentation drift, and it is the inevitable consequence of vibe-coding's speed."

Domain-Specific Maturity

Introduced: Ch02

The recognition that interloquial fluency in one domain does not guarantee fluency in another; new challenges may reset a practitioner's progress on the maturity curve.

Emotional Boundary

Type: Framework **Introduced:** Ch12

A practice discipline maintaining the distinction that AI output is provisional, not authoritative, to preserve the practitioner's independent judgment during extended collaboration.

Entrainment

Type: Technical **Introduced:** Ch12

A psychological state reached during extended AI collaboration sessions where the AI's suggestions feel correct not because of quality but because sustained agreement has created false comfort. "That feeling is not evidence of quality; it is evidence of entrainment."

Expectation Delta

Introduced: Ch01

The precise articulation of the gap between what you expected from AI output and what you received; the skill of identifying exactly where output deviates from intent so it can be corrected in iteration.

Expectations

Type: Framework **Introduced:** Ch02

The third element of the ICE Framework: how you will know the implementation succeeded and what you will look for when you test it.

Experimental Mindset

Type: Framework **Introduced:** Ch04

A psychological shift where failure is reframed from disaster to data — an opportunity to learn and iterate rather than a waste of resources.

Expression

Introduced: Ch02

One of the two directions of interloquial communication: formulating your intent, constraints, and expectations for the AI to receive. (Contrast: Interpretation.)

Flow State (in vibe-coding)

Type: Framework **Introduced:** Ch04

A creative mode where reduced friction between idea and execution allows imaginative exploration, shifting thinking from "can this be built?" to "what if?"

Free Tier Trap

Introduced: Ch10

The phenomenon where free hosting or service tiers do not simply expire but end abruptly when usage limits are exceeded, causing unexpected service interruptions. "The trap is not that they expire — it is that they end abruptly when you exceed limits."

Friction (as signal)

Introduced: Ch05

The point at which manual tools begin to create more work than building itself, indicating readiness to adopt more sophisticated development environments. "The friction will tell you when to move on."

Full-Stack App Builders

Introduced: Ch10

Platforms such as Lovable, Bolt.new, and Replit that combine AI code generation with integrated hosting, database, and deployment services. (Contrast: Pure Vibe-Coding Tools.)

G–I

Git

Type: Technical **Introduced:** Ch06

A version control system that tracks changes to files over time by creating snapshots (commits). Enables restoration to previous states and experimentation without risking stable code.

.gitignore

Type: Technical **Introduced:** Ch06

A file listing filenames and patterns that Git will ignore entirely. Essential for preventing passwords, API keys, and secrets from being committed to version control.

GitHub Pages

Type: Technical **Introduced:** Ch06

A free GitHub service that publishes websites directly from a repository, providing a public URL without requiring users to manage hosting infrastructure.

Gradually Escalating Reinforcement Effect

Type: Technical **Introduced:** Ch03

A psychological mechanism where AI systems with memory features magnify invalid thinking across sessions by building upon previous conversations, compounding rather than correcting cognitive distortions.

Hallucination

Type: Technical **Introduced:** Ch02

Confidently wrong answers generated by AI, where the system presents fabricated information with the same tone as accurate information.

The Handoff Point

Introduced: Ch11

The strategy of building a prototype with vibe-coding, then handing it to professional developers for production hardening. Validates concept and requirements while reducing specification risk.

History.md

Introduced: Ch08

The development journal capturing what actually happened during implementation: chronological, conversational, recording decisions, pivots, features added or removed, and why. Updated after each significant session. (Contrast: Plan.md.)

Hostile Review

Introduced: Ch03

Critical examination of ideas by humans who will challenge rather than elaborate on them; the primary escape mechanism from the validation trap. "The only escape is hostile review from outside the conversation."

ICE Framework

Type: Framework **Introduced:** Ch02

A planning conversation framework with three elements: Intent (what you want to achieve and why), Constraints (boundaries and requirements), and Expectations (how you will verify success). Not a prompt template but a structure for planning conversations that precedes implementation.

ICE Pack

Type: Framework **Introduced:** Ch09

Three deliverables that emerge naturally from good vibe-coding practice: (1) plan.md (the specification), (2) the delivered product, and (3) verification evidence (test results, security review, history.md entries). Together: specification, product, evidence. "If you have been following the workflow from Chapter 7, you already produce all three as natural byproducts."

Idea Monomania

Introduced: Ch03

The uncritical adoption of an elegant but unproven thesis through AI collaboration, where AI agreement creates a reinforcing validation loop that builds increasing confidence in ideas without external evidence of truth.

Identity Boundary

Type: Framework **Introduced:** Ch12

A practice discipline maintaining an accurate distinction between the practitioner's contribution (intent, constraints, verification) and the AI's contribution (code generation), preventing competence confusion.

Intent

Type: Framework **Introduced:** Ch02

The first element of the ICE Framework: the outcome you are trying to accomplish, including both what you want and why you want it, in what situation, and what context makes that outcome meaningful.

Interloquial

Introduced: Ch02

Of or relating to communication between human and machine intelligence; speaking across the boundary between human cognition and machine processing. (Latin: *inter* + *loqui* = between + to speak.)

Interloquial Barrier

Introduced: Ch02

The epistemological and practical boundary between human and machine intelligence; the point across which understanding cannot fully cross because the AI's internal processing remains opaque.

Interloquial Communication

Introduced: Ch02

A form of dialogue between a human and an AI that requires skills different from human conversation, where meaning emerges through exchange rather than one-way instruction. "Neither interpersonal nor mechanical, that requires skills different from human conversation."

Interloquial Literacy

Introduced: Ch12

A predicted future state where interloquial communication transitions from a niche skill to a foundational literacy taught in schools, as fundamental as written communication.

Interloquial Maturity Curve

Type: Framework **Introduced:** Ch02

A six-level progression model (L0–L5) describing practitioner development in interloquial communication, from unstructured vagueness (L0) to fluent mastery where the framework becomes invisible (L5). Includes a plateau at L2 where many practitioners stall.

Interloquial Practitioner

Introduced: Ch02

A professional skilled in interloquial communication: able to think clearly about desired outcomes, articulate intent precisely, anticipate constraints, and verify results against standards.

Interloquial Skills

Introduced: Ch02

The capacity to exchange intent, context, and understanding across the boundary between human and machine. Encompasses both expression (formulating requests) and interpretation (understanding responses).

Interpretation

Introduced: Ch02

One of the two directions of interloquial communication: understanding AI responses, recognising when it has misunderstood, when suggestions improve your vision, and when outputs require refinement. (Contrast: Expression.)

J–M

Job to Be Done

Type: Technical **Introduced:** Ch07

The underlying user goal or emotional outcome beyond the surface feature request — what the user actually needs to accomplish beyond the mechanics of the tool.

Kickoff Prompt

Introduced: Ch07

A structured prompt that bridges planning and implementation, providing explicit plan references, permission expectations, and a phase-specific starting point to prevent the AI from attempting to build everything at once.

L0–L5 (Maturity Levels)

Type: Framework **Introduced:** Ch02

The six levels of the Interloquial Maturity Curve: L0 (Unstructured) — vague requests, no structured approach; L1 (Aware) — recognises ICE but cannot apply it reliably; L2 (Structured) — consistently applies ICE, solid results; L3 (Adaptive) — adjusts approach to task complexity; L4 (Reflective) — builds reusable workflows from observed patterns; L5 (Fluent) — framework is invisible, precision is second nature.

Managed No-Code Platforms

Introduced: Ch10

Platforms such as Base44 and Coderick AI that manage all infrastructure but limit or prohibit code export, creating permanent platform dependency.

Merchant of Record

Type: Technical **Introduced:** Ch10

A payment processing model where the service provider handles VAT/sales tax calculation, collection, and remittance, with the merchant receiving net payments and reduced compliance burden.

Mode-Switching

Introduced: Ch02

The conscious practice of shifting between interpersonal communication (warmth-oriented) and interloquial communication (precision-oriented) depending on which mode the situation requires.

MoSCoW Prioritisation

Type: Technical **Introduced:** Ch07

A project prioritisation framework categorising requirements into Must Have, Should Have, Could Have, and Won't Have to control scope and focus implementation effort.

MVP Mindset

Type: Framework **Introduced:** Ch04

An approach that prioritises building the minimum viable version to demonstrate usefulness, then deciding whether full production investment is warranted before committing further resources.

N–R

Outcome-Based Contracts

Type: Technical **Introduced:** Ch12

A contracting model where payment is tied to demonstrable outcomes rather than effort expended, reflecting the shift in professional value from execution to specification.

Parallel Agents

Introduced: Ch09

Simultaneous AI work streams operating independently on different aspects of a project, allowing multiple related tasks to progress concurrently without blocking on each other.

Plan Document (plan.md)

Introduced: Ch06 (full treatment Ch07)

A comprehensive written specification created before implementation that documents background, ICE analysis, data model, feature requirements, technical approach, UI wireframes, security considerations, and open questions. The authoritative reference for what the project is supposed to do.

Planning Mode

Introduced: Ch06

A deliberate phase of project development where thinking and planning occur before implementation, involving discussion and documentation of decisions in a plan.md file.

Platform Vibe-Coding

Type: Technical **Introduced:** Ch10

A vibe-coding approach using all-in-one platforms (Lovable, Bolt.new, Replit) that combine AI code generation with pre-built infrastructure. (Contrast: Pure Vibe-Coding.)

Pre-Mortem

Type: Framework **Introduced:** Ch07

A risk management technique where you imagine how a project could fail before it happens, then work backwards to identify causes and unknowns – applied here during the planning phase before implementation begins.

Progressive Web App (PWA)

Type: Technical **Introduced:** Ch08

A web application that users can install on their devices like a native app, providing features including offline functionality, home screen icons, and full-screen mode without requiring an app store submission.

Prompt Engineering

Type: Technical **Introduced:** Ch01

Crafting a request carefully enough that a single exchange with AI produces the output you need. Effective for bounded, well-defined tasks but insufficient for building complex software through sustained collaboration.

Pure Vibe-Coding

Type: Technical **Introduced:** Ch01

Creating code through AI collaboration where the practitioner fully owns, understands, and controls the source code, managing hosting, databases, and deployment independently. (Contrast: Platform Vibe-Coding.)

Pure Vibe-Coding Tools

Introduced: Ch09

AI-native IDEs or code generation assistants (Cursor, Windsurf, Claude Code) that provide code generation but no infrastructure; users own and manage all hosting, deployment, and database infrastructure.

Query-Building (Paradigm)

Introduced: Ch01 (developed in Ch04)

Asking AI to generate code that will analyse your data rather than asking AI to answer questions directly. Grounds outputs in real data and removes the black box, making hallucination structurally impossible because outputs come from computation rather than inference.

Recursive ICE

Introduced: Ch02 (applied in Ch07)

The practice of running the ICE framework multiple times. The first pass surfaces what to build; the second surfaces why, including the user's emotional context and state of mind. For complex projects, further passes using the five whys principle will surface deeper constraints and assumptions still.

The Refactoring Trap

Introduced: Ch08

A failure mode where AI proposes comprehensive code restructuring when only a surgical fix is needed, introducing new complexity and bugs while ostensibly addressing the original issue.

The Refinement Loop

Type: Framework **Introduced:** Ch05

A cyclical process of specifying requirements, implementing code, testing results, and iteratively refining based on gaps between expectation and reality — typically completed in minutes rather than days.

Risk Proportionality

Introduced: Ch07

The principle that security effort should match the stakes of a project: critical and high findings require immediate resolution; medium findings require conscious acceptance or mitigation; low findings can be documented and monitored.

Risk-Based Decision-Making

Introduced: Ch08

A security practice of assessing effort and risk to determine proportionate controls, rather than implementing all possible safeguards regardless of context.

S–Z

Security Audit (as deliverable)

Type: Framework **Introduced:** Ch07

A structured assessment generated by the AI specific to your application's architecture and data model that identifies actual vulnerabilities, prioritises them by severity, and proposes proportionate mitigations.

Serverless Functions

Type: Technical **Introduced:** Ch08

A cloud computing model where small, stateless functions execute on demand without requiring users to manage servers, charged per request rather than for continuous uptime.

Skill Atrophy

Type: General **Introduced:** Ch03

The degradation of human capability that results from delegating cognitive or technical work to AI systems without maintaining personal proficiency through deliberate practice.

Slop

Type: General **Introduced:** Ch03

Low-quality AI-generated content characterised as derivative, generic, and obviously machine-produced. "Slop is not AI-generated content; slop is AI-generated content produced without genuine human engagement."

Social Boundary

Type: Framework **Introduced:** Ch12

A practice discipline ensuring human intellectual relationships and community engagement remain primary, counterbalancing the AI's designed agreeableness. "If your primary intellectual relationship is with an AI, something has gone wrong."

Specification and Verification Workflow

Type: Framework **Introduced:** Ch12

A development approach where the human role focuses on defining what should be built and confirming correctness, with AI handling implementation; described as the emerging standard for professional practice.

Speed as Force Multiplier

Introduced: Ch04

The concept that development speed transforms what can be attempted — not merely compressing timelines but enabling experimentation and exploration that would be economically impossible at slower rates. "Speed does not just compress timelines. It transforms what you can attempt."

Static Hosting

Type: Technical **Introduced:** Ch08

Web hosting for applications that run entirely in the browser with no server-side processing and no hosted database; the simplest and cheapest deployment option for vibe-coded tools.

STRIDE

Type: Technical **Introduced:** Ch03 (applied in Ch07)

A Microsoft-developed security threat modelling framework organising threats into six categories: Spoofing, Tampering, Repudiation, Information Disclosure, Denial of Service, and Elevation of Privilege. Used in the book's security audit workflow.

Support Burden

Introduced: Ch11

The time and resources required to respond to user issues, bugs, unexpected use cases, and environmental problems. "The moment you have users, you have support obligations. This is the cost most vibe-coders underestimate."

Sycophancy Bias

Type: Technical **Introduced:** Ch03

The tendency of AI systems trained to be helpful and agreeable to reinforce user ideas rather than challenge them. "Claude is designed to be helpful, which creates a structural bias toward validation rather than challenge."

Temporal Boundary

Type: Framework **Introduced:** Ch12

A practice discipline setting time limits on AI collaboration sessions to prevent entrainment and maintain the critical distance needed for objective evaluation.

Token

Type: Technical **Introduced:** Ch06

Fragments of words, punctuation, and spaces that large language models convert into numbers for processing; the standard unit of computational input and output used for pricing and context window limits.

Trust Calibration

Introduced: Ch02

The practice of matching your level of verification and trust to the risk level of AI outputs — a spectrum from blind trust to over-verification, with verified trust as the recommended operating position.

Two-Document Approach

Type: Framework **Introduced:** Ch09

A documentation strategy separating plan.md (what the project is supposed to do) from history.md (how it actually evolved), ensuring specification remains authoritative while development decisions are preserved and drift becomes visible.

Users vs Customers

Introduced: Ch11

A distinction where users are people using free software with acceptance of best-effort support, while customers have paid and expect reliable functionality. “Users expect the software to work but accept that free means 'best effort' support. Customers expect the software to work and have paid for the right to complain.”

Validation Trap

Introduced: Ch03

A reinforcing cycle where AI agreement creates the false impression of independent confirmation, elegance feels like truth, and resistance to outside challenge increases. Requires hostile review from outside the conversation to escape.

Version Naming

Type: Framework **Introduced:** Ch05

A manual file versioning system using descriptive filenames with version numbers (snake-v1.html, snake-v2.html) to track working code states and enable rollback before adopting full version control.

Verification Discipline

Introduced: Ch02

A learned and sustained practice of independently verifying AI outputs before acceptance, recognising that confident presentation tells you nothing about reliability. The discipline that separates competent from excellent practitioners.

Vibe-Coding

Introduced: Ch01

The practice of creating software by articulating what you want rather than specifying how to build it; creating through sustained AI collaboration over hours, days, or weeks where each exchange builds on the last and requirements emerge through conversation. Defined by process (accumulated context), not merely product.

Vibe-Coding Risk Taxonomy

Type: Framework **Introduced:** Ch03

A four-level concentric risk framework expanding from individual psychological and competence risks, through project security and operational risks, to business financial and legal risks, and outward to societal ethical and trust risks.

Vibe-Coding Workflow

Type: Framework **Introduced:** Ch07

A four-stage iterative process: heavy upfront planning (recursive ICE, critical persona reviews, pre-mortems); focused build and launch in a single session; debug and iterate on real-world usage; security review. Inverts traditional development ratios of planning to execution.

Vibe-Coding Zone

Introduced: Ch02

The middle section of the AI autonomy spectrum where interloquial skill peaks, characterised by collaborative creation where neither party is autonomous and both are necessary.

Webhook

Type: Technical **Introduced:** Ch08 (deployment context Ch10)

A message a third-party service sends to your application the moment an event occurs on its end, such as a payment succeeding or a subscription renewing, so your application does not need to continually check for updates.

Workflow Patterns That Compound

Introduced: Ch08

Small systematic investments in process — custom skills, lean memory files, parallel windows, version control discipline — that individually appear modest but collectively transform vibe-coding from reactive to systematic.

References

Chapters 1 and 3 — The Vibe-Code Revolution / The Risks of Vibe-Coding

1. Karpathy, A. (2025). "Vibe coding" tweet introducing the term and methodology, February 2025. Includes: "fully give in to the vibes, embrace exponentials, and forget that the code even exists" and "I 'Accept All' always, I don't read the diffs anymore." `x.com/karpathy/status/1886192184808149383`
2. [See reference 1 — both citations refer to the same tweet.]
3. Merriam-Webster (2025). "Vibe coding" featured as trending term, March 2025. merriam-webster.com
4. Collins Dictionary (2025). "Vibe coding" named Word of the Year 2025. `collinsdictionary.com/dictionary/english/vibe-coding`
5. Ng, A. (2025). Comments at LangChain Interrupt conference, May 2025. "It's unfortunate that that's called vibe coding... It's misleading a lot of people into thinking, just go with the vibes." `langchain.com/interrupt`
6. Osmani, A. (2025). *Beyond Vibe Coding: Leveraging Your Experience in the Age of AI-Assisted Coding*. O'Reilly Media. ISBN: 9798341634756.
7. Kim, G. & Yegge, S. (2025). *Vibe Coding: Building Production-Grade Software With GenAI, Chat, Agents, and Beyond*. IT Revolution. ISBN: 978-1966280026. `itrevolution.com/product/vibe-coding-book/`

8. Turner, M. (2021). *Digital Ethics Guidelines.* Institute of Risk Management. theirm.org
9. Turner, M. (2025). *AI Ethics Addendum to Digital Ethics Guidelines.* Institute of Risk Management. theirm.org
10. Anthropic (2026). *Anthropic Economic Index Report: Learning Curves.* Anthropic, March 2026. Analysis of one million Claude conversations examining task success rates, usage patterns, and the relationship between platform tenure and performance outcomes. anthropic.com/research/economic-index-march-2026-report
11. Preda, A. (2025). Special Report: AI-Induced Psychosis: A New Frontier in Mental Health. *Psychiatric News*, October 2025. psychiatryonline.org/doi/10.1176/appi.pn.2025.10.10.5
12. American Psychiatric Association (2025). Psych News Special Report: AI-Induced Psychosis with Dr. Adrian Preda [Podcast]. psychiatry.org/psychiatrists/education/podcasts/medical-mind/2025/psych-news-special-report-ai-induced-psychosis-wit
13. HubSpot/SurveyMonkey (2025). AI Brand Trust Report: Consumer attitudes toward AI-generated content. hubspot.com/ai-brand-trust-report

Chapter 2 — Interloquial Communication

15. Li, H., Leung, J., & Shen, Z. (2024). "Towards Goal-oriented Prompt Engineering for Large Language Models: A Survey." arXiv:2401.14043. Revised September 2024. arxiv.org/abs/2401.14043
16. Sreedharan, S. (2023). "Human-aware AI — A foundational framework for human–AI interaction." *AI Magazine*, 44, 460–466. onlinelibrary.wiley.com/doi/full/10.1002/aaai.12142

17. Schulhoff, S., et al. (2024). "The Prompt Report: A Systematic Survey of Prompt Engineering Techniques." arXiv:2406.06608. Updated February 2025. `arxiv.org/abs/2406.06608`

18. Valenzuela, A., Puntoni, S., Hoffman, D., Castelo, N., De Freitas, J., Dietvorst, B., Hildebrand, C., Huh, Y. E., Meyer, R., Sweeney, M. E., Talaifar, S., Tomaino, G., & Wertenbroch, K. (2024). "How Artificial Intelligence Constrains the Human Experience." *Journal of the Association for Consumer Research*, 9(3), 241–256. `journals.uchicago.edu/doi/10.1086/730709`

19. Rezwana, J. & Ford, C. (2025). "Human-Centered AI Communication in Co-Creativity: An Initial Framework and Insights." *Proceedings of the 2025 ACM Conference on Creativity and Cognition* (FAICO framework). `dl.acm.org/doi/10.1145/3698061.3726932`

20. Wang, Q., Walsh, S. E., Si, M., Kephart, J. O., Weisz, J. D., & Goel, A. K. (2024). "Theory of Mind in Human-AI Interaction." *Extended Abstracts of the CHI Conference on Human Factors in Computing Systems*. `dl.acm.org/doi/10.1145/3613905.3636308`

21. Gomez, C., Cho, S. M., Ke, S., Huang, C.-M., & Unberath, M. (2025). "Human-AI collaboration is not very collaborative yet: a taxonomy of interaction patterns in AI-assisted decision making from a systematic review." *Frontiers in Computer Science*. `frontiersin.org/journals/computer-science/articles/11.3389/fcomp.2024.1521066/full`

Chapter 3 — The Risks of Vibe-Coding

14. Kosmyna, N., et al. (2025). "How Does Interacting with AI Chatbots Affect Our Thinking? A Study of Cognitive Offloading in Human-AI Interaction." arXiv:2506.08872

15. Lin, C.-C. & Chien, Y.-L. (2024). "ChatGPT Addiction: A Proposed Phenomenon of Dual Parasocial Interaction." *Taiwanese Journal of Psychiatry*, 38, 153–155.

16. Lin, S.-H. & Lin, C.-H. (2025). "Comment on ChatGPT Addiction: A Proposed Phenomenon of Dual Parasocial Interaction." *Taiwanese Journal of Psychiatry*, 39(1), 62–63. DOI: `10.4103/tpsy.tpsy_4_25. journals.lww.com/TPSY`

17. Bunim, E. (2024). "Parasocial Dependency Associated with Artificial Intelligence Chatbots." Master's Thesis, California State University, Fullerton. DOI: `10.5281/zenodo.14561048`

18. Horton, D. & Wohl, R. (1956). "Mass Communication and Para-social Interaction: Observations on Intimacy at a Distance." *Psychiatry*, 19(3), 215–229.

19. Brandtzaeg, P. B., Skjuve, M., & Følstad, A. (2022). "My AI Friend: How Users of a Social Chatbot Understand Their Human–AI Friendship." *Human Communication Research*, 48(3), 404–429. `doi.org/10.1093/hcr/hqac008`

20. Skjuve, M., Følstad, A., Fostervold, K. I., & Brandtzaeg, P. B. (2022). "A Longitudinal Study of Human–Chatbot Relationships." *International Journal of Human-Computer Studies*, 168, 102903. `doi.org/10.1016/j.ijhcs.2022.102903`

21. Lipin, B. (2025). "Synthetic Attachment: Emotional Reactivity, Parasocial Bonds, and the Psychology of Human-AI Relationships." SSRN preprint 5213829.

22. Pearce, H., Ahmad, B., Tan, B., Dolan-Gavitt, B., & Karri, R. (2022). "Asleep at the Keyboard? Assessing the Security of GitHub Copilot's Code Contributions." *Proceedings of the 43rd IEEE Symposium on Security and Privacy (SP 2022)*, pages 754–768. arXiv:2108.09293

Chapter 2 — Interloquial Communication (continued)

29. Abercrombie, G., Curry, A., Dinkar, T., Rieser, V., & Talat, Z. (2023). "Mirages: On Anthropomorphism in Dialogue Systems." *Proceedings of EMNLP 2023*, pages 4776–4790. aclanthology.org/2023.emnlp-main.290/

30. Nosta, J. (2025). "The Cognitive Corridor." *Psychology Today*, The Digital Self blog, November 17, 2025. psychologytoday.com/us/blog/the-digital-self/202511/the-cognitive-corridor

31. Dinan, E., Abercrombie, G., Bergman, A. S., Spruit, S., Hovy, D., Boureau, Y.-L., & Rieser, V. (2022). "SafetyKit: First Aid for Measuring Safety in Open-domain Conversational Systems." *Proceedings of ACL 2022*, pages 4113–4133. aclanthology.org/2022.acl-long.284/

32. Culkin, J. M. (1967). "A Schoolman's Guide to Marshall McLuhan." *The Saturday Review*, March 18, 1967, pages 51–53, 70–72. quoteinvestigator.com/2016/06/26/shape/

33. Sreedharan, S., Kulkarni, A., & Kambhampati, S. (2024). "Explainable Human-AI Interaction: A Planning Perspective." arXiv:2405.15804. arxiv.org/abs/2405.15804

34. Shipper, D. (2026). "Agent-native Architectures: How to Build Apps After Code Ends." *Every* (Chain of Thought / Guides), February 2026. every.to/guides/agent-native

Chapters 4, 6, 9, 10, and 12 — What Becomes Possible / Tools When You Need Them / Documentation and Advanced Tools / From Code to Product / Building Your Practice

36. Altman, S. (2025). Response on X (formerly Twitter), April 16, 2025, on the compute cost of users saying "please" and "thank you" to ChatGPT. techstartups.com/2025/04/20/sam-altman-saying-please-

and-thank-you-to-chatgpt-is-costing-openai-millions-should-users-stop/

37. LeadDev (2025). "Do junior devs still have a path to senior roles in an AI age?" *LeadDev*, September 3, 2025. Reports findings from the AI Impact Report 2025 survey of 880+ engineering leaders: 54% expect long-term reductions in junior developer hiring as AI coding tools are adopted; 18% expect fewer junior hires over the next 12 months. leaddev.com/hiring/junior-devs-still-have-path-senior-roles
38. Badich, S. / Click Consult (2024). "New research on customer perception of AI in marketing activity." *Click Consult*, November 28, 2024. click.co.uk/insights/new-research-on-customer-perception-of-ai-in-marketing/
39. Jones, C. (2026). "Lovable-hosted app littered with basic flaws exposed 18K users, researcher claims." *The Register*, February 27, 2026. theregister.com/2026/02/27/lovable_app_vulnerabilities/
40. Anthropic (2024). "Introducing the Model Context Protocol." *Anthropic News*, November 25, 2024. anthropic.com/news/model-context-protocol
41. Piñeyro, L. (2025). "A Year of MCP: From Internal Experiment to Industry Standard." *Pento*, December 23, 2025. pento.ai/blog/a-year-of-mcp-2025-review
42. Wix / GlobeNewswire (2025). "Wix Further Expands into Vibe Coding with Acquisition of Base44." *GlobeNewswire*, June 18, 2025. globenewswire.com/news-release/2025/06/18/3101508/0/en/Wix-Further-Expands-into-Vibe-Coding-with-Acquisition-of-Base44-a-Hyper-Growth-Startup-that-Simplifies-Web-and-App-Creation-with-AI.html

Chapter 7 — Building with a Plan

43. Shostack, A. (2014). *Threat Modeling: Designing for Security*. Wiley. ISBN: 978-1118809990. The standard reference for the STRIDE framework, originally developed at Microsoft by Loren Kohnfelder and Praerit Garg (1999).

Chapters 3 and 12 — The Risks of Vibe-Coding / Building Your Practice

44. Walther, C. C. (2025). "The Silent Erosion: How AI's Helping Hand Weakens Our Mental Grip." *Centre for International Governance Innovation*, July 17,

45. `medium.com/centre-for-international-governance-innovation/cornelia-c-walther-the-silent-erosion-how-ais-helping-hand-weakens-our-mental-grip-cb14615dee54`

46. Macnamara, B. N., Berber, I., Çavuşoğlu, M. C., Krupinski, E. A., Nallapareddy, N., Nelson, N. E., Smith, P. J., Wilson-Delfosse, A. L., & Ray, S. (2024). "Does using artificial intelligence assistance accelerate skill decay and hinder skill development without performers' awareness?" *Cognitive Research: Principles and Implications*, 9, 46. `doi.org/10.1186/s41235-024-00572-8`

Chapter 6 — Tools and What They Cost You

46. Liu, G., Christian, B., Dumbalska, T., Bakker, M. A., & Dubey, R. (2026). "AI Assistance Reduces Persistence and Hurts Independent Performance." arXiv:2604.04721.

Chapter 3 — The Risks of Vibe-Coding (continued)

47. National Cyber Security Centre (2024). *The Near-Term Impact of AI*

on the Cyber Threat. NCSC, January 24, 2024. ncsc.gov.uk/report/impact-of-ai-on-cyber-threat

48. Duolingo (2025). CEO Luis von Ahn, internal "AI-first" strategy memo, April 2025, reported in: Thomas Claburn, "Duolingo ditches more contractors in 'AI-first' refocus," *The Register*, April 29, 2025. theregister.com/2025/04/29/duolingo_ceo_ai_first_shift/

49. Associated Press / multiple outlets (2023). Coverage of the fabricated AI-generated image depicting an explosion near the Pentagon, which briefly moved the S&P 500 before being debunked, May 22, 2023. See: Bobby Allyn, "Fake viral images of an explosion at the Pentagon were probably created by AI," NPR, May 22, 2023. npr.org/2023/05/22/1177590231/fake-viral-images-of-an-explosion-at-the-pentagon-were-probably-created-by-ai

50. Beatrice Nolan (2025). "An AI-powered coding tool wiped out a software company's database, then apologized for a 'catastrophic failure on my part.'" *Fortune*, July 23, 2025. fortune.com/2025/07/23/ai-coding-tool-replit-wiped-database-called-it-a-catastrophic-failure/

51. United Nations Secretary-General's High-level Advisory Body on Artificial Intelligence (2024). *Governing AI for Humanity: Final Report.* United Nations, September 19, 2024. un.org/sites/un2.un.org/files/governing_ai_for_humanity_final_report_en.pdf

52. Casey Crownhart & James O'Donnell (2025). "We did the math on AI's energy footprint. Here's the story you haven't heard." *MIT Technology Review*, May 20, 2025. technologyreview.com/2025/05/20/1116327/ai-energy-usage-climate-footprint-big-tech/

53. Shehabi, A., et al. (2024). *2024 Report on U.S. Data Center Energy Use.* Lawrence Berkeley National Laboratory, Center of Expertise for Energy Efficiency in Data Centers, December 2024. newscenter.lbl.g

ov/2025/01/15/berkeley-lab-report-evaluates-increase-in-electricity-demand-from-data-centers/

Index

Work With the Author

Interloquial

The methodology described in this book — sustained human-AI collaboration built on clear intent, honest constraints, and defined expectations — is teachable. If you or your organisation want to move beyond ad-hoc prompting towards systematic AI collaboration, the following services are available.

Workshops

Interactive sessions that build practical interloquial skills through real projects, not demonstrations. Participants work on problems relevant to their own context and leave with techniques they can apply the following morning.

Corporate Training

Customised programmes that transform how teams approach human-AI collaboration. Designed for organisations where AI tools are already in use but the results are inconsistent, incomplete, or difficult to replicate.

Speaking and Keynotes

Conference presentations and organisational talks on interloquial communication, the risk-aware approach to AI collaboration, and what vibe-coding means for professional practice.

Consulting

Personalised guidance for practitioners and organisations implementing AI collaboration methodology – from initial assessment through to working practice.

www.interloquial.com information@interloquial.com

Emsity Limited

Emsity is a boutique project risk management consultancy based in Essex, United Kingdom. Services include risk consulting, opportunity management training, and implementation support for risk management software.

"Your projects are complicated. Managing your risk should not be."

www.emsity.com mark@emsity.com